THE UNVEILED NUMEROLOGY

VOLUME ONE

You do not necessarily carry the name you think...

Numerology Charts & Resources
Including our free tool for calculations
www.numeyoga.com

Our powerful online Numerology Software
www.numeyoga.pro

Learn more about sidereal and karmic astrology
www.nostredame.com

Discover our online Astrology Software
www.astrozeus.pro

Photo illustration: God council in Olympus: Hermes with his mother Maia.
Detail of the side B of an Attic red-figure belly-amphora, ca. 500 BC.
Part of a photo by Nikoxenos-Maler.

Michel Pirmaïer is the discoverer of the method Maia.
Method registered by Michel Pirmaïer and Wilfrid Pochat at the I.N.P.I. (France)

Wilfrid Pochat & Michel Pirmaïer

THE UNVEILED NUMEROLOGY

VOLUME ONE

You do not necessarily carry the name you think...

&
Nostredame.com Publishing

Special thanks to

Translators of the Translated.net Team

And for their final read-through and help

Gerri Lyn Becker
Françoise Cadoux
Gigi Caouette
Vera Mazur Caouette
Pascale Rotchin

To all angels disguised as humans,
prisoners and captors of the Village,
and especially Number 6…

Foreword

Thanks to my friend and colleague Wilfrid, who is grateful to the numerology enthusiasts from the other side of the Atlantic (who managed so brilliantly to bring this science into the popular consciousness), I am delighted to reveal this work to the English-speaking world. This book outlines the fundamental ideas of a clear and concise method to create a precise and relevant numerological chart.

I am eternally grateful to my inquisitive friend for having discovered numerous important American works and especially for having taught me that, thanks to them, numerology is a science in its own right.

As Frenchmen, we are profoundly attached to our European cultural values. In the specific domain of numerology we are evidently very aware of our Greco-Roman heritage. We are delighted and also pleasantly surprised that this awareness is also present in American culture.

When you question established knowledge, especially in the so-called esoteric domains like numerology, you expose yourself to strong reactions from the knowledge bearers. As a practitioner of sidereal and karmic astrology, I am only too familiar with the brick walls I faced when trying to convince people that my ideas were sound. There is nothing more difficult than trying to rethink the improbable in these sciences because many of the practitioners have an impressive track record with masters, gurus and teachers, a history linked to their own past lives. Therefore it is very easy to offend the people belonging to that idealistic world.

I am not trying to start a debate. I simply want to re-examine the aspects of this science that do not work. I am not a numerologist. Before making the discovery that was the catalyst for this book, I had always distanced myself from numerology and been confused by it, having never really recognized myself in any charts or information given to me. I had always considered the astrology I practice to be much more precise, effective and relevant. I had always thought that a numerological analysis should be as similar as possible to an astrological chart, a real one... This had never been the case.

This book is the result of an enormous amount of research on behalf of my friend Willy. The years he spent researching this subject culminated in his Numeyoga software and in this book. He was relentless in his quest to fix the parts that didn't "fit". His labors should be praised as should his unrelenting desire to prove the value of numerology to me. We discussed it constantly; naturally he was aware of the inherent inconsistencies and mistakes and could only agree with me when I said that there was something "not right"...but what was it?

Jokingly I often told him that one of these days I was going to apply myself to the problem and resolve it. Of course it was only a joke and I was making fun of him a little, he who could not fail to recognize the power of astrology.

Then, thanks to him, the problem was resolved. He handed everything to me on a silver platter, and, since, over time, he has become an excellent numerologist (don't tell him – he doesn't know yet!), he gave me a top-notch education in numerology. He deserves all of the praise for this discovery.

Now, as far as numerological and astrological readings go, it must never be forgotten that we all possess all of the attributes of the angel incarnate on our dear planet. Therefore we all potentially carry all numbers, aspects, indicators, elements, planetary positions and more.

So why do this type of reading? Simply because the elements of a chart, such as the different facets of the personality matrix, are not present in every person in an equal quantity. It is all a question of degree and it is this that defines the mosaic of our incarnate identity. This is a very important point because the argument used by critics of this type of personalized work is that every person is able to recognize him/herself in every reading. This is undeniably true if the reading is stuffed full of generalizations. I am not in any way trying to convince uninterested parties to believe in esoteric sciences. However, it must be acknowledged that numerology and astrology, such as they are practiced in the vast majority of cases, are actually only a shadow of their true selves. This allows a rational and logical person to think "either this reading doesn't mean anything and so it is pointless to continue or there is truth in it and so we need to be as precise as possible".

However, the majority of these readings suffer from a terrible lack of precision. Throughout my life, through meetings with various practitioners, numerologists and other specialists, I have noted that most of them do not really believe in their science. This is why they end up being happy with generalizations, setting out in multiple directions and each thinking they have found the Holy Grail.

Why then, you might ask, does this book not also suffer from the same problem? I grant you that we only find solutions through experimentation. The only way to prove a hypothesis is by working hard, thoroughly "investigating" and, above all, being precise, extremely precise. That is the purpose of this book even though we acknowledge that it is only a prelude to other, more in-depth, works.

At this stage, as a quick aside, let me point out an undeniable fact: these sciences will always attract a number of critics who will claim, *ad infinitum*, and even when presented with the most relevant and unmistakable readings, that all of this is just rubbish. Well bully for them. It would do them good to get a serious reading done to find out what is missing in their emotional lives. This is not a criticism but rather an encouragement.

The charts must describe the person, but, more than that, they must also reveal the finer points of the task chosen by the entity for this incarnation.

That is where the truth of the reading emerges because looking in the mirror helps you to understand the things that are preventing your life from being harmonious. This type of reading is not a succession of criticisms and judgments but rather another way of discovering the karmic obstacles you need to overcome.

Before going any further, it is important to think about the reasons why a person who wants to know which direction his future is going to take would approach numerology, astrology or any other similar science.

Over the course of our incarnations on earth, most humans have forgotten the first commandment, to love one other. While admittedly it is generally acknowledged that love cannot be disregarded and that it is necessary for the harmonious and balanced evolution of humanity, the incarnate souls that we are have forgotten the most important part of this sentiment. It is impossible to love another person if you do not love yourself first. Ignoring this evidence, human beings look for love outside of themselves, as if the other can give them the thing they think is missing – self-love. Seeing your own reflection in the loving eyes of a soul mate – how beautiful! Not only that but how can you love yourself when all day long you hear people saying that we must get rid of our overpowering egos!? What a dilemma!

A reading of this kind brings out all of the so-called negative points but also sheds a light on the positive points, the points that allow us to be good people and love ourselves!

Therein lies the paradox of our existences. We all know very well in our heart of hearts what we do not like about ourselves, we know what we think are the bad points in the way we behave. Furthermore, these assumptions are the very reasons why we are not able to respect and consequently love ourselves and appreciate other people. The things that we do not like in another person and which sometimes offend us are often the very traits that we possess ourselves, the traits that we do not like to admit to and cannot forgive in ourselves. This is what we call the mirror effect. The famous "pot and kettle"! It is no more profound than that!

So these readings, even if they are sometimes disturbing and hurtful, touch the deepest emotional state of being and are designed to find out what needs to be healed. A doctor must make a precise diagnosis in order to treat a patient. We can only be healed if we face up to what is bothering us, if once and for all we decide not to judge this problem and if we treat these open wounds with the miracle ointment called love. Did He not also say, "Thou shall not judge"!?

Returning to the ego and self-love, there is a world of difference between the two concepts. The first tries to be seen in a false light while the second unconditionally accepts who you are. If we agree to look at ourselves lovingly in the mirror, without any pretense, then perhaps we can also accept the other as he is.

I believe that is where the real journey of profound discovery and transformation can begin.

This is the aim of the much criticized esoteric sciences. They would not have survived centuries and centuries, always attracting more and more followers, despite being rejected, often violently, by self-righteous people, if they did not contain a deeply rooted and unmovable truth.

To summarize, this book may open doors closed long ago which may lead to hurt and offence, at least on the surface. If you feel like that then close this book quickly as it is not for you. If not then be forgiving towards yourself and others. Try to consider and examine the path you have already begun towards your divinity rather than judging the things that are not yet perfect. We are all impatient to become Gods again but our lack of confidence in life often obscures our vision.

No doubt that at the dawn of this new emerging world, this type of reading will become one of the most appropriate, even indispensible, methods of soul therapy.

As for the science of numbers, I will let Wilfrid introduce this in his own way.

Michel Pirmaïer
Astrologist
Discoverer of the Maia method

Introduction

The original French version of our book was published in February 2010. In the space of a year we received a huge amount of positive feedback and this American version incorporates the discoveries we have made since then. My friend Michel and I have also decided to translate the professional version of our online numerology software (www.numeyoga.pro) into American because this program is used by numerous professional numerologists. It generates in-depth readings focusing on the personality and life path of individuals.

First let me give you a bit of background information.

I discovered numerology at the end of the 80's through the first popular works published in France. I found the idea that you could calculate a person's profile and his/her destiny through the so-called properties of numbers both amusing and exciting.

However, at first glance it seemed too easy. After all, how could a few numbers translate the psychological complexity of a person? I wanted to firm my own opinion on the subject and leave any preconceived ideas at the doorstep.

This resolution led me to explore the hidden side of numbers with great determination.

At that time I had just discovered the techniques of past life regression advocated by Patrick Drouot and Ian Stevenson. Once again I decided to rethink and experiment with voyages into the subconscious, all the while keeping a critical eye on what I was learning. Having hundreds of regressions and having written an account of my research, I decided to verify the results of several of these past life explorations against historical fact. The latter was to verify if I was having waking dreams or if I was actually uncovering memories of real past lives.

At the same time I continued reading numerology manuals, still eager to verify the precision and depth of the suggested analyses. Furthermore, even though the calculations needed to create a numerology chart were not difficult, I found it preferable to use a computer.

At the time, I couldn't find any satisfying software for the Atari ST and so I decided to create my own program. Numeyoga was born.

I remember that in 1993 I submitted my account on reincarnation in French to various publishers at the same time as I sent my software to several magazines. In the end it was my software that found favor with the editors and so Numeyoga was reported on in the now defunct magazine Start Micro No.11 in the November 1993 edition. As I couldn't find a publisher for my account I made it available to download from the early days of widespread internet use where it gradually attracted numerous readers.

Since then, I have been continually improving my software which has been translated from French into English and Italian. Today my program is widely available as one of the principal driving forces behind the growth of public interest in numerology. In this respect, I have a duty as to its content. Consequently I try my best to systematically deliver a synthesis of work by other numerologists. However, I am aware that there will always be more work to be done.

That work made me realize that the specialists disagree on a number of important points. They could not agree on which data should be used to construct a numerological chart.

Even now, a method called "French" or "European" dictates that, in addition to the person's date of birth, his/her birth name and customary first name must be taken into account when casting a chart. This is the method that I used at first without really knowing whether I should use my current surname or the one I was given at birth before I was registered. I created two charts and compared them. Apart from the generalizations contained in the two charts that would apply to anybody, it seemed that using the name I had at birth instead of my patronymic gave a clearer result.

I then tried the "American" method and finally discovered what appeared to me to be the most appropriate one. I had to use my date of birth and my birth surname but also all of the first and middle names listed on my birth certificate.

I subsequently encountered the works of Françoise Daviet in French and Matthew Goodwin in English which opened my eyes to more interesting interpretations. Then, later on, Dan Millman's in-depth study on life purpose convinced me of the extraordinary power of the number in defining a person's psychological profile.

At that time I did not yet have a reason to write this book. After all, what good was yet another book on numerology? Everything there was to say had already been repeated many times. Additionally, it seemed that the main points on interpretation had already been written, and well written, notably by Daviet, Goodwin and Millman.

I hadn't counted on the arrival of one of life's little practical jokes.

To tell you the truth, while I could not find fault wither my chart nor my wife's chart, I sometimes spotted mistakes or missing elements in charts, some of which were created using my software. Users praised the qualities of the program but also confessed to being confused about some of the analyses. No chart was completely wrong but there were sometimes important differences regarding aspects of the personality, whichever method was used.

It is obvious that a computer analysis can never be a perfect substitute for an analysis carried out by an experienced professional. The software cannot construct a chart with the same relevance or finesse as a numerologist. That said, in a certain number of cases, with or without the software, the chart was completely off-target for any elements directly related to first or last names.

I spent many years questioning these discrepancies to the point where I never felt like I could claim to be a numerology expert despite my growing experience. Something was wrong. It was like there was a missing link or master key that once found would finally allow me to dedicate myself professionally to teaching the symbolism of numbers.

Until I discovered this missing link, I limited myself to creating a program as conscientiously as I could. I defined my work as a synthesis and defined myself more and more frequently as a referee between opposing ideas. I did hundreds of readings and every day I felt more and more impatient to understand the reason behind the inaccuracies, when there were no real contradictions that I could see.

In 2008 I suddenly saw the light in the most unfitting way possible.

At the time I was working regularly with my astrologer friend Michel. One day I was messing around, casting a chart for him using the latest version (5.0) of my software which was still under development. I was determined to show him that numerology was not the poor relation of the esoteric sciences compared to the all-powerful sidereal astrology in which he was an expert.

In his case, the American method revealed a dominant 4. His life path 6 came from a 24. The Expression and Aspiration numbers also reduced to a 4 just like his birth date. I knew that for the American numerologist Goodwin if 3 of the 4 numbers were the same then this was a dominant number, which in Michel's case was 4. My friend's personality should be marked by the characteristics of this number more than any other.

However, while it was undeniable that this surprising character led an orderly and meticulous life, that he was a trusting person in need of security, he had nonetheless travelled where the wind took him, undertaken all sorts of experiences, pushed several limits and was also very happy to sometimes be able to take time out. Something mysterious was constantly pushing him to break out of his secure surroundings, to push his own limits and, often, to question everything he thought he knew.

Michel told me that what bothered him in numerology such as it was practiced at the time was that a part of his personality remained hidden. He confirmed the aspects revealed by the 4 but his exploring, restless and adventurous side was not revealed. There was a hole in the analysis! Furthermore, he often joked that one day he was going to add his two cents worth to the subject. However, as he was not a numerologist he kept his distance, no doubt preferring the astrology he held so dear!

I knew that he was right about an essential point when he said that a numerological chart should not be far removed from an astrological chart… a sidereal one of course. Where was Aquarius, the sign that appeared so often in his astrological chart? There was surely something crucial missing in the fundamentals of numerology.

However, for Michel, logic and common sense always prevail. Numerology either is or is not. It does not allow for approximation.

Faced with this loss, it was clear to me that the number 5 was missing from his chart. Where was it? In him it was striking: sometimes 4 and 5 worked together and sometimes they were in opposition. Moreover, his perfectionism was signified in a large part by his life purpose 24/6.

For all that, Michel did not refute the analysis of his life path, no more than he denied the influence or the correspondence of 4 in his character. However, there were one or two pieces missing from his personality jigsaw.

That day, while he was preparing one of his secret recipes for us to eat, and without imaging the consequences of his words, he shared an important fact with me. He had been surprised to discover that he had not been given his father's surname at birth, but that apparently he had been given his mother's. He had ordered a copy of his birth certificate on the internet and noticed that his father's surname had only been registered a few days after his birth. Consequently, he had originally been given his mother's surname.

I immediately reacted, "Michel, this is crucial information for the construction of your chart!"

As he stood there amused by my reaction, I changed the surname used in my reading and obtained the new results, wondering whether the 4 that partially suited him was going to disappear and perhaps my faith in numerology along with it …

The result was conclusive. The Expression of my friend became 9. It was modified by an Aspiration (Soul Urge) 5 and a Potential (often unfairly referred to as the Hidden Self) 22/4. All of a sudden, everything was clear. The master number 22 was a bonus, a way of describing the power of his knowledge.

Then Michel had a moment of incredible intuition which was, believe me, far from being his first. It was one of those magic moments. It was the spark that led me to look at numerology with fresh eyes. Perhaps at this stage you can already predict the incredible revelation that was going to result from our discovery which I will reveal to you in detail in chapter IV.

It took me almost 20 years to encounter this method and stop juggling with different theories depending on which one corresponded the most to any given person. As with astrology, there is only one method. It is precise, rigorous and relentless because numbers are never approximate. Either numerology is pure speculation or it is a real science.

In an attempt to settle this issue, this book will reveal to you, above all, a method. This method must be taken into account if we want to have full access to our road map and our attributes because, until now, some aspects have remained hidden to numerous natives, and probably not without reason. However, we must acknowledge that a vast cosmic plan has been out of our reach…

On the other hand, I will not devote very much of this book to interpreting the influence of each number on a core element. I will, however, provide an outline and suggest works for the reader to refer to on the subject written by my favorite authors. Nevertheless I will attempt to clearly define the influence numbers have on the chart parameters by summarizing the interpretations that I found to be the most accurate throughout my years of research.

When using this unique method, I have noticed that some charts remain the same while others can be seen in a whole new light. Descriptions that originally constituted the major part of the most obvious, most social aspect of a person came to define his innermost trait. In other cases, accurate aspects remained so through a subtle repositioning of elements. For example, the

Expression number became the Potential number or the Aspiration number became the Expression number. No analysis has missed the target. How can we fail to see the Number behind each life? That would be like thinking that some people breathe from birth without having lungs!

Some numerologists will have trouble admitting that the error has been a human one. I have myself perpetuated this aberration in good faith. Once they have recovered from the shock, I promise that each one can, in all honesty and without prejudice, test and validate my idea.

I know that we all have reasons to prefer one profile to another. Often our ego wins out because it likes to see itself in a certain light. This is made all the easier by the fact that we have the potential to be all the numbers. At one time or another we have all taken on the characteristics of a number to experiment with, even if the personality trait that it refers to is not natural to us. Who has not rebelled a little against nature at a certain point in his life? For example, a situation could arise in which a being has to show authority and courage when he usually prefers to remain in the background to maintain his comfort, calm and serenity.

However, we must avoid this bottomless pit filled with interpretations that are so vague and general they apply to every single person. The science of numbers reveals a general human truth:

Every person lives the destiny that corresponds to his archetype, by expressing in his own way, and achieving through his own means, his deepest aspirations.

That is exactly what numerology describes. It allows us to identify the foundations and supporting walls of our personality. It reveals the key numbers which show us how to apprehend our life path in the right way and how to discover and understand the part that we are here to play.

I hope this book will help you get there.

CHAPTER I

In the beginning there was the number

"Always ensure that the laymen do not find out about this, for there is possibly no doctrine more ridiculous than this one for the common people; but the same may be said for those minds which are richly gifted with the most admirable and most inspired qualities"

(Plato 427-348 BC – secret letter to Denys the Younger)

What is a number? Faced with the difficulty of giving an exhaustive definition, some authors, even those who compile dictionaries, admit that this is an almost impossible task. Of course we talk of counting, comparing, classifying and coding. Numbers can be ordinal or cardinal depending on how we use them. However, those terms only describe methods for using the numbers.

The idea that the number is a concept, a simple representation made by the brain, is soon found to be insufficient because, concept or not, the number exists. Whether the human brain is aware of it or not, the number is present as soon as an object exists. The two things are inseparable. The number is like intimately linked energy. This is true whatever convention dictates about naming the object in letters as well as in numbers.

From the moment of its creation, an object is One. If an identical object is created from the same mould then it is also One because it has its own existence, individuality and its own limits. It does not matter where it comes from or whether or not it is aware of its own origin; it is unique. The number is present from the very moment that the object comes into existence. In the Epinomis, Plato communicates this association when he tells us that "*the number gives its nature to all things*".

On an esoteric level, the number is a link between the spiritual world and the material one. It is not less linked to the material just for being intangible. By analogy, it resounds with all of the elements of the universe. Its absolute nature allows humans to share a common heritage with their creator(s). It was used to create the world and then given to humans so that they too could become creators.

The number is both universal and intangible. Mathematics is a language shared by all people and all cultures.

Numerology is the study of the properties and symbolism of numbers within the experiment of human incarnation. This study started a very long time ago and has been called various names such as arithmancy. It is almost impossible to determine its origin. However, we are sure that the Egyptians, Phoenicians and Chaldeans all already had ideas on the subject many centuries before Christ because we know that some of their thinkers taught Pythagoras during his many travels.

Before them, the Sumerian civilization had already recognized the divine power of numbers. The Mesopotamians used a sexagesimal system with 60 as its base and venerated the number 7 in particular as it was the first number not to be a divisor of 60.

The idea that the first 9 numbers (with the exception of 0) are of specific importance dates back to Ancient Egypt. According to the pyramid texts, the Ennead comprised the nine Gods of the Egyptian pantheon and therefore constituted all of the forces present in the universe. The ennead is also symbolized by a square made up of 9 signs grouped 3 by 3.

A bit closer to us, we know that the Greeks transposed letters into numbers by using values in groups of 9. The first 9 letters are worth 1 to 9, the following 9 are worth 10 to 90 and the last 9 are worth 100 to 900. At that time, before numerological interpretation even existed, it was fashionable to write short poems containing 2 verses in which the sum of the letters comprising each verse was the same.

In the 5th century before Christ, the Pythagorean School argued that everything was related to numbers. The influence of Pythagoras, who studied the doctrine of numbers for twelve years with the Chaldean mages, was undoubtedly behind that idea. Furthermore, he propagated the idea that the world can be represented through the first 9 numbers.

Philolaus, one of his disciples, taught that numbers are the key to all knowledge. He was fascinated by the number 1 and said that it was a perfect number because when added to any other number it transformed it from odd to even or vice versa.

Nowadays, it is widely acknowledged that 9-number recursive numerology i.e. reducing any sum obtained to a single digit ($34 \rightarrow 3 + 4 = 7$), originated in the Pythagorean school of thought.

The legacy left by Pythagoras and his followers goes far beyond the theories and tables taught by teachers in schools. The Pythagorean School studied numbers in an attempt to penetrate the mysteries of the Cosmos. Numbers were classed according to various properties that you needed to know in order to fully understand the meaning attributed to each one. Almost all of us know about prime numbers but there are also other categories such as sacred numbers, perfect numbers, and so on. This means that the qualities attributed to numbers are not arbitrary or the result of a subjective choice made by some obscure author, but have been determined through observation of the attributes and results of number interaction.

The aim of this book is not to present all of the discoveries from that time. For readers who want to know more about that subject, I have provided a bibliography at the back of this book. I will, however, sum up the thinking of the researchers from that time: they were trying to deduce the structure of nature from the metaphysical. Nowadays we do the opposite. Scientific research is about observing real objects and it is often forbidden to make any conclusions whatsoever on the transcendent energy at their origin.

That said, we must bear in mind that symbolism is intimately linked to the human mind and its imagination. Therefore

23

the definition of the characteristics of each number should not be seen as a fixed portrait. There is also a certain amount of feeling involved. I would go as far as to say that it is a balance of reason and intuition.

We also have to include human activity, our discoveries and new disciplines which require adjustments and classifications. When computers, environmental science, genetics and so forth appeared, they too needed to be combined with the energy of numbers. At the same time, these new disciplines brought nuances and forced reconsideration and widening of existing analogies.

Since its origins, Judaism has also been immersed in the relationship between letters and numbers. Hebrew partially inherited the Phoenician alphabet. Each of its letters corresponds to a number (*Aleph* is worth 1, *Beth* is worth 2, and so on). In this sense Hebrew is a coded language at the root of Kabbalah. Gematria, one of the components of the latter, is the art of finding the hidden meaning behind a word's numerical value. This technique became widespread from the 2nd century AD.

The symbolism attached to Hebrew letters corresponds to the original meaning of the word represented by the letters e.g. *Aleph* means Bull, *Beth* means House, and so on. By extension, *Aleph* is an analogy for the progenitor and his strength. This first letter refers to the father and creator. The One. *Beth* reflects shelter and therefore refuge. Is the maternal womb not in fact our first home? The second letter (2) relates to the mother.

This Hebrew correspondence table largely applies to the letters and the ordinal value of letters belonging to the Latin alphabet that we use today.

Later, following the arrival of Islam, Muslims also became very interested in the relationship between numbers and words. In the 12th century, the mystic Ibn Arabî wrote a theory of numbers and letters.

It is true to say that over the centuries numerology has remained an esoteric discipline used by mystics. It fascinated the Church from the 4th century onwards with Saint Ambrose, Saint Clement of Alexandria, Saint Atanase and Saint Augustine. It was passed on through the work of alchemists, fellows and disciples like Cagliostro (18th century). In the 19th century, Christian established occult methods of interpretation, combining Hebrew culture with Latin letters.

Finally, it wasn't until the beginning of the 20th century that the science of numbers was rediscovered through the works of three women who made it available to the wider public. In 1911, L. Dow Balliet, the first of the three, established the value of each letter used in English by taking alphabetical order into account. She explained the importance of vowels and master numbers. Juno Kapp introduced the ideas of cycles, pinnacles and challenges. In 1931 Florence Campbell wrote a work of reference, republished many times since, called "Your days are numbered". Then in 1974, Kevin Quinn Avery brought out the bestseller "The Numbers of Life". A little later, Matthew O. Goodwin wrote the indispensable "Numerology The Complete Guide" in two volumes. It would not be possible to exclude from that list the subsequent contributions of Lynn Buess and Dan Millman.

There were also the famous readings by the visionary Edgar Cayce on numerology. Why would we close the door to information conveyed through channeling if it turned out to be relevant?

Modern numerology finally took off in a real way in France in the 80's. Yet in 1948 Doctor René Allendy had already developed the symbolism of numbers in a work of the same name. After him, Jean-Pol Kersaint and Georges Jouven wrote more specifically about esoteric arithmancy. Then, Jean-Daniel Fermier and François Notter opened a door that many subsequent people were to pass through. I also want to mention Georges Guilpin's book entitled "La vie au fil des chiffres" (Life through numbers) that develops elements related to the more social aspects of a personality.

Finally, I hold a special place in my heart for the French work of Françoise Daviet which in the 90's considerably enriched the understanding of the rules of interpretation by delving further, in particular, into the interaction between numbers. She also contributed to the link between the various numerological elements and psychological complexes and developed the significance of the association between personal years and astrological houses. This was crucial work.

Nowadays, interest in numbers has also given rise to other very similar disciplines. Pentanology considers the first 9 numbers and the number 10 by placing them symbolically around a pentagram. By focusing on the date of birth and avoiding the choice of which first and last names to take into account for a reading, this approach avoids the pitfalls of traditional numerology which I will describe later.

Dan Millman also avoided this problem in his in-depth study of the core numbers revealed by the date of birth alone. Other specialists, such as Doctor Roger Halfon, have explored the possibility of a numerology with a base of 12 which would resonate with the 12 signs of the zodiac.

In another context, the enneagram describes nine psychological profiles numbered from 1 to 9 but the number retained does not correspond to its real numerological significance, with the exception of 2 and 8. That said, the descriptions of these profiles could not fail to be noticed by the practiced numerologist. Thus profile 3 of the enneagram which describes a fighter, an entrepreneur and a competitor who constantly embarks on new projects seems to have been copied straight from the definition of number 1. Therefore, so as not to add to the confusion, I have included a correspondence chart between these numbered profiles and the real numbers to which they can be associated in the appendix to this book.

Finally, it is possible that these methods are only reactions to the errors inherent in numerology. In the science of numbers field, different ideas have given rise to different schools. Thus an element found using one calculation will be given different names by different authors. Nothing is simple. The different recommended methods and techniques are often in opposition with each other. While numerology is certainly attractive due to the relative simplicity of its calculations, the beginner is quickly confronted with a multitude of options and definitions.

Until now, knowing that the aim of this esoteric science is to study the energy of numbers as applied to the personality, it has been agreed that all of an individual's identifying data needs to be taken into account such as first names, middles names, last names and dates of birth.

This premise is very old. For a long time, every person in the Oriental and Western Greek civilizations was named with a number. Before figures were used and since Hebrew and Greek were numeric alphabets (each sign had a numerical equivalent), it was customary to add letters to a man's name. The Greeks call this numeric evaluation *isopsephy*, the Hebrews call it *gematria* and for the Muslims it is described in the expression *Hisab al Jumāl*.

In his very enlightening book available in French *"Les Nombres cachés"*, Georges Jouven reminds us that this practice is justified in the Bible, where it is written in Genesis (2:19) *"Now out of the ground the Lord God formed every beast of the field and every bird of the heavens and brought them to the man to see what he would call them. And whatever the man called every living creature, that was its name"*. Later in his book he uses the following example of an inscription found on a wall in Pompeii to illustrate that the use of numbers for identifying people has been around since the Antiquity, *"I love 545"*. He also cites this posthumous riddle on a Messenian epitaph: *"Search and you will know who I am, lying in the land that has nourished me. I am 1354"*.

Nowadays, by applying this technique, a correspondence table between each letter in our alphabet and a number has been established, taking into account alphabetical order (A equals 1, B equals 2...J equals 10, etc.). This table is the logical consequence of how things were done in the Antiquity. Thus Plutarch (46-125 AD) reports that Eustrophos, the Platonic philosopher, said that the golden Epsilon engraved in the centre of the facade of the Apollo temple in Delphi was worth 5. Epsilon is the fifth letter of the Greek alphabet which refers to our letter E, which is also the fifth letter of the Roman alphabet.

Despite the above, questions still remain. Should we use the 26 letters of the Roman alphabet that correspond to the alphabets used in English and French? What is the status of the accented letters in French? What should a German person do with Ä Ö Ü ß? Knowing that in Italian, the letters J, K, W, X and Y do not exist, does that mean that L (tenth letter in the alphabet) is worth 1? ...

We should not forget Chaldean numerology either which casts a different light on the subject. This is probably the most ancient numerology and there are but a few books on the subject, including one by Leeya Thompson. Chaldean numerology is based on the association between letters and sounds; this is contrary to modern numerology which, as we have just seen, associates the value of a letter to its rank in the original Roman alphabet.

Once the numerologist has taken these considerations into account, he must decide how many times a number must appear in order to be considered insufficiently or excessively present in a chart.

As a final point, there are specialists who claim that W should be treated as a vowel when it is pronounced as such. I am a bit disturbed about this as some people pronounce my name *Ouilfrid* (the word "oui" in French) and others pronounce it *Vilfrid*. And what about the rule that Y should be treated as a consonant?

The main advantage of this chaos is that every person is free to mix up the different ideas he sees fit, arranging and rearranging the subtle mechanisms to fit a profile as well as possible to its subject even when there are clearly some characteristics missing. I have used these strategies myself in several charts that evaded reason using traditional interpretation, always with the feeling that something was missing in numerology, like a key that would reveal the universal characteristic of this science.

Contrary to astrology, the science of numbers does not really possess a direct Tradition in which the fundamentals have been passed down through the centuries. We have already seen how recent its rediscovery has been. Moreover, it does not depend on observable facts. Whether or not you believe in the science of stars, you cannot deny that a map of the sky does not contain any approximation (I do not mean interpretations of that map). Sidereal astrology relies on the accuracy of astronomical calculations.

As for numbers, we have seen that the parameters used seem to be arbitrary. Yet, there is a certain logic to it. You do not, for example, use the name of your cat to make your chart but it's true that there are subjective points. The date of birth depends on the system used in your society. Some alphabets are not syllabic and so it is impossible to associate a letter with its rank, etc.

Some opponents argue that numerology claims legitimacy because it's old and therefore must be true. While it is true, as we have just seen, that the hidden meaning of numbers has always spoken to man, no old knowledge, no solid manual, has ever materialized to show us the way. However, it is possible to deduce the qualities of numbers from the esoteric study of numbers which has been practiced since the Pythagoreans, for example, then Plato.

At this stage it must be noted that numerology depends on certain assumptions. It is a deductive system that is enriched by experiences and observations. It is called an esoteric science because its deepest meaning is hidden. It is one of the tools given to man to allow him to evolve during his physical incarnation. It cannot be understood outside of the mystical dimension of life. Numbers tell us who we are, where we come from and where we are going. They link us to the invisible, to that which escapes reason whilst also being intimately linked to every other object in our world.

Numbers are intangible. They are spiritual. Yet no object in this world can exist without them. That is what links them to the human mind. Can an object exist if it has not been planned? Who is behind the code and the process of creating the living? Who is behind the number?

In conclusion...

- Everything is a number.
- Numbers are intrinsically intangible.
- Numerology is the study of the properties of numbers and their interaction with man and matter. These numbers reveal the native's road map, which was drawn up before his creation, and the nature of the personality he has chosen to complete it.
- A figure is not a number, but a way of writing the number.

CHAPTER II

The road map

"I do not come from a specific time or place. My spiritual being experiences its eternal existence outside of time and space and if I dive into my thoughts by travelling back through the ages, if I extend my mind to an existence far from the one perceived by you, I become the person that I desire to be."

Joseph Balsamo, Count of Cagliostro – (Report of his trial)

We have our parents to thank. However they behaved towards us, it was probably perfect because it allowed us to follow our chosen itinerary.

Numerology, like many other esoteric disciplines, cannot be disassociated from the concept of reincarnation. It is not within the scope of this work to argue this belief. Therefore, I would ask the reader to please excuse the presumptuous tone that follows.

From our earthly, that is linear, point of view, our soul experiments with this physical reality through successive lives. We choose to be embodied in order to carry out an experiment, the grand design of which escapes us on this side of the veil for the simple reason that, if we were fully conscious of the reasons for this experience, we could not carry it out. In summary, a sort of amnesia

31

must accompany our various travels in order for us to achieve our aim.

That said, this suppressed memory can gradually be brought to the surface depending on our level of awareness. From being a simple oblivious actor, we can become actors who are aware of our roles, or even directors. Let us not forget that we are the authors, actors and audience of the show in which we are performing. This means that we can wear whatever costume we choose. Furthermore, nothing stops us from changing and/or assuming these three roles all at the same time.

These faculties can be acquired. If we so desire, we can access our past lives. We have at least two ways to do so. The direct path is to directly access these memories using techniques for past life regression. The other path is indirect. It relies on tools that help us to read the past, e.g. numerology and astrology, amongst others.

The first path allows us to focus on an echo from the past which is posing a problem in our current existence by manifesting in our life in an unwanted manner, often creating obstacles. Regression allows us to identify the past life that has left this echo and to free ourselves from its influence. A more recent approach consists of finding a potential that was developed in a past life and reactivating it in the present life. I work with this objective when I guide regressions.

The second solution offers us a different approach. A chart, whether it is numerological or astrological, is a snapshot taken at birth that reveals our road map by providing indications about our past lives and their consequences.

Our road map is dynamic. It clearly states our aspirations and potentials. Aspiration is the intention of the soul, its primary desire. The ego, weighed down by karma, can oppose this desire by imposing desires of its own. As for our potentials, they are the legacy of our past acquisitions. If we confine our lives to our current existence then we could speak of gifts. But is the innate not in fact the result of our past life experience?

Finally our expression is influenced by two essential characteristics: our aspiration and the means we have to realize it.

Before we incarnated on this earth, we had decided to follow a path. This path is punctuated by tests, lessons and questions that will force us to use all of our intrinsic qualities. This dive into the alchemist's crucible allows us to reshape our identity by means of this path which can be difficult, even perilous, but which is always right because it was chosen.

Negotiating, adapting and sublimating all of the trials we encounter is a delicate matter, but do those trials not allow us to gain awareness, push our limits and discover ourselves? Humans have a tendency to dramatize their existence during incarnation. Yet, it is not against the rules to try to make life easier for yourself.

When he is not aware of this truth, man is quick to cast himself as the victim and to point to an executioner when he encounters a difficult situation. He is unaware, however, that those roles were already distributed and agreed to before he was born.

Western civilization is immersed in Judeo-Christianity which has twisted the true meaning of reincarnation. In broad terms, we are paying for our past actions. We reap what we have sown. However, any farmer knows that he does not necessarily reap what he has sown. Unforeseen events can change everything (climate, infestations, etc.).

No-one forced us to reincarnate, no more than we are forced to take on the role of the victim. We so rarely adopt the role of the executioner probably because it is the role that disturbs us the most. However, seen in this light, every trial helps us to evolve and so both victims and executioners must be named. Even so, I would praise the world that does not rely on this strange dynamic.

It is true that trials can help us to move forward so long as we understand their true reason. If not they can become real trapdoors, holes of depression for some and mountains of guilt for others. That can seem cruel but, on the other hand, the soul always has the freedom and the possibility to begin these experiences again, in as many lives as it wants, in order to evolve.

At this point I would like to pay homage to Harold Ramis' film "Groundhog Day" that came out in 1993. In this film, a journalist (played by Bill Murray) who is rather "full of it", is reporting on a local festival. He finishes recording then, due to bad weather, he finds himself stuck in the town where he was filming and ends up having to stay over. To his great astonishment, the next day and all subsequent days, he wakes up to exactly the same day, the 2nd of February. He has to continually repeat everything while the other characters he meets are not living the same nightmare as him. For them, and his journalist partner (Andie MacDowell) in particular, this is a unique day and so nobody has any idea what the main character of the film is going through.

I do not know what the scriptwriter intended but the film is a metaphor for reincarnation. The main character starts his day over and over again, as if at the end of every night, a force (his soul) made him start again until he let his heart speak with sincerity in the place of his ego. Thus, each day is an opportunity for him to improve himself, to enrich his knowledge and to think about the meaning of life.

Some days, so completely discouraged by the situation, he commits suicide... Yet he still wakes up the next day fresh and ready to go in the same conditions. He finally understands that escape is not a solution. At that moment, he reaches an important stage in our human condition: acceptance.

Seen as a metaphor for reincarnation, this fable is full of lessons. The ego brings us nothing, except selfishness, while we are never more fulfilled than when we are sincere and accept to recognize our imperfections. It is exactly that ability that frees our character at the end of the film.

If this planet is a school, it exists to teach us about tolerance. We wander off path when simply we have not been able to express the true nature of our hearts. We often react to gestures, words and behavior that we deem inappropriate because of the separation caused by our binary nature. This separation is due to the dichotomy between the left and right sides of our brain. It is the heart that unites them.

So just like the journalist from the film, we keep returning down to Earth until we finally understand that our desire for other people to act according to our aspirations is the cause of all suffering. That does not mean that we have to become yes people; tolerance does not mean breaking our promises or renouncing our values. In fact it is quite the opposite. It means that, as every action is a reaction to something else, we must understand, help and commit to others.

Seeing life in that way is rich in perspective. On some level it's true that it can be disturbing to think that everything, or almost everything, is predetermined. One day a close friend said to me that fortunately our road maps are written in pencil. We are entirely free to transform and modify our script as we evolve. We have even more freedom when it comes to the way in which we experience events. Are we going to dwell on our role of victim, spend our lives lamenting and throw in the towel or are we going to rediscover ourselves and give meaning, even potential, to the opportunities that come our way? Do we know how our trials may have touched the lives of other people by giving them the opportunity to obtain awareness?

If something bothers us then sooner or later someone will come along to reflect it back at us. Life is a mirror that puts us in contact with people who reflect our images back at us; these are people that we have chosen, before incarnation, to meet.

Numerology is a formidable tool for rereading and exploring our script. It uses the prism of numbers to describe the part we are here to play. In the next chapter, we shall discover its properties. Let us keep in mind that every human being is capable of playing all of the characters. It is important not to confine anyone to a single energy. Everything interacts. Everything penetrates everything else. Everything flows. Everything is movement. Everything is here for a reason. There is no such thing as chance.

The values revealed in a chart are like the skeleton of a musical composition in which we can improvise as much as we like within the framework that has been decided in advance for our lives. The numbers watch over us and constantly remind us of the objective that we have set for ourselves. They are here to help us.

To summarize

Just as the genome contains all of a person's genetic material, so does numerology, in the same way, contain the sequence, in numbers, of the aspirations, potential and destiny of that same individual.

CHAPTER III

Properties of numbers

"There are two excesses: excluding reason entirely and admitting reason to the exclusion of everything else."

Pascal (Pensées IV-253)

Numbers accompany us in the duality of our universe. Their energy (unless you prefer to talk of their potential or even their properties) embraces the specter of this duality. The positive or negative attributes of numbers (which will be presented later on) are linked to the ability to emit light. Numbers can just as easily be characterized by an energy that connects and builds as by the opposite. In the latter case the number releases energy that breaks up, disconnects and separates. Even so, it is sometimes necessary to break up, disconnect and separate in order to rebuild. It is important not to confuse the idea of positive and negative with the idea of good and evil which is linked to what we like and dislike and is defined according to the cultural norms in place at a given time.

In the first chapter we saw that the specific choice to use the first 9 numbers dates back to the Egyptians. This was because the nine Egyptian deities represented the whole of creation but also because of the correspondence with the Pythagorean idea of a world constructed to the power of 9, represented by a square made up of 9 smaller squares.

1	4	7
2	5	8
3	6	9

Representation of the enneagram in figures

In this enneagram, the 5 is placed in the centre of 4 pairs of numbers (1-9, 2-8, 3-7, 4-6). The sum of each of the four pairs is 10. 10 was a sacred number for the followers of Pythagoras for whom it represented the expression of the divine macrocosm. It is the sum of the first four numbers (1 + 2 + 3 + 4). The Pythagoreans named it tetractys. Ten is the first double-digit number in the decimal system.

The number 5 also occupies the central position in the Sator square that we are about to discover and study. This square contains remarkable associations between letters and numbers and makes it possible to envisage a partly metaphysical link between the Latin alphabet and numbers.

THE SATOR SQUARE AND LATIN LETTERS

This magic square is made up of 5 Latin words (SATOR, AREPO, TENET, OPERA, ROTAS), each one made up of 5 letters that can be read right to left or left to right. Many squares like this have been discovered. Some examples are accompanied by the letters A for alpha and O for omega. The oldest one to date was created before the eruption of Vesuvius that buried Pompeii in 79 AD.

What was the secret intention of the people who engraved those words? There have been many attempts at interpretation. In addition to the explanations relating to emerging Christianity, the most recent theory expounded by Nicolas Vinel linking the squares to a Jewish tradition must not be ignored. Vinel advances the

Pythagorean origin of these magic squares as revealed in a work by Iamblichus (Syrian writer from the 2nd century AD).

Each person can reach their own conclusions depending on their translation but be aware that TENET and AREPO do not have direct equivalents in current Latin dictionaries. Some people believe that Arepo is the name of the Sower: *"Arepo, the Sower holds the wheels by his means"*. Others believe that this palindrome warns us that *"The Creator holds your destiny in His hands from the moment you are born to the moment you die"*.

SATOR means planter, creator, father and author.

AREPO is a *hapax* i.e. a word that draws its meaning from its sole occurrence in literature. Is it a proper noun, the equivalent of a Gaulish word for plough or, as other people claim, an allusion to the sacred bull of the Egyptians, the god Apis?

TENET is a sort of conjugated form meaning he who holds, directs, etc.

OPERA means action, help, competition, work that produces a result, troubles, service and attention, but also leisure. However, it also contains the backward journey from Omega to Alpha: O through to A. The inscriptions Alpha and Omega that accompany some Sator squares serve as a reminder of this. Remember that all of the words contained in this square can be read from right to left and also from left to right.

ROTAS (from ROTA) means wheels, chariots and the sun disc in the singular.

S	A	T	O	R
A	R	E	P	O
T	E	N	E	T
O	P	E	R	A
R	O	T	A	S

At our level, the interest of this square becomes obvious when we transcribe the words that compose it in numerical values. In order to do this, we will use the alphabetical order of each Latin letter, using the definitive Latin alphabet composed of 26 letters, as the letters that arrived after the Sator square was created, like the W, occupy a higher rank and so will not influence the final result.

	19	28	19	28	19	
19	S1	A1	T2	O6	R9	19
28	A1	R9	E5	P7	O6	28
19	T2	E5	N5	E5	T2	19
28	O6	P7	E5	R9	A1	28
19	R9	O6	T2	A1	S1	19
	19	28	19	28	19	

The Sator square
and its numeric transcription
by fadic addition based on the 26 letters of the current Latin
alphabet

Once again, it is striking to note the central position of the 5 which forms a cross with the other 5's. The sum of the lines and columns is either 19 or 28. Both of these numbers reduce to 10, the Tetractys held in such esteem by the Pythagoreans. The sum of all of the numbers is 113 which reduces as follows $1 + 1 + 3 \rightarrow 5$.

Is it not surprising to see that the order of the Latin letters produces such a symmetry and perfection in their corresponding numbers and that they all correspond to the meaning given to them by the followers of Pythagoras?

It is just as remarkable that, if you use the strict correspondence with the alphabetical order of the 19 letters comprising the archaic alphabet, you will yet again find a beautiful harmony. In that case, A equals 1, E equals 5, N equals 11/2, O = 3, P = 4, R = 6, S = 9 and T = 8.

	25	19	37	19	25	
25	S7	A1	T8	O3	R6	25
19	A1	R6	E5	P4	O3	19
37	T8	E5	N11	E5	T8	37
19	O3	P4	E5	R6	A1	19
25	R6	O3	T8	A1	S7	25
	25	19	37	19	25	

The Sator square
and its numeric transcription
by fadic addition based on the 19 letters of the archaic Latin alphabet

The similarities are incredible. The middle 5 is replaced by the master number 11 (N is the 11th letter of the archaic Latin alphabet). The total 25 that is reached can also be reached using the 26 Latin letters by adding up the diagonal line (top left to bottom right). The total of 37 can also be reached by adding up the other diagonal in the 26-letter version (bottom left to top right).

8 letters are used. The fadic addition of these letters results in 36 in both versions of the alphabet. This signifies that although the ranks of some letters have been changed, a strange alchemy has allowed the numerological values to be conserved. In the archaic Latin alphabet, the 8 letters all have a different value between 1 and 8 and the total 36 (3 + 6) reduces down to 9 (the only value that is not present).

In summary, the Latin alphabet may have evolved but the metaphysical dimension of the square lives on. There is still a lot to say on harmonious metamorphosis. Will one book be enough?

This square invites questions on the hidden dimension of the Latin alphabet and some of these remain unanswered to this day. Despite its known historical origins, what should we think about this perfect unity found both in the 19 archaic letters and in the 26 definitive Latin letters? I do not know of any other Sator Square created using the vocabulary of our current languages. While it is certainly possible to create magic squares, there are none, to my knowledge, that will result in a fadic sum of such perfection and symmetry.

Let us now turn to the origin of Latin letters.

The first known use of alphabetic writing (using 22 letters) was by the Phoenicians in the 11th century BC. This invention was probably the result of a thousand-year long adaptation of Egyptian hieroglyphs. These 22 letters cannot fail to remind us of the symbolism invoked by the number 22 that we will look at later on. The Hebrew alphabet also contains 22 letters.

Our own alphabet later inherited these letters following numerous adaptations and transformations by ancient civilizations. This alphabet is called Latin because it was used by the inhabitants of the region *Latium* in which Rome was the major city.

In its early days, the Latin alphabet contained 19 letters all written in upper case: A, B, C, D, E, H, I, K, L, M, N, O, P, Q, R, S, T, V and X. G appeared around 250/300 BC (this was in fact the reappearance of a letter already used first by the Phoenicians and then the Greeks). The letters F, Y and Z were also reintegrated from the 1st century BC. U and V were interchangeable for a long time before U became a letter in its own right. J was linked with I then gradually became a separate letter. W was a little bit like the odd one out. Of Germanic origin, it was integrated much later into the Latin alphabet, appearing only at the end of the 12th century. It was a shortened version of the double V but the English preferred to refer to it as a double U.

All that said, this Latin alphabet seems well-adapted to conveying numerological information as we saw with the SATOR square which reveals a remarkable harmony behind the rank attributed to each Latin letter. And what about now? Should we retain the value of the 19 archaic Latin letters or the value of the 26 definitive letters? I shall reply to that question with another question. Do you not think that the arrival of a new letter reflects the current state of evolution, in the same way as the discovery of new planets beyond Saturn allowed astrologers to interpret profound mutations in our civilization?

You might ask why we have this order and not another. Maybe the human spirit is generating this force by defining it, in the same way as it did for dates. What if, by doing this, man was only following his intuition?

From a metaphysical point of view, it can be considered that all transformations and additions correspond to the evolution of societies. From the triumphant Roman Empire to its decline, then under the authority of the all-powerful Catholic Church, Latin letters have worked their way into Western Europe by combining with local influences. In a way, the expression "to the letter" suggests the scope of their power.

We will see later how the shape of letters can have a symbolic interpretation which echoes the meaning of the associated number. By its very design, its inherent geometry and its history, A must correspond with 1 and B with 2, etc. Place B before A and you lose the echo.

On a related matter, what about the current dominance of the Latin alphabet? It is at the origin of most European languages. Moreover, it is English, alone amongst all of the Romance languages, that has the most faithfully preserved it by not removing any letters or adding any accents. It is striking to note that English has become the international reference language. It is as though a silent force has been helping it along. Thanks to the English language, Latin letters are found everywhere in the world, even in China and Japan. We even find evidence of their universality in website addresses in which accents cannot be used…

From the Roman Empire to the powerful influence of the British Empire and then to that of the United States, there has been one alphabet which, once it had fully evolved, comprised 26 upper case Roman letters! It could be concluded that this alphabet is gifted with certain properties, that it protects a hidden meaning and that it is sacred…

While the French language also uses these 26 letters, it has evolved to include accented characters. Other European alphabets that have evolved from the Latin alphabet have either added new letters or letters have fallen out of use.

As for the decimal system, it has been widely used since the Antiquity by the Egyptians, the Greeks, the Hebrews, the Latins, the Indians, the Chinese, and so on. Its particularity is that it is divisible by 2 and 5 and there is a strong possibility that using fingers for counting (2 x 5 fingers) also contributed to its development. The 0 appeared later, finally making it possible for large numbers to be written down.

With some rare exceptions, the use of the decimal system seems to be a constant throughout the ages and civilizations. It is as if a higher power had whispered in the ear of human beings that they were only to use this process.

A very similar variation on the decimal system can be found in Mayan civilization. Maya use a base number of 20 when counting. Numbers 1 to 4 are represented by as many dots in a line and 5, 10, 15 and 20 by as many horizontal bars.

The figures used in the current day to write down numbers were imported from India by the Arabs and became widespread in the West from the 15th century onward. With globalization their usage has become universal, even if other notations are still used in some places.

Finally the decade symbolizes unity. The number 10 contains all of the single digit numbers because they can all be added to another single-digit number to make 10 (1 + 9, 2 + 8, etc.). Its written representation symbolizes both what is visible (1) and what is invisible (0). Alternatively, the vertical line of 1 represents the masculine while the circle evokes the feminine.

Nowadays, the decimal system and the Latin alphabet are intricately linked with the phenomenon of globalization. They have become universal references.

This is why the evidence of a relationship between the order of the Latin alphabet and the numeric value of each letter means that, in modern numerology, this correspondence table must be taken into account in readings. This is naturally done for people born in Anglophone or Francophone countries.

Furthermore, over the last few years, the Romance languages have begun to be standardized. Since 1990, Portugal has reintegrated three letters into its alphabet so that it now has the 26 letters found in the English and French alphabets. This is strange, don't you think?

However, some alphabets like Spanish or German have additional letters with their own rank which then modifies the value of other letters. The letter/number correspondence is also different in alphabets that do not use all 26 letters such as Italian and Dutch. In that case, should the specific order of each official alphabet be taken into account? Probably. That study would require a thorough examination which takes into account the Maia method that we will look at later.

On the other hand, the 26 Latin letters contained in the English alphabet seem to be in a stable, if not necessarily definitive, phase of its evolution. This assessment is confirmed by the worldwide use of that alphabet.

1	2	3	4	5	6	7	8	9
A	B	C	D	E	F	G	H	I
J	K (11)	L	M	N	O	P	Q	R
S	T	U	V (22)	W	X	Y	Z	

Value of each of the 26 letters of the English alphabet

Before beginning to explore the hidden meaning of numbers, let us remind ourselves that the following definitions have been created using the mathematical properties, representations and symbolism of each number. Thus the 5 tends to be self-centered because it is at the centre of the enneagram. Furthermore, arithmancy says that it is at the centre of two worlds. The Divine symbolized by the four numbers before 5 and the Earthly symbolized by the four numbers after 5.

0

The 0 represents both the invisible and everything. It bestows power or weakness upon individuals. It symbolizes hidden gifts and unexploited potential.

When it is present in a compound number (like for the life path), it intensifies strength, intuition, sensibility and expression in accordance with its accompanying number (10, 20, etc.). The individual usually reaps the benefits of this potential when he reaches maturity (around the age of 40).

1
I AM

1 represents the beginning, the affirmation of self through action and body. It corresponds to the astrological signs Aries and Leo. It is the very principle of individuality. It must not be confused with Unity which is better represented by the number 10, sum of the 4 principal creators of matter (1 + 2 + 3 + 4) that we will look at later.

The number 1 is Yang, the sun, the sky, the masculine archetype, the creator and the father. It is the beginning. It is self-sufficient and can only be divided by itself. It is its own roots and powers. 1 to the power of x always equals 1. It symbolizes the being and the ego. It emanates light. It is both the giver and the destroyer of life. The square power of numbers created entirely from several 1's produces a strange harmony. The whole number made up of nine 1's, i.e. 111,111,111, to the power of 2, produces a whole number with 17 particularly astonishing digits: 12,345,678,987,654,321.

On the positive side, Ones are creative, imaginative, bold, confident, radiant, self-educated, independent, enthusiastic, determined, lively, strong, they are full of vitality and love of life, generous, capable of self-healing, original, innovative, pioneering, sexual, courageous, ambitious, combative and competitive whilst also being organized.

On the negative side, they are individualistic, egotistical, narcissistic, boastful, proud, arrogant, touchy, wrathful, aggressive, dominating, violating, stubborn, quick-tempered, infertile, oversensitive, paranoid, impatient, inhibited, obsessive and schizophrenic.

One teaches us to have confidence in ourselves and to develop our creative sides. It makes us understand that skills are acquired by trying and fighting and that we must not be discouraged if the results are not immediate.

2
I AM NOT ALONE

2 expresses association, cooperation and balance but also separation. As soon as 1 appears then 2 can exist. The individuality of 1 is only complete when another 1 appears and reflects its identity back to it. In order to exist, the individual needs the other, either through cloning or mating. For man, the promise of a separate individual cannot be upheld without a specific link to the mother during gestation. There is no individualization without the presence of the other. I exist because the other also exists. The other allows me to differentiate. It can all be resumed in the following paradox: which came first, the chicken or the egg? Answer: neither one! The 1 and the 2 are intimately linked. They were created simultaneously.

Thus the 2 translates the duality we need to differentiate between beings, states and objects. Without opposites any basic judgment is void of meaning. Even and odd, presence or absence, hot or cold, light and dark, and so on. This simple binary distinction is sufficient for us when programming all of the universe's information into our daily log. All numerical recording can be resumed in the expression of 2 successive states (1 or 0).

However, this 2 is paradoxical and ambivalent. 2 is not enough to count the sides of a simple geometric figure (2 dimensions) but it can be used to count the number of distinct surfaces of a cone (3 dimensions).

It refers to the astrological signs Cancer and Libra. The pair 1 & 2 is intimately linked to the Aries/Ascendant axis (the I) & Libra/Descendant axis (the other). In the same way, all the evidence suggests that 1 and 2 echo the pair Leo (Sun – masculine trait) & Cancer (Moon – feminine trait).

2 is Yin, the Earth, the moon, the feminine archetype and the mother. It also refers to the subconscious, desires, emotional memory, childhood and the masses.

On the positive side twos are strong, fertile, intuitive, resistant, perseverant, balanced, delicate, sensitive, harmonious, cooperative, understanding, considerate, adaptable, sociable, loyal, generous, friendly, popular, diplomatic, devoted and altruistic.

47

On the negative side, they risk becoming a slave, incapable of saying "no" or fixing their limits, negligent, devoid of tact, impressionable, lost in their dreams and illusions, self-sacrificing, dependant, stubborn, egotistical, unfair, merciless, irritable, frigid and powerless.

Two teaches us to work with others (without being a slave) and to be aware of our responsibilities. It teaches us that we must leave space for the other. It shows us that we are filled with contradictory feelings and values, and that we must integrate this duality into our daily lives.

3
I CREATE

3 logically appears with 1 and 2. It is the space separating two distinct entities and the path that must be followed if we wish to enter into contact with the other in order to become acquainted or even pair up.

Therefore the 3 represents communication, relationships, expression, expansion, extension, transmission and creation resulting from the addition of the first distinct numbers 1 (the father) and 2 (the mother) = 3 (the child). This illustration of the trinity is found in divine representations within numerous religions.

The 3 allows us access to an infinite variety of shades using the primary colors red, blue and green. It is associated with the fundamental plans of the incarnate being combining physical, emotional and intellectual aspects. It refers to a new state distinct from the two conflicting aspects found in the positive, negative and neutral forces. It is the 3 fundamental bodily humors called *doshas* belonging to Indian medicine (*Vata, Pitta* and *Kapha*). It allows us to situate ourselves on a line pointing in two opposite directions. Past, present and future. It is the first geometrical surface: the triangle with its three sides.

In astrology, it is naturally associated with the planet Mercury. Mercury is the fast-moving messenger of the Gods. This task definitively links 1 and 2. The child by incarnating is himself a messenger from the beyond. Mercury is the ruler of Gemini and Virgo and so 3 corresponds to those two signs.

The 3 also signifies intellectual skills (analysis, method and organization), studies, siblings, cousins and adolescence. Its double nature (it oscillates between 1 and 2) gives the impression of inconsistency which may be interpreted as a U-turn or betrayal.

On the positive side threes are expressive, cerebral, charming, sociable, capable of healing through their words, good speakers, interactive, constructive, talented, optimistic, enthusiastic, charismatic, strong-minded, determined, instinctive, spontaneous, joyful, affectionate, light, funny, young and full of sprit and voluble.

On the negative side they can be quarrelsome, confused, prone to overreact, dependant, introverted, dilettante, scattered, superficial, featherbrained, gullible, plaintive, misunderstood, rarely inclined to express emotions, hiding them behind a criticism or mocking, even cynical, front, obsessive, depressed, depressive, polemic and opportunistic.

Three teaches us to act naturally and spontaneously while retaining a rational and organized mind and without taking offence too easily. It is the promise of the discovery of a feeling of youth and freshness, even purity.

4
I AM SETTLED

The 4 is present in all of the first three numbers at the same time. It is the time needed to cross the space (3) separating two distinct entities (1 and 1). While the 3 gave us the means to describe a surface, the 4 represents the first polyhedron: the 4-sided tetrahedron.

It is the first number to not be a prime number. It is also the first single-digit number (apart from 1) to result from a square power: 2 to the power of 2. This makes it a square number.

Therefore the 4 represents time and materialization.

It is intimately linked with matter and space: the 4 cardinal directions, the 4-dimensional universe including time, the 4 nitrogen bases of DNA, the four elements Earth, Water, Air and Fire, the 4 types of matter (solid, liquid, gas and liquid crystal), the 4 sectors created by two axes (latitude and longitude or in astrology

Ascendant/Descendant and Medium Coeli and Imum Coeli for example). That is the fixed aspect of 4.

However, 4 is also associated with cycles. The four phases of the lunar cycle, the four seasons, the four phases of a sinusoidal curve (positive increasing, positive decreasing, negative increasing and negative decreasing), and so on. In this respect it represents the notion of non-random progression because it moves forward in a precise direction and order (autumn does not follow winter and water does not transform from gaseous matter into solid matter without passing through a liquid state). Therefore you cannot ask 4 to change the established order of things.

The tempo of the metronome represents it well. It has 4 stages. The needle swings to the left, returns from the left, swings to the right, returns from the right. The movement of 4 is inevitable, predictable and reassuring. It implies a wait, a necessary period before the next stage begins.

It always contains the idea of a return to the beginning, even though the time that it represents seems to always travel in the same direction. Seasons succeed each other in a cyclic motion. A new summer may only begin once the previous summer is over. This solid progression is reassuring. Its markers and reference points are certainties in a world that becomes so uncertain once the 5 arrives. Finally, if I dare say it, is the paradox of this "cyclic" square not in fact that of squaring the circle?

4 symbolizes the phase in which the individual finds his bearings, makes himself secure and carefully settles into his environment. It reflects our fears, accepted educational methods, the need to feel secure, our limits, waiting time and our ability to build. It is the expression of the signs Taurus and Capricorn which are earthly and temporal signs.

On the positive side, fours are practical, logical, methodical, pragmatic, patient, hard-working, stable, committed, considerate, consistent, persevering, stubborn, enduring, solid, authentic, established, loyal, faithful to their roots, their values and authority, concrete, realistic, concentrated, disciplined, honest, profound, accomplished, thrifty and constant.

On the negative side, they can be nostalgic, old-fashioned, conservative, lazy, inhibited, frustrated, fatalistic, obstinate, rigid, untrusting, spiteful, closed-minded, devoid of imagination, stubborn, can act in bad faith and be ruthlessly ambitious, obstinate and blinded.

Four teaches us to put our trust in time. Everything comes to those who progress methodically.

THE PYTHAGOREAN LEGACY
THE WORLD IN 4

Finally, with the 4, we have everything necessary for the creation of a world:

- individualisation (the 1)
- the separation of All and/or the other (the 2)
- the space separating 2 entities (the 3)
- the time needed to evolve in that space (the 4)

The sum total equals the Unity (1 + 2 + 3 + 4 = 10). However, behind this 10 that is so dear to the Pythagoreans, there is also the 5 (the man) because in a number system with a base of 5 (i.e. 4 one-digit numbers and 0 used to write all numbers: 0, 1, 2, 3, 4), 10 is the way of writing 5 i.e. 1 set of 5 and 0 unity. This way of thinking is also used by the Mayans whose numbering system distinguishes between the first four numbers symbolized by the corresponding number of dots and the 5 symbolized by a horizontal line.

Understanding this key shows us why the decimal system is universal by its very nature. We have just seen how beyond 0 (which is not created), 4 numbers are needed to create the world. Their vibrations can be combined to create all other single-digit numbers. We must bear these associations in mind when considering the symbolism and relationship between numbers:

6 associations of 2 different numbers are possible
Creation of 3 numbers: 5, 6 and 7

$$1 + 2 = 3$$
$$1 + 3 = 4$$
$$1 + 4 = 5$$
$$2 + 3 = 5$$
$$2 + 4 = 6$$
$$3 + 4 = 7$$

Sum of all possible associations of 2 distinct numbers
$$3 + 4 + 5 + 5 + 6 + 7 = 30$$

4 associations of 3 different numbers are possible
Creation of 2 numbers: 8 and 9
$$1 + 2 + 3 = 6$$
$$1 + 2 + 4 = 7$$
$$1 + 3 + 4 = 8$$
$$2 + 3 + 4 = 9$$
Sum of all possible associations of 3 distinct numbers
$$6 + 7 + 8 + 9 = 30$$

And the association of the 4 numbers of creation
$$1 + 2 + 3 + 4 = 10$$
No other number can be created
after the first 4 numbers.

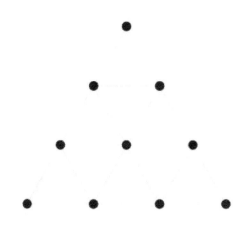

The symbolic Pythagorean Tetractys figure

5
I DISCOVER
1 + 4 or 2 + 3

First different number to appear by combining the vibrations of the 4 created numbers. On the axis 1-2-3-4, it is the sum of the extremes (1 + 4) or the middle numbers (2 + 3).

Now it is the turn of man! The 5 represents the totality of the means given to the soul to achieve its incarnation experiment in this world based on 4 (individualization, duality, space and time).

As we have seen, man lives out his destiny in this material and temporal world (4), by expressing in his own way (3), through his own means (1), the deepest aspirations of his soul (2).

Man has the free will to discover, explore, and always push, the limits. Independent and free, beings experience this universe through the feelings and tools at their disposal: 5 senses, 5 fingers on each hand and sexuality.

The freedom of 5. It is a prime number and so neither the result of a fadic sum (adding the previous successive numbers from 1) nor a square number. It is the centre of the enneagram. The pentagonal numbers 5, 12, 22, etc. (number of dots needed to create a pentagon in which each side has the same number of dots) when reduced, create all of the numbers between 1 and 9. Therefore 5 has access to the entire possible universe.

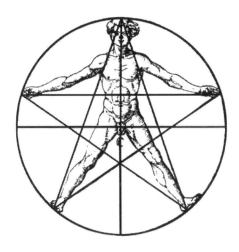

Sexuality (mating) is symbolized by 5. The addition of 1 (odd number) and 4 (even number) or of 2 (even) and 3 (odd) make 5. The human being's sexual organ is at the centre of the circle inside the pentagram in which the arms, legs and head occupy the 5 points of the star.

5 represents involuntary events, which are nonetheless consequences of man's actions on his environment. It represents profound experiences, changes in the course of existence and awareness.

5 is in the sign of Virgo.

On the positive side fives are free, interested, impassioned, available, focused, like experimenting, independent, in love with the world, high-spirited, agile, mobile, rapid, spontaneous, curious, observant, optimistic, kind, good humored, a little bit teasing, sensual, active, devoted, enthusiastic, pioneering, adventurous, astute, bold, imaginative, innovating, perceptive, intuitive and clairvoyant.

On the negative side, they can be self-centered, complacent, risky, agitated, scattered, slippery, dependent or the opposite i.e. detached from everything, easy, volatile, irresponsible, bitter, undisciplined, tense, impetuous, reckless, agitated, reactive, impatient, devil-may-care, hedonist, excessive, mocking, intolerant, chameleons and opportunistic.

Five shows us that freedom, knowledge and consciousness are born of our own experiences. Nothing is more real for five than experimentation on earth. More than all the other numbers, fives know that independence and freedom of action and spirit are the essential and indispensable values in the game of life.

The Mind had fun with the 5 and used it to explore different facets. 4 single-digit numbers preceded it and it is followed by 4 other single-digit numbers which invite man to return to his source. However, it is more difficult to find the link between the numbers from 6 to 9 than it was with the numbers from 1 to 4. Created from associations between the preceding numbers, 6, 7, 8 and 9 share certain properties with them. Their attributes are also revealed when people associate them with cultural elements.

6
I ACCEPT MYSELF
1 + 2 + 3 or 2 + 4

Notice that, just like the 5, the 6 does not exclude any of the 4 creation numbers (1 + 2 + 3 or 2 + 4) but that both of those combinations depend on the 2. From this we glean a numerological rule: the 6 always needs the other to express itself.

The preceding exploration of the 5 taught us to be aware of the consequences of our actions. Now, man must enjoy his existence while respecting the freedom of others. He must create rules of play and be aware of his responsibilities. He understands that the perfection of this world consists of maintaining a permanent balance in order to survive. That every effect has a cause. That every action has a reaction.

6 is the first perfect number according to the Pythagorean school because, according to their definition, it is the sum and result of its divisors (itself excluded) so 1 + 2 + 3 = 6 and 1 x 2 x 3 = 6. In the book of Genesis, and also in the Qur'an, it is written that this world was created in 6 days. Does that mean that 6 symbolizes the ideal number of days we need regardless of the earthly length of that "day"?

An individual displaying a 6 undertakes to achieve perfection and become irreproachable. He tends to want to harmonize his life, his relationships and his home. The family, in existence from the birth of the first child, is represented by 6. The fadic addition of 3 gives 6 (1 + 2 + 3). It reflects choice, hesitations and promises. The balance that is sought is present in the geometrical shape of the hexagram in which two equilateral triangles perfectly fitted over each other symbolize the harmony between mind and matter (Star of David). 6 is associated with Virgo, the sixth astrological sign, as well as Libra (justice/the other) because 6 needs the other (2).

On the positive side, sixes are fair, equitable, conciliatory, measured, balanced, gentle, calm, pacifists, aesthetes, principled, pure, incisive, devoted, perfectionists, mediators, protectors, responsible, cultivated, rational, logical, sympathetic, sociable, friendly, charming, tender, loving and attentive.

On the negative side, they can be detail obsessed, selective, demanding, compulsive, ambivalent, unsatisfied, submissive, victimized, self-conscious, cold, sad, disenchanted, disillusioned, hesitant, skeptical, bitter, critical, judgmental, worried and easily manipulated in relation to their projected image, dependant and irresponsible.

Six teaches man to accept differences, to seek reconciliation and to preserve the harmony of this world.

7
I MATURE
3 + 4 or 1 + 2 + 4

7 is a link to the Mind. Like 5 and 6, it does not exclude any of the 4 creation numbers (3 + 4 or 1 + 2 + 4) and always needs the 4.

The number 7 is associated with the Gods. It reports to us knowledge that comes from the stars. There are 7 Sumerian Gods at the origin of our world, 7 Pleiades sisters of which Maia is the eldest, 7 visible "errant" stars (Sun, Moon, Mercury, Venus, Mars, Jupiter and Saturn). Seven reflects time (the 7 days of the week). It represents doors and passageways. With the exception of the eyes, the human body has 7 orifices which allow direct access to the outside. It provides access to more subtle dimensions (the 7 chakras) and feeds the soul through painting and music: the 7 fundamental colors of the rainbow and the 7 notes in a musical scale.

While 4 was the only number to not be prime in the series 1, 2, 3 and 4, 7 is the only one to be prime in the series 6 to 9. These opposing singular qualities represent the spirit of 11 (4 + 7).

Like 5, 7 is independent. It is not the result of a fadic sum and it is not a square number. It is the only single-digit number that is not a divisor of the circle. However, unlike 5, its exploration is interior. Then again, there is a connection between the two. Does the sexuality of 5 not allow us to reach the seventh heaven?

7 signifies reflection, hindsight, awareness, faith and open-mindedness when faced with differences, ruptures and internal transformations. The individual can now consider the impact of his actions and access a higher state of consciousness. Do we not say

that when a child reaches the age of 7 he has entered the age of reason?

The King of the Gods, Zeus, is the ruler of Sagittarius (sign associated with 7).

On the positive side, sevens are kind, generous, open, spiritual, wise, profound, believe in healthy living, respect morals and ethics, remain faithful to their values and promises, cultivated, full of faith and passion, open, autonomous, independent, researchers, perceptive, original, intuitive, inspired, compassionate, transcendent and have tasks to complete.

On the negative side, they can be oversensitive and susceptible and therefore proud, agitated, anxious, sarcastic, overly critical, rebellious, confused, impressionable, frustrated, misunderstood, betrayed, victimized, solitary, introverted, sullen, polarized, resigned, cold, disobedient, mythomaniac, antisocial, cynical, can suffer from an inferiority complex, detached and disconnected.

Seven teaches us to live and accept our true nature, to respect our commitments and to bring together body and Mind. It teaches us how to trust and listen to ourselves and to have self-esteem in order to find the inner faith that we can use to enlighten others.

8
I CONTROL
1 + 3 + 4

This is the first of the numbers to exclude one of the first 4 numbers (the 2) in its creation. Therefore it is free from duality and, in some way, from the other. It is the number of incarnation. While individualization (1) needs 2 in order to exist, 8 is the direct incarnation of the soul.

8 represents transformation, development of individual powers and the individual's control over the rules of life which allow him to create abundance. It is the only single-digit number to be the result of a number raised to the power of three (2 cubed). It reflects two fundamental aspects of life, sex (5) and the birth, death, rebirth cycle (3, the child created through sexuality), 5 + 3 = 8. It is

the number of karma. It reflects all forms of death, i.e. transformations that allow us to abandon one situation in order to access a new stage of evolution.

The famous Chinese book of changes, I Ching, alone contains all of the force of 8. We have seen that 8 is 2 cubed. I Ching uses 2 replies, Yes (unbroken line) and No (broken line), combined in groups of three, which results in 8 possibilities called trigrams revealing the on-going changes undergone by the world so that it would be maintained. These trigrams are grouped into pairs, giving 64 combinations $(6 + 4 \rightarrow 10 \rightarrow 1 + 0 \rightarrow 1)$.

8 is also a double 4 (4 x 2 or 4 + 4). This aspect is everywhere, e.g. the cardinal directions: North-West, North-East, South-East, and South-West. In the same way, dividing a plane with two axes creates 4 zones and dividing a volume with three axes (including depth), creates 8 parts.

The octagon is the geometrical shape associated with 8 and it comprises of one square laid on top of the other; both squares share a centre point and their corners are 45° apart.

From this point of view, it is important to consider affinities shared by different numbers. 8 is linked with 2, 3 and 4.

From the symbol representing infinity (an 8 on its side) to the four loops of the two facing snakes wrapped around Hermes' caduceus, the symbols associated with 8 represent the idea of a cycle, eternity, strength and duality. Like an echo, 8 has always inspired man to create paths to free himself from an endless cycle, e.g. the 8 limbs of yoga, the 8 beatitudes of Christ, the 8 principles of I Ching, the noble eight-fold path of the Buddhists, and so on.

Finally, 8 is naturally the eighth astrological sign, Scorpio.

On the positive side, eights are instinctive, lucky, ambitious, determined, persistent, confident, famous, looking for respect, influential, determined, enterprising, powerful, courageous, efficient, practical, realistic, capable of making choices, calculating (in the good sense of the word), leaders, Masters of the occult, assertive, prosperous, generous, erotic, brave, philanthropic, sincere, easy to please and good children.

On the negative side, they can be blasé, inaccessible, impervious to human nature and/or too materialistic, money-grabbing, lying, manipulating, unsatisfied, grudge-holders, difficult, uncompromising, unfaithful, intimidating, tough, hard, irritable, authoritarian, aggressive, either dominating or submissive, thoughtless, disbelieving, easily influenced, obsessed with a fear of failure, insatiable, sadistic, morbid and self-destructive.

Eight teaches us to explore and use all of our abilities in a bid to control the force of these two polarities thereby achieving success and generating abundance.

9
I AM ONE WITH THE OTHERS
2 + 3 + 4

While 8 does not need the other, 9 is free from the ego. It does not need 1 to be created.

9 signifies the accomplishment of the self, transcendence through knowledge, integrity, ideals, wisdom, faith and universal love. It is the expression of the Egyptian enneagram, the 4 couples face to face above which One ensures protection. It is the last of the single-digit numbers before we reach the decade which symbolizes the return to unity.

The 9 does not influence the final result of a fadic reduction. Added to any number, the sum can be reduced back to that same number. $8 + 9 = 17 \rightarrow 1 + 7 = 8$. With the exception of 1, 9 is the second square number after 4 (3 to the power of 2). It also has other remarkable properties. The difference between two numbers comprised of the same figures but inversed, e.g. 14 and 41, is always a multiple of $9(41 - 14 = 27 \rightarrow 2 + 7 = 9)$. The fadic reduction of a multiple of 9 is always 9. It is as if, when all is said and done, any number stamped with a 9 cannot be reduced to any other number. This infers completeness, the end of something. It is like the final square in the game of cosmic hopscotch. It is a return to the skies but also a birth following 9 months of gestation.

In this cycle that is reaching its end, man has the possibility of envisaging new projects, or dreaming of future enterprises. 9 connects us to our imagination and our psyche, and finally to our soul, because it is the soul that controls our future.

9, which is the final single-digit number, corresponds both to the last sign of the zodiac, Pisces, but also to the ninth sign, Sagittarius.

On the positive side, nines are idealistic, sensitive, inspired, intuitive, accomplished, exemplary, ethical, honest, profound, sincere, open, empathic, philosophical, mystical, wise, compassionate, generous, poetic, gifted in arts, healing, altruistic, luminous, harvesters and guides.

On the negative side, they can be unrealistic, emotional, confused, nonchalant, disorganized, disturbed, inconsistent, gullible, superstitious, pessimistic, easily influenced, susceptible, exploitable, aimless, slippery, limited, quarrelsome, easily led astray, indiscrete, intolerant, "parochial", drug-users and schizophrenic.

Nine teaches us to join our words and actions. It helps us to show integrity by talking sincerely from the heart. Linked to the astrological signs Pisces and Sagittarius, 9 can just as easily be a mystic (Pisces) as a guru (Sagittarius) depending on the other aspects of the chart and the sub-number behind it.

THE MASTER NUMBERS

After the 9 single-digit numbers, a particular importance is given to numbers comprised of two identical figures, for example 11, 22 and 33. These numbers are called master numbers. They doubly express their trait.

4 numbers for creation: 1, 2, 3 and 4.

3 master numbers: 11 (1 decade + 1), 22 (2 decades + 2) and 33 (3 decades + 3). The master numbers are associated with the mind and the Creation. The 4 represents the body and so 44 is not a master number.

11 and 22 should never be reduced when they appear in the calculation of a core number. But the real reason is that you cannot add the same principle. Yang (1) + Yang (1) = Yang (1). Yin (2) + Yin (2) = Yin (2), while 3 is the result of their addition (Yang + Ying). In practice, unlike 33, 11 and 22 can be directly found both in letters (K and V) and in a date of birth (11th or 22nd day of the month and November, the 11th month).

The master numbers 11 and 22 should never be reduced in any numerological calculations for another simple reason, i.e. the difference between each Master Number and its fadic sum is always a multiple of 9. That is why any calculations involving a master number will have the same result whether or not the master numbers have been reduced. On the other hand, and this is key, the sub-number changes and so changes the nuance of the single-digit number.

$$11 \rightarrow 1 + 1 = 2 \text{ with } 11 - 2 = 9$$
$$22 \rightarrow 2 + 2 = 4 \text{ with } 22 - 4 = 18 \ (2 \times 9)$$

11
I RISE

11 is special because its most remarkable property is that it is both the first number after the decade and also the first two-digit number written using the same number twice. 11 seems to be a troublemaker adding an extra dimension to the unity represented by 10. Suspect, don't you think?

In any event, it doesn't seem to find grace either in the eyes of Saint Augustine for whom "*the number 11 is the armory of sin*" or later on for Dr René Allendy who found it unfavorable "*because it puts the cosmic Whole in the presence of an element that can only be disturbing*".

This is obviously only one side of the story. No number is inherently good or bad. It simply adjusts itself in accordance to the formulated intention. With 11, we are definitely in the presence of a new element which is intending above all to reveal the existence of something extra, another dimension. It is certain that another truth exists outside of the established order. This rebellious side, this loose cannon (partly due to the fact that it has to confront the other) is, in a way, excluded from the circle. Furthermore, 11 is not a divisor of the circle.

The assertion of this originality is not without consequence. It represents the gift of being able to free yourself and the inspiration needed to foretell revelations and thereby shake up the established truths.

11 helps us to develop holistic consciousness and connect different levels of reality. It is difficult to imagine that we can do this without risking harsh changes, internal struggles or

transgressions. Those potential confusions are due to 11's ambivalence when the sub-number 20 is also present in results.[1]

It is difficult for 11s to harmonize their inspiration and creative spiritual impulses (reflecting Virgo, the 11th sign of the Zodiac) with their powerful instincts. 11 is a double 1, a double "I", an Aries/Leo. What a packed program it has!

On the positive side, 11s are strongly intuitive, creative, full of initiative, aware of their capacities, stimulated, curious, open, forging their own paths, courageous, strong, gifted in arts and esoteric sciences, friendly, devoted, altruistic, revealing, healers of the soul, inspired, modern, visionary and they explore and report on new spiritual paths.

On the negative side, they can be tense, torn between two extremes, excessive, irritable, megalomaniac, paranoid, hot-tempered, vindictive, proud, jealous, contemptuous, hung-up on various issues or have a superiority complex, egocentric, inflammatory, eccentric, embittered, neurotic, indecisive and oversensitive.

Eleven teaches us to free ourselves from the restrictive framework of our lives, to take a step towards future potential and to not always accept the established norm. It shows us that we have the power and energy necessary to make advances and create something in accordance with our deepest feelings. It also teaches us to stop procrastinating, to not underestimate our abilities and to be doubly confident in ourselves

22
I SHINE

22 is a number extremely marked by differentiation (20 + 2). It brings twice the ability to add something different to the structure (2 x 11) with a desire to turn dreams into reality. In a sense it is an accomplished number, resulting from the addition of the decade and 12 (Yang and Yin).

---

[1] See Chapter V, the calculation of the Life Path.

It encompasses the world and creates it in its totality. The Phoenician alphabet originally comprised 22 letters. The Tarot deck contains 22 major arcana. 22 is the culmination of the magnum opus. It is the tangible manifestation, if not the perfect finished product, of the being's potential incarnated in the body. The 360° of the circle has 22 divisors.

While 11 can give rise to trouble with its revolutionary ideas (11 is the fadic sum of France), 22 builds. 22 is a link between tradition and modernity and a bridge between the past and the future. It reflects the interior dimension and the necessity of accepting and transcending our limits and the things that we have repressed in order to build on new foundations without renouncing the old ones. Unlike 11, 22 finds itself torn between preserving/respecting that which already exists and demolishing everything in order to start again.

It controls the 4 numbers of the body (1 + 2 + 3 + 4). This unity represented by the 10 is reflected in the tenth astrological sign to which it refers: Capricorn.

On the positive side, 22's are physical, solid, resistant, persevering, concrete, gifted with extraordinary powers, able to benefit from empirical knowledge, good leaders, hard-working, full of ideas, builders, visionaries, wise, enlightened founders and explorers… There is genius here to be awakened.

On the negative side, they can be proud, hard, unfair, blinded, anguished, unstable, distressed, deaf to advice, inhibited, cold, distant, sexually excited, obsessed, impotent, destructive and have lots of hang ups.

22 teaches us to establish solid foundations in our life and to respect that which is established while looking to change that which does not work. It teaches us that time is our ally, that life's challenges and difficulties are not our enemies but springboards for us to evolve.

33
I GUIDE

33 represents the spirituality in the heart of human beings. The individual is intuitive, creative and wise, all at the same time. This energy represents emerging spirituality; it is not present in the alphabet because there is no letter in the 33rd position.

On the positive side, 33's are joyful, radiant, generous, healers, guides, instinctive, selfless, team-spirited and they are able to appreciate and manage all sorts of situations.

On the negative side, they can be utopian, crafty, liars, can crumble under the weight of their responsibilities, excessively self-critical, can play the victim and be self-sacrificing.

SUB-NUMBERS

All numbers that are not the first 9 single-digit numbers, the 0 or the master numbers are sub-numbers. They all related by fadic addition to a single-digit number. The sub-number 25 is related to 7 because $25 \rightarrow 2 + 5 = 7$.

The interpretation of a sub-number is the synthesis of the properties of the combinations. The light and dark aspects of each number either reinforce or oppose each other. The energies combine from left to right and from the past to the future. In 18, for example, the 1 exerts its influence first and masks the effects of 8 if the energy is not balanced. Once you are familiar with the properties of the numbers 0 to 9, it is relatively easy to determine the force of other numbers. The interpretation of sub-numbers is discussed later, as well as the aspects formed by the combination of numbers.

THE 26 LETTERS OF THE LATIN ALPHABET

When the Roman alphabet disappeared, it bequeathed us its letters. Each European alphabet that inherited these letters managed and modified its legacy in accordance with the evolution of the people using it. While, like man, languages are mortal, the letter is not. It is capable of adapting, metamorphosing and reproducing.

The Archaic Latin alphabet only originally contained 19 letters. As this alphabet evolved it reintegrated 7 letters, some of which had already existed in Greek or in Hebrew, while others were the result of the mutation of existing letters, changing *de facto* the numerical value of the following letters. The modification of their rank led to a change in their values; this change in significance was the natural consequence of the evolution of the collective consciousness.

Fundamentally, the study of a letter's form is only concerned with its upper case version which was the only form originally used by the Romans. The lower case form appeared later in the evolution of the alphabet. However, the upper case form also changed over the centuries, as did the value of certain letters.

Echoing the collective consciousness, the letter contains the energy of the number that corresponds to its rank. This rank changed over time. The geometric form of a letter contains the properties that can change the expression of its value.

The shape of the letter speaks to us; let us listen to what it has to say. Is it created using vertical, horizontal or diagonal lines? In which direction are the lines pointing? Towards the top (the sky), the bottom (the earth), from right to left (the past) or, the opposite, from left to right (the future)? Does it contain acute, obtuse or right angles? What is the balance between straight lines (sending) and curves (receiving)?

A
1
Creative – Mental

Alpha before omega: "The beginning".

This first letter immediately tells us about our origins. It also indicates the only direction in which we are going, i.e. to the sky, up there, with the Father. Is it for this reason that the Greeks rotated this letter, which originally represented the ox (*aleph*) in the Phoenician alphabet.

The legs of the A show us the importance of having a firm grip on the ground. Not only are they firmly entrenched but, what's more, its two legs are joined. The A invites us to use this horizontal bar to lift ourselves up.

In is unarguably worth 1. It is the 1st Greek letter (*alpha*) and the 1st Semitic letter (*aleph*). It is 1st letter of both the archaic and current Latin alphabets.

General meaning: Creation. Possibility of a new departure. A well thought through initiative. Reasoned action. Balance. Solidity. Trust. Progression. Elevation.

B
2
Dual – Emotional

Just as the first letter was masculine, salient, virile and pointing upwards, this second letter is concerned with the feminine. Bulging, full and rounded, with its upright back, it represents the breast, maternal stomach and also the lips. It is welcoming and motherly but also precariously balanced… It needs the other and in return it has a lot to offer.

At its origin, in a different form, it represented the house for the Phoenicians; the Greek *Beta* is the transformed version of it.

It is unarguably worth 2. It is the second Greek letter (*beta*), the second Semitic letter (*beth*) and the second letter of the Latin alphabets (archaic and current).

General meaning: Gentleness, protection and conciliation. Link with the mother, nourishment, gestation, the home and house.

C
3
Balanced – Intuitional

From its origins to the current day, one element has characterized the form of the third letter: openness.

Its archaic form, similar to the < sign, suggests an open mouth. It symbolizes the need to communicate. Its current form also hints at the possibility of bridging the gap between its two extremities. This incomplete space suggests a hole, like emptiness or an incomplete form; by analogy, it reflects the expression of 3, the number which, in its current form, is like two Cs turned over and stacked one on top of the other.

The letter C originates in the third Phoenician letter which represents the neck of a camel. Over time, it was considerably changed by the Greeks and the Etruscans.

There is little doubt that it is worth 3. It is the third Greek letter (*gamma*), the third Semitic letter (*gimmel*) as well as the third letter of the Latin alphabet (archaic and current). It was sometimes confused with the G.

General meaning: Open-mindedness and direction to be taken and reached. Movement. Travel. Projection. Expression. Communication. Progression. Sharing.

D
4
Balanced – Physical

Originates in the Phoenician letter *Daleth*.

The expression of its different meanings reflects earthly nourishment (breast, fish, and so on), just as its shape suggests a rounded stomach.

It is undoubtedly worth 4. It is the fourth Greek letter (*delta*), the fourth Semitic letter (*daleth*), as well as the fourth letter of the Latin alphabets (archaic and current).

General meaning: Indicates the need to respect the constraints and demands of the physical body and to take earthly realities into account. Nutrition. Food. Structural and archetypal memory.

E
5
Creative – Physical

Fifth letter representing the *Epsilon* of the Greek alphabet that was carved into the pediment of the Delphi temple.

Its definitive form dates back to the sixth century BC; it was bequeathed to us by the Greeks who had themselves borrowed it from the Phoenicians. The latter's representation of the E was of a man holding his arms open to the sky. By turning this letter 90° to the left, does it become a representation of a being imploring the Gods? What kind of information does he hope to receive from the cosmos?

There is no doubt that it is worth 5. It is the fifth Greek letter (*epsilon*), the fifth Semitic letter (*he*), as well as the fifth letter of the Latin alphabets (archaic and current).

General meaning: Thirst for knowledge and self-discovery. Pushing one's limits. Projecting into the future. Freedom from archetypes. Exploration. Openness. Avant-garde and futuristic mentality.

F
6
Dual – Intuitional

It integrated the Latin alphabet in the first century BC, but it actually originated in an earlier time.

The Phoenician *waw* represented hooks used in navigation, but also evoked a phallus... Its current angular form comprised of lines is very masculine.

When it was integrated into the alphabet, in the 6th rank, the value of the subsequent letters shifted. However, its Latin meaning implies the idea of a link, the "and", defined as a coordinating conjunction in English. This letter is worth 6 which expresses this need to link, reconcile and assemble.

At the beginning, the Phoenician letter *waw* gave Greek the consonant *digamma* which was worth 6. *Digamma* is formed by the overlapping of 2 gammas (3 + 3), but it disappeared from the archaic Greek alphabet, only to reappear in the Etruscan alphabet. The resulting shape was very similar to an F.

General meaning: Linking and joining. Anchoring. It indicates a real determination to harmonize and bring together. To attract to itself. To concentrate on what is necessary to succeed. It is a perfectionist and critical which can make it fail. Is not without a sarcastic edge.

G
7
Balanced – Mental

This letter only appeared in the Roman alphabet towards the third century BC and it served as a way of pronouncing the letter C more softly.

It was placed seventh in the alphabet, taking the place of the then defunct Z. As for Z, it corresponded to the seventh Greek and Phoenician letters *zeta* and *zaïn* and was later reintroduced at the end of the Latin alphabet.

General meaning: Hermeticism. Difficulty accepting difference. Progression. Thirst for often hidden knowledge. Maturity. Elitism. Gnosis. Independence.

H
8
Dual – Mental

The letter H appeared in the Phoenician alphabet lain on its side. For those people, it represented a barrier, an enclosure and a limitation, in the same way as it now expresses the limitations of incarnation.

The expression 8 conveys the archetype of karma. The design of the H implies a ladder allowing man to climb up to heaven or down to hell. It represents the birth/death/rebirth cycle.

It is undoubtedly worth 8. It was the eighth Greek letter (*heta*) and the eighth Semitic letter (*eth*). When the letters F and G were added to the Latin alphabet, it finally reclaimed the position it had previously occupied in the Greek and Phoenician alphabets: the eighth.

General meaning: Free will. Rise or fall. Transformation and metamorphosis. Freedom or obstacle. Determination. Awareness. Stage. Passage. Lock. Liberation. Force. Infinity.

I
9
Creative – Emotional

Verticality represented in its purist form.

A single line; the dot only appeared in the 11th century. Phallic symbol, emitting and receiving antenna, exemplary unapologetic uprightness; it manifestly links heaven and earth.

It comes from the Hebrew letter *yod* which means hand. It then became *iota* in Greek and was the tenth letter of both of these alphabets. The Latin I was used to express both the vowel I and the consonant J.

In the French language, the I was only disassociated from the J in the 16th century, while in Italian, the distinction was never made. Thus in French the I became the ninth letter, leaving the tenth position (its value in Greek) to its alter ego, the J. By adding I (9) + J (10), we obtain 19. The written form of this number is comprised of the first (1) and last (9) single-digit numbers.

General meaning: Clarity, precision, aspiration, inspiration, channeling, sowing and attentiveness to celestial paths. The man "with a mission", reaches up to heaven. Uprightness, integrity and immutability.

J
1 (10)
Dual – Mental

In order to understand the origins of J, the origins of I, referred to above, must be taken into account. A rounded base is the only difference in form between a J and an I. This base gives it more sensitivity.

General meaning: Accomplishment. Rebirth. Aspiration and inspiration. New opportunities. Oscillation. Conservatism.

K
11
Creative – Intuitional

This is a male letter, formed exclusively from segments. There is symmetry in its written form between the top and the bottom. By drawing an imaginary horizontal line at the point where all the lines meet, we obtain symmetry between the top and bottom of the letter, in the image of 11, its value. It is fixed in both heaven and earth while also turning itself resolutely towards the future.

It is the descendant of the eleventh Hebrew letter *kaph* which represented the palm of the hand. This letter became *kappa* in Greek. While it was not used very often before the 12th century, the Latin K remains closely associated in different languages with words describing strength and vital energy.

General meaning: Radiance, exaltation, revolution and evolution. Renewal. Freedom (in relation to the past). Circulation of multiple energies. Strength and will.

L
3 (12)
Balanced – Mental

It is represented by two lines that form a right angle at its base.

Its energy is masculine even though its pronunciation is soft. It comes from the Semitic letter *lamed* signifying a goad and later became the Greek *lambda*. In those alphabets, L is worth 30. Nowadays, its twelfth position also reduces to 3 (1 + 2 = 3).

General meaning: fairness, gentleness and determination. Openness, communication, expression and education. Restitution and projection.

M
4 (13)
Balanced – Physical

Letter containing numerous meanings of which the most significant is no doubt its human expression. Its symmetry recalls the link uniting two beings as if they were holding hands. With its sharp corners turned towards the top and the bottom, it also suggests antagonism between the mind and the body as well as a definition of the present moment, neither looking to the past or towards the future. It is reminiscent of mountain peaks and the crests of waves.

Its Phoenician form contained many undulations reflecting the waves of the sea, the moving water. *Mem* in Hebrew means water. The Greeks called it *Mu* and gave it a value of 40, which is can be reduced by fadic addition to its current value, 4 (4 + 0).

The sound it makes refers to very human and earthly notions of pleasure, e.g. "mmm that's good…". It symbolizes primordial and nourishing water from both the sea (*mare* in Latin) and the mother, the fluid in which the journey began. It finds its natural place at the beginning of the words mother, maman, mamma, mama, Mary and of course Maia.

General meaning: Strength of creation, cyclic movement, duality, gestation, materialization and realization. Meeting point between the spiritual and the material.

N
5 (14)
Dual – Mental

This letter is formed from three lines and two corners, one turned towards the mind and the other towards the body. It is a masculine letter and was originally the fourteenth Phoenician letter *noun*, the meaning of which is similar to the word fish. This is logical after the M which is all about water!

The fourteenth position of this letter in the Latin alphabet, which is worth 5, corresponds to the fadic reduction of 50 (5 + 0), i.e. the value of *noun* in Hebrew and of *nu* in Greek.

General meaning: Intimacy, introspection and secrets. Negation and fleeing reality. Restriction. Adaptability. Influence. Change. Fracture.

O

6 (15)

Creative – Emotional

A letter that is by its very nature extremely feminine; it is completely round and reminiscent of the circle formed by persons around a fire or a table.

It originally represented an eye, which is the meaning of the Hebrew word and letter *ayin* worth 70 → 7. However, this value does not correspond to its Latin position. The Greeks had two forms of this letter, *omicron* (little o) worth 70 and *omega* (big O), placed at the end of their alphabet, worth 800. By adding *omicron* (70) to *omega* (800), we get 870 → 8 + 7 → 15 → 1 + 5 → 6, which corresponds to its Latin position and value. What surprising evolutionary gymnastics!

It should be noted that [o] followed by [m] corresponds to the sacred sound *aum* or *om*. O (6) + M (4) equals 10, i.e. rediscovered unity.

General meaning: Circle, groupings, family, home and intimacy. Reassuring. Delimitation or limitation. Expression of surprise or astonishment. Imprisonment. Closing in. Restriction (going round in circles).

P

7 (16)

Dual – Mental

The form of this letter expresses a precarious balance as well as a dual nature since it contains both masculine and feminine elements.

The peak recalls bridging which seems to prevent the energy from circulating directly from bottom to top. This form implies lack of certainty. It is true that its shape has changed many times since its Phoenician and Egyptian origins.

The original letter seems to be the Phoenician *pé* which then became the Greek *pi*. Its original value was 80 while in the Latin alphabet the P is worth 7 (1 + 6).

General meaning: Change, uncertainty, imbalance, restriction and renunciation. Speaker. Weight of destiny. Constraint.

Q
8 (17)
Dual – Intuitional

Letter formed using an oval at the bottom of which there is a sort of appendage, sometimes stuck with the oval and sometimes not depending on the different typographies in use over the ages. Here harmony is emphasized, broken or prolonged according to the form of the line.

The Phoenician *qoph* that is used in Hebrew (with the value of 100) is at the origin of the Greek *goppa* which is worth 90 and so not the same as its Latin value of 8 (17th position). Specialists agree that in the early days of the Phoenician alphabet, the sign was represented by an 8 either standing up or on its side. How ironic history can be since nowadays we attribute the value of 8 to the letter Q which was originally written as an 8!

General meaning: Success achieved through a wise and spiritual approach. Germination. Intention. Intuition. Separation or distance from a circle of people (family in the broad sense of the word). Freedom. Pushing limits.

R
9 (18)
Creative – Emotional

Unlike P, the letter R finds balance and stability by extending the bottom of the loop to its base. This was not always the case as the form of this letter has changed throughout the ages.

The Semitic form *resh* (worth 200) symbolized the head, but it also recalls principles and causality just like the Greek letter *yod* (the I). Note that in Latin, the I (*yod*) and the R are both worth 9. On the other hand, the R was the Greek *rho* and was worth 1 (it had a value of 100).

General meaning: Inspiration, vision, reason, affirmation, prudent determination, projection, creation and conciliation. Separation.

S

1 (19)

Dual – Emotional

This letter represents the winding life path, characterized by a shape that moves in every direction. From left to right, you travel from the past towards the future and vice versa. Its primitive form was very different from its current form; the Phoenicians wrote it as a W and pronounced it *shin*. It was worth 300 in Hebrew. The Greeks turned it 90° to the right and named it *sigma* (200). The Phoenicians had two other letters *sameth* [ks] and *tsadé* [ts] which became *xi* and *san* respectively in Greek and were pronounced in a hissing way like an S. On the other hand, the numerical correspondences are very different.

General meaning: Adaptation. Pragmatism. Alternative. Winding. Indistinguishable. Indefinable. Artist. Memory. Duplicity. Delay. Protection. Sensuality.

T

2 (20)

Dual – Emotional

Masculine letter that seems balanced in its verticality and which possesses a horizontal line that seems to block out communication with heaven. Its two stretched out arms link the past with the future.

This is the final letter of the Semitic alphabet (*taw*, worth 400) and it became the Greek *tau*. Another Phoenician letter phonetically similar to T became *teth* in Hebrew and *theta* in Greek, both worth 9. However, as this letter was of no use to the Romans, it was not retained.

General meaning: Gathering, cooperation, support, shelter, protection of goods, conservatism and rigidity. Hesitation between two directions and blockade.

U

3 (21)

Dual – Intuitional

Entirely turned towards heaven, this letter suggests both determination and gentleness. Just like a magnet, it seems to attract spiritual energy to its seemingly unstable base which also serves as a receptacle.

Its origins, which are often confused with that of the V, are found in different adaptations of the Hebrew *waw* and the Greek *upsilon* that the Etruscans remodeled in accordance with the requirements of their language.

The Latin V was used to express both the vowel U and the consonant V. These letters were differentiated around the time of the Renaissance.

General meaning: Sensitivity, receptiveness, attraction, listening, welcome, comfort, warmth and magnetism but also uncertainty, circle of influence and oscillation.

V

22

Balanced – Intuitional

While very similar to the letter U in its form and origins, the absence of curves gives it a masculine polarity. The V is represented as the point of a heaven-sent arrow that is stuck in the ground.

The sexual connotations of this letter, symbolized by its form, is obvious. It represents the female pubis; vagina, vulva, virgin and virility all begin with the letter V.

The male and female principles evoked by this letter reflect the number 22, the value of its position, which symbolizes the double polarity of the world in its entirety.

General meaning: Access, culmination and truth. Sensuality. Realization. Reception. Transmission. Strength. Radiance. Energy.

W
5 (23)
Dual – Physical

Its form represents a double V. The symbolism of the V is retained but it has gained duality as evidenced by its three triangles. One points upwards and the other two point downwards.

It appeared around the 12th century and was placed after the V. It is pronounced as double U in English but double V in French due to the differentiation of the U and the V.

General meaning: Openness. Imagination. Alternative. Transfer. Duality. Separation. Power. Exaltation. Recklessness. Affirmation of the self and of differences. Pride.

X
6 (24)
Dual – Emotional

Masculine, the unambiguous form of this letter expresses alternately a barrier, a crossing, an intersection, a sort of trestle and a signature. It gives the impression of opening itself up in all directions.

The corresponding Hebrew letter *samekh* signifies support. It is worth 60 like its originating letter, the Greek *xi*, which is reduced to 6 ($60 \rightarrow 6 + 0 = 6$), the current value of X.

General meaning: Solidity. Supports. Construction. Multiple choices. Obstacle. Sign. Target. Need to refocus.

Y
7 (25)
Dual – Intuitional

This letter is reminiscent of a funnel. Its shape is comprised of a V placed on top of an I, which expresses cohesion rather than duality. The V recalls the female pubic hair and the I symbolizes the phallus; Y clearly expresses the meeting of these two polarities. This double aspect can be seen in the French language in which the Y acts both as a vowel and a consonant e.g. *noyer, payer*.

The form of the Y represents a receptacle that channels energy from up above to down below, from the spiritual to the material. Its shape also suggests a tree trunk with its two branches reaching towards the sky.

It was referred to as the "Greek Y" which harks back to its Hellenic origins as *upsilon* (worth 400). However, the Y only took its place in the Latin alphabet in the middle of the first century BC and its Latin value changed over time as new letters were added.

General meaning: Progression and choice. Growth. Elevation. Development. Judgment. Synthesis. Channeling. Concentration. Love. Gaiety. Joy. Hope.

Z
8 (26)
Creative – Emotional

A masculine letter represented by sharp corners and brutal changes of direction that give it an aggressive and unpredictable temperament, like a lightning bolt zigzagging across the sky.

This letter comes from the seventh letters in the Semitic and Greek alphabets, *zayin* and *zeta* respectively. It was integrated into the Latin alphabet in the first century BC and so, like the Y, it was relegated to the end of the alphabet. Of course, like the Y, its value (8) is the result of letters being added to the alphabet. There is a parallel between a people's potential for enlightenment and the need to integrate new letters into their alphabet. These new letters are like an echo of the people's evolution and growing awareness.

General meaning: Strength and the ability to incite fear, aggression, violence and respect. Sudden event. Consequence. Need for control. Change of direction. Change of course. Transformation. Mystery.

Different causes produce the same effect
or
the same effect is not necessarily due to the same causes

Fundamental rule: the apparent expression of a number may seem identical to that of another number even when it is not the same. Different people do not necessarily have the same motivation to explore a particular domain. A number's energy determines motivation.

Take drug use for example. It is 5's curiosity that leads him to experiment with the effects of the drug, whilst 9 is more concerned with seeking refuge in an artificial paradise.

To summarize...

- A native's personality is revealed by the value of all of the numbers comprising his numerological chart.
- A property can be redundant in various numbers.
- Each single-digit number from 0 to 9 possesses a unique spirit.
- A number containing many digits is interpreted by considering the numbers behind each digit (e.g. 41 would be analysed in relation to the 4 and the 1).
- The numbers 11, 22 and 33 are called master numbers and have their own vibrations. 11 and 22 must <u>never</u> be reduced.

CHAPTER IV

The Maia method

"There are many authorities (so called) upon numerology. Study same, if ye would know same; yet rely upon the spirit of truth, ever, that may make itself manifest in its own way unto thee."

Edgar Cayce (reading 261-15)

Now we are about to tackle the fundamental question of this book: Which data should a numerologist take into account when constructing a numerological profile?

Is it possible that until now certain essential data, and not just minor details, have not been taken into consideration?

Have you ever read numerological charts that more or less corresponded to your true nature or, if not, to a close friend's nature, without there being a reason for this correspondence?

In the introduction to this book, we saw that, historically, two methods have been used in modern numerology to describe an individual. There is the method called "French or European" and the method called "American".

They agree on one point, that, in all cases, the date of birth of the subject must be taken into account.

Nothing difficult about that, you might say. Well you would be wrong! I have a very illuminating example to share with you. I know someone who was born on the 31st of October 1957 just before midnight but her father registered that she was born on the 1st of November 1957 just after midnight. The birth certificate clearly states that she was born on the 1st of November. Which date should be used?

I gave my friend two readings to look at without telling her which one was based on which date. The analysis dealt with the life path as affected by different cycles and realizations, nuanced by challenges she may have to face and missing numbers.

In fact, she had difficulties deciding which numerological chart was most applicable to her, possibly reflecting the ambiguity of her double birth date. If you think about it, this is logical. All numerologists agree that an influence in a cycle gradually declines to make way for the next vibration, like in astrology when the sun or another object is on the cusp, i.e. between the end of one sign and the beginning of the next sign.

In the case of this person born a few minutes before midnight but whose date of birth was registered on the next day, it seems normal that there would be a double influence. This would imply that a numerologist also needs to know a subject's hour of birth in order to take the impact of these two energies into consideration: the energy that precedes a birth and the energy that follows a birth which takes place just after or just before midnight.

Upon rereading the charts, it seemed to my friend that the 1st of November, i.e. the official date, resounded more with her current state, while the earlier date corresponded better to the beginning of her existence. This implies that there is even a question mark over the date of birth.

In the French method, both the name given at birth and the assumed name are taken into account. In my opinion, and through my experience, the results of this method are inconclusive. At most, this information determines the social personality of the subject, his appearance, the one that he displays to others which resounds with the assumed surname and first name he was given at birth and still uses if they have not been changed.

However, people frequently change their name for various reasons and in these cases the apparent personality is determined by using the subject's current surname with his assumed first name or nickname, if the latter is used more in practice.

Nevertheless, as we shall see later, there are certain cases which seem to yield an excellent result using the French method thereby encouraging some numerologists to pursue this path.

The American method takes into consideration all of the information declared on the civil register, i.e. the date of birth, the surname at birth, the first name and all of the middle names in the order in which they were registered.

The immense advantage of this method is that it considers the first name and all of the middle names. Françoise Daviet clearly defined the correspondence between the positions of the first name and middle names and the associated areas of existence. Would you make a potato gratin only using potatoes and salt? In the same way, a numerological chart which did not take the assumed name into account would be missing essential elements. Furthermore, middle names often produce a vibration charged with family history. It could be the name of a godfather, a grandmother or a close family friend who has often been treated as one or both parents. An emotional connection is therefore conveyed through middle names.

All that being said, in many cases the American method also suffers from approximation, as if it were missing information necessary for the correct construction of a chart. I have often seen readings that have not corresponded exactly to my perception of close friends. Starting with my own children! My wife and I naturally chose their first names because we liked how they sounded but I also made sure that they were not missing any numbers from the numerological chart. Welcome to wise children...

Yet, over the years, the behavior of my cherubs seemed to cry out the absence of a number in their true personalities. I was aware of it without being able to explain it because in my mind I had constructed a perfect numerological birth certificate! It is only much later, when I was enlightened by the discovery of a new method that I was finally able to explain and understand the reasons why there was a discrepancy in my children's charts, when my chart and my wife's chart gave excellent results using the American method!

I can admit that destiny was teaching me a lesson about how we all stick to our certainties and close off other options. Yet, does science not evolve more efficiently in the face of doubt? I am not arguing that we should automatically question everything but it is necessary to keep an open mind, especially when little grains of sand get caught in the wheels and make them squeak.

This door had been left partly open for me and allowed me to welcome in, even if it wasn't easy, the key information that Michel had whispered to me.

Let us go back to the precise moment that I touched on in the introduction, when I explained how I became aware that my friend was not initially given his father's surname at birth. This information allowed me to take his true birth surname into account, that is, his mother's surname, to discover through numbers that which I had often observed of his true personality. The new chart finally brought to light key numbers that had been missing until that moment.

But Michel did not stop there. While he was very happy to have finally found a numerological chart that corresponded to him, he said to me in a serious and calculating tone, "Your thing isn't logical!"

In response to my interrogative look, he explained himself, "If you apply my mother's maiden name to your numerological analysis then that system must apply to everyone, without exception, don't you think?"

Then in response to my dubious look, he added, "If you are telling me that my mother's surname must be taken into account even if I only had it for a fraction of a second, then, as we are all born of our mothers even before our births have been registered, everybody's mothers' surname should be taken into account in an analysis!"

That really shook me up. I returned to my computer and tested a large number of charts that I had saved by changing the birth surname to the surname of the native's mother, if I knew it. The results were enlightening!

Dare I add that even faced with the information emerging before my very eyes, it was difficult for me to question all of the books and teachings by major numerologists who are the masters of this science. It was not easy to take that step!

And yet…

Our society, even if it has kept its largely phallocratic tendencies, has more recently started to give feminine expression back its rightful place. This has not always been the case. In the past, a certain narrow-mindedness created a rule whereby a child is always given the father's surname.

Yet, how can we not have realized that numbers could express the preponderant female role in a being's incarnation? On a biological level, and probably on much more subtle levels, the substrate that allows an entity to take on a bodily form is provided by the mother. Whether we like it or not, it is the woman that provides a womb for this developing body. Our first feelings, our first impressions and the growing awareness of our environment have to pass through the mother. The individualization of 1 needs this other 1, which is the mother (the 2).

Was this a planned pregnancy? In what conditions did it occur? The information absorbed by the fetus impregnates the cells of its developing body in an important way. A large range of emotions leave their first indelible marks.

Heredity may be shared with the father but it is the mother that impregnates the unborn child with her entire being. Furthermore, in the majority of cases, this privileged connection is reinforced in early childhood (breastfeeding, childcare, etc.).

By way of analogy, it is clear that it is in the maternal name that we should find all of the ascendance of the mother. No other data is capable of representing this particular vibration. For the child, the mother's name is very often the name of the maternal grandfather, but it could also be the grandmother's surname if the latter was an unmarried mother. It is undeniable that this name carries the family history.

Furthermore, by taking into account the child's mother's birth surname, we are necessarily integrating a paternal influence and so the masculine vibration is still very much present. The father influence is present in the name passed on by the mother because she herself has the name of her father or of a more distant male ancestor in the case of unmarried mothers. Therefore, masculine and feminine components are both represented.

We must not forget that a female fetus develops all of her ova containing half of the gene pool during gestation whereas a man only develops his spermatozoa during puberty. The latter are regularly renewed because they have a limited life span (a few weeks). The ovum is the most important transmitter of hereditary material because it is both at the centre of the fetus and in the energy field of the mother carrying it.

Fortunately, the numerous cases of people registered with their mother's name have allowed this primordial influence to come to light. Thanks to the unmarried mothers who passed on their birth name to their children it has always been possible to construct accurate charts and so to validate the impact of numbers. This is how we finally found the missing key.

In order to convince you of this, I invite you to redo your own chart, replacing your father's surname with your biological mother's birth surname. I say "birth" because you must use her real maiden name and in no case any name that she may have subsequently received.

If there is any doubt over the real surname that your mother was given at birth then only a full (photo)copy of her birth certificate from the civil register will reveal the truth. Be aware, however, that in some countries the certificate you receive may have been changed to include updated information, e.g. following legitimization. It is therefore essential that you obtain a copy of the original certificate.

While that document can remove all ambiguity, there are still two specific cases to consider. It is impossible to know my mother's birth surname if my parentage is unknown or if I was adopted by a woman who is not my biological mother but I am unaware of that fact. It is possible that, in good faith, I believe I know my mother's surname but I am wrong. The inaccuracy of my chart would almost certainly lead me to doubt the effectiveness of numerology.

A native who is aware that he does not know his mother's birth surname may still be able to find the most likely fadic sum by trying out all combinations. By comparing the Expression number obtained with all of the possible values of his mother's surname, he may be able to find the one that corresponds to him. This is the method used by astrologists to discover the time of birth when the latter is unknown or too approximate.

All that said, other names and nicknames that we have throughout our lives are not without consequence, as we shall see later. I am certainly not suggesting that an adoptive mother does not heavily influence the evolution of her adopted child. It's just that this is not important to each member of the family in question. Considering the biological mother's birth name, even if she was a surrogate mother, allows us to pinpoint the energy that indelibly marked the native at the moment of his incarnation.

The method that takes into account this crucial imprint is called the Maia method. We gave it this name as a nod to something else that will be revealed later.

The Maia method has always existed in practice. There are cases in which the numerologist has already unwittingly applied it.

This method was already implicitly used by the so-called French method in the cases where a person was born and registered with their mother's birth surname and only one first name. Same thing with the American method for people who have their mother's surname, a first name and one or more middle names. That is why the criteria used by these methods and the resulting interpretation have been accurate. This was the case for both me and my wife when I used the American method because we were both given our mothers' surnames, a first name and one or more registered middle names. This was why I had no real reason to doubt the accuracy of our charts. Without realizing it, like many others, I was already using the Maia method.

As for the other cases, the people who were not given their mother's maiden name, I simply invite them to construct a new chart in light of this new method. In order to be as objective as possible, chapter VIII is entirely dedicated to demonstrating the relevance of the Maia method by looking at the lives of four well-known figures.

Additionally, you will find all the information you need to construct a numerological chart in chapter V.

If you cannot initially recognize yourself in a reading done through the Maia method, then ask a sincere and frank person who knows you well to read it. We all occasionally have difficulties accepting some of our own personality traits. Oh ego, how you hold us in your grasp! But be careful because, as we have seen, the problems could be due to an error in your mother's birth name.

So why did we choose the name Maia for this method? You can ask my friend Michel who discovered it.

For many years Michel has been working on a new method of astrology that will be revealed in good time in a new work by him. Having named this method Hermes, he thought it natural to find a name with a link to Greek mythology. He was naturally inspired by Maia, the mother of Hermes. Do you see the relationship between using your mother's surname and the link between numerology and astrology? The science of Numbers is the mother of all sciences. Just ask Pythagoras. For me, astrology is a sort of geometry of the number.

Furthermore, in this time of profound mutation leading to earth shattering revelations, it is like a nod to the stars that are frequently cited in channeling. Maia is the eldest of the Pleiades, the daughters of Atlas and Pleione. She was seduced by Zeus and Hermes was born of their union. Maia can also be translated by "the nursing mother", a name traditionally associated with the grandmother, the wet-nurse or even the midwife.

Later on, the Romans purportedly named the fifth month of the Gregorian calendar after Maia; we now call this month May. Situated in the middle of spring, it corresponds to the Northern hemisphere of the Roman Empire, to the maternal and nursing symbols of the goddess.

Elsewhere, in Hindu mythology, Maia represents the female pole of the main creator. In Central America, the homonymy with the Maya civilization is not surprising.

Using the Maia method

- Use the first name and all of the middle names registered with the civil registry, the native's date of birth and <u>his biological mother's birth surname</u>.
- Use the alphabet correspondence table for the language that was used to officially register the native's first and middle names: English for an American, French for a French person, Italian for an Italian person, and so on. Be careful, the value of

the letters is not the same from one alphabet to another. English and French use the same alphabet. French accented letters do not hold a separate rank, e.g. an é has the same value as an E.

- Use the alphabet correspondence table for the language that was used to officially register the mother's maiden. Very often it is the same as the native, but there are special cases.
- Never reduce the master numbers 11 and 22.
- In English and French, consider K as a letter worth 11 and V as a letter worth 22 (their respective position in these alphabets)
- Consider that a number is missing if, and only if, there is no letter corresponding to that value.
- Consider that a number is excessively present when more than 9 letters have that value.
- Recognise the importance of the intensifier (most common number in the inclusion chart called Intensity number).
- Find the native's Active number by fadic addition using all first and middle names.
- Find the Heredity number by fadic addition using all of the birth surnames of the native's biological mother and father.
- Do not reduce the day, month and year of birth when calculating challenges and personalities so that sub-numbers and challenges 9, 11 and 22 are revealed where relevant.
- Only consider three challenges: The two "minor" challenges and the major challenge of existence which is equal to the birth year, reduced to a single digit, minus the birth month.
- Complete the chart with the numbers revealed by the native's sole assumed first name (or nickname if more commonly used) and the family name; this reflects the native's social personality.

CHAPTER V

The numerological core elements

> *"Everything relating to knowledge bears a number; it is neither possible to comprehend nor to apprehend anything without it."*
>
> Philolaus (Pythagorean philosopher)
> born before 440 (possibly 470), died after 399 BC

In this chapter I am going to list the core elements that are essential to the Maia method. The references to Astrological Houses are crucial and they have been brilliantly defined in the very detailed works of Françoise Daviet.

The list of elements is not exhaustive; some numerologists explore other avenues and suggest other "collections". However, I deliberately chose to dedicate this chapter to the elements that I have found particularly probing in light of my own experience and comments made by the users of my Numeyoga software. Let us first review the data needed to construct a numerological chart. We need to know the native's first name and all of his middle names in the order in which they were registered in the civil register, his current surname (patronymic) which may be his birth name or one acquired later in life (e.g. following marriage or legitimization), his date of birth and his biological mother's birth surname.

We need an example and so let us use the data of an imaginary person. Therefore, as the expression goes, any resemblance to persons living or dead is purely coincidental.

Imagine that our subject is called Pamela Natalie Scarlet Vellin and that she was born on the 16th of October 1965. The place of birth is not important to us, unlike in astrology.

Let us assume that Pamela got married in 1998 and took her husband's surname, Smith. Pamela's mother had also taken her husband's surname at marriage, Vellin, but her true birth name was Brown.

We do not have to take any nicknames into account because we have created her without one.

Using the Maia method, we will consider the following information:

Her mother's birth surname: Brown

Her first and middle names as declared at birth: Pamela Natalie Scarlet

Her current patronymic: Smith (even though she received her father's surname Vellin at birth)

Her date of birth: 10/16/1965

In most cases, we must consider the alphabet of the language that was used when reporting on the civil status registers, normally it's this that is the mother tongue.

In our example, Pamela is American like her mother. The declaration made in the civil status registry of the American state has been written in English. In this case, which is after all the most common, there is no problem, and we will use the English alphabet.

If a person is American but his/her mother is of another nationality, we will use the English alphabet for first and middle names of the person and the mother's alphabet for the mother's maiden name.

Example: an American called Andrea Laura whose mother is Mexican has the maiden name of Rodriguez. The numerological calculations will be done with the English alphabet with the first names Andrea and Laura and the Spanish alphabet on her mother's maiden name, Rodriguez.

To find out the value of each letter of the main Latin alphabets, see Appendix 1 of this book.

1	2	3	4	5	6	7	8	9
A	B	C	D	E	F	G	H	I
J	K (11)	L	M	N	O	P	Q	R
S	T	U	V (22)	W	X	Y	Z	

Value of each of the 26 letters of the English/French alphabet

To calculate the numerological value of a name, just add the value of each letter according to its position in the alphabet. Then reduce the result, as many times as necessary, to obtain a number between 1 and 9 or a master number 11 or 22.

BILL (B worth 2, I worth 9, L worth 3)

$2933 \rightarrow 2+9+3+3 = 17 \rightarrow 1+7 = 8$

In this case, the 8 comes from a 17 (1+7). 17 is the sub-number of 8.

Sometimes, two steps are required.

$78 \rightarrow 7+8 = 15 \rightarrow 1+5 = 6$

The core elements linked to mother's birth surname and native's first and middle names

The Aspiration Number (sometimes called Soul Urge or Heart's Desire)

This number reveals the soul's aspirations which exist to help it achieve a higher state of consciousness. It teaches us about the nature of the assistance given by the people who will influence the native's destiny and who will definitely have the corresponding value in their core numbers. This number expresses the unflagging desire of the soul to live in accordance with its ideals during its passage on earth.

Even though the ego can be reluctant to comply with this soul urge, the latter is so powerful that we often have no choice but to accept its chosen path. Therefore it is better to understand the imperative desires of our soul as quickly as possible. This number is the soul's way of showing us the best and quickest path to take in order to achieve wisdom, even happiness and to access our true nature (Life Path), whether we like it or not.

The Aspiration Number is obtained by reducing the sum of all the vowels, taking the sub-numbers into account. Vowels effectively contain the music of the soul.

In English (see table above for vowels), A worth 1, E worth 5 and so on...In our example, we find:

```
        PAMELA NATALIE SCARLET BROWN
Vowels  -1-5-1 -1-1-95 --1--5-  --6--
```

Aspiration: 1+5+1+1+1+9+5+1+5+6 = 35
                 35 → 3+5 = **8**

A challenge[2] on this number or the absence[3] of this number in the inclusion chart indicates that this aspiration will be hindered. See this as one more reason not to give up.

Aspiration	1	2	3	4	5	6	7	8	9	11	22
See page	130	143	155	170	182	197	211	224	239	253	261

The Potential Number (sometimes called Latent or Quiescent self)

This number expresses everything we possess, i.e. our gifts, our inherent nature. It indicates the being's skills. It informs us of our past life acquisitions and all of the potentials that will surface, or not (is it our aspiration?) in this life.

---

[2] See below for the definition of challenges.

[3] See below for the definition of missing numbers in the inclusion.

For these reasons I do not think that we should call it the Hidden Self but the True Self. This number reflects the Life Path that we will look at a bit later.

The Potential Number is obtained by reducing the sum of all the consonants, taking the sub-numbers into account. In a way, the consonants are the architecture around the sound. Alone, they do not represent anything; they need the vowel in order to express themselves. By way of analogy, they are the human body and its potential which need the soul's music (the Aspiration Number) to come alive.

Don't forget that if you obtain an 11 or a 22 when reducing the separate sum of the first name, middle names and surname then the master number must be conserved. This is not the case for Pamela.

In English (see table above for consonants), B worth 2, C worth 3 and so on... In the case of Pamela:


```
         PAMELA NATALIE  SCARLET BROWN
Consonants 7-4-3- 5-2-3--  13-93-2 29-55
```

Potential: 7+4+3+5+2+3+1+3+9+3+2+2+9+5+5 = 63
63 → 6+3 = **9**

A challenge[4] on this number or the absence[5] of this number in the inclusion chart reveals a need to use this potential in a fairer and more balanced way than before.

Potential	1	2	3	4	5	6	7	8	9	11	22
See page	130	144	156	170	183	198	212	225	239	254	262

---

[4] See below for the definition of challenges.

[5] See below for the definition of missing numbers in the inclusion.

The Expression Number

This number is obtained by reducing the sum of all of the letters in the native's first name and his mother's birth surname. You must consider all sub-numbers obtained from adding the consonants and the vowels respectively. This number logically corresponds to the sum of Aspiration Number + Potential Number.

This parameter is one of the most important in the chart along with the Life Path, the Maturity, Aspiration and Potential Numbers. It is the synthesis of the being's motivations and capabilities and the driving force behind his journey along his Life Path. This number describes the native's attitude and the way he behaves towards other people. It is like his signature, the energy behind the evolution of his personality.

Let us find Pamela's Expression Number:

PAMELA NATALIE SCARLET BROWN
All letters 714531 5121395 1319352 29655

```
  PAMELA : 7+1+4+5+3+1 = 21
 NATALIE : 5+1+2+1+3+9+5 = 26
 SCARLET : 1+3+1+9+3+5+2 = 24
   BROWN : 2+9+6+5+5 = 27
```

Expression: 21+26+24+27=98 → 9+8=17 → 1+7=**8**

You should also be aware of the importance of any sub-number revealed by adding the Aspiration number to the Potential Number.

This is the case for Pamela for whom we obtain:

8 (Aspiration) + 9 (Potential) = 17/8 (Expression).

Let us see how many possible combinations there are for an 8 in Expression:

Aspiration 1 + Potential 7 = 8
Aspiration 2 + Potential 6 = 8
Aspiration 3 + Potential 5 = 8
Aspiration 4 + Potential 4 = 8
Aspiration 4 + Potential 22 = 26/8
Aspiration 5 + Potential 3 = 8
Aspiration 6 + Potential 2 = 8

Aspiration 6 + Potential 11 = 17/8
Aspiration 7 + Potential 1 = 8
Aspiration 9 + Potential 8 = 17/8
Aspiration 11 + Potential 6 = 17/8
Aspiration 22 + Potential 4 = 26/8
Aspiration 22 + Potential 22 = 44/8

There are 13 combinations of aspirations and potentials of the soul expressed through this 8! It is important to not simply lump these together; the Expression number can be obtained by combining various different numbers and so specific combinations contain important nuances that need to be interpreted.

We have just worked out the Aspiration Number, the Potential Number and the Expression number using all of the mother's birth surname, first and middle native's names. But these core numbers are also present inside each surname, first name or middle name. The vowels of each name reveal a sort of mini Aspiration number which reveals something about that name according to its position. It is the same with the consonants and the Potential Number. The sum of the two (the Expression Number) reveals specific information about a particular area. Let us look at these influences in detail:

Expression	1	2	3	4	5	6	7	8	9	11	22
See page	130	143	155	170	182	197	211	224	238	253	261

The First Name

PAMELA	PAMELA	PAMELA
714531	-1-5-1	7-4-3-
7+1+4+5+3+1	1+5+1	7+4+3
21/**3**	**7**	14/**5**
All letters	*Vowels*	*Consonants*

In our example, the fadic sum of all of the letters of the first name Pamela gives a first name Expression Number 3 (from 21), a first name Aspiration Number 7 (no sub-number) and a first name Potential Number 5 (from 14). Using the Aspiration, the Potential and the Expression Numbers of the first name alone, we can gain an insight into the behavior of the native in her everyday life. This area corresponds to the idea of service, work, healthcare, hygiene, day-to-day health, small problems, subordinates and co-workers, etc.

If you practice astrology, it will not have escaped your attention that the first name controls the same areas as the sixth House.

First name	1	2	3	4	5	6	7	8	9	11	22
See page	131	144	156	171	183	198	212	225	239	254	262

The first Middle Name

NATALIE	NATALIE	NATALIE
5121395	-1-1-95	5-2-3--
5+1+2+1+3+9+5	1+1+9+5	5+2+3
26/**8**	16/**7**	10/**1**
All letters	*Vowels*	*Consonants*

The Aspiration, Potential and Expression Numbers obtained from the first middle name Natalie are 7 (16), 1 (10) and 8 (26) respectively. The interpretation of these results relates to associations, unions, spouses, contracts, justice and more generally the native's positive and negative relationships with her partners and/or colleagues. This area is clearly of importance to Pamela in this existence because her first middle name 8 refers back to the general Aspiration and Expression Numbers 8 and to her Growth number.

In astrology, this is the seventh House.

1ˢᵗ Middle Name	1	2	3	4	5	6	7	8	9	11	22
See page	131	144	156	171	183	198	212	226	239	254	262

The second Middle Name

SCARLET	SCARLET	SCARLET
1319352	--1--5-	13-93-2
1+3+1+9+3+5+2	1+5	1+3+9+3+2
24/**6**	**6**	18/**9**
All letters	*Vowels*	*Consonants*

For the second middle name Scarlet, we obtain an Expression 6 (24), an Aspiration 6 (no sub-number) and a Potential 9 (18). These numbers shed light on everything in the area of creativity, love, children, pleasures, leisure activities, distractions and games as well as speculation and hobbies.

This is the fifth House in astrology.

2nd **Middle Name**	1	2	3	4	5	6	7	8	9	11	22
See page	131	144	157	171	184	199	213	226	240	255	262

If, by chance, the native has more than one first name and two registered middle names then, apart from the fact that they need to be integrated into the calculations, you also need to decide their significance in the numerological chart. Research is essential to numerology. It is only through experimentation and statistical evidence that we can prove the accuracy of analyses. In this case, as so few people have more than two middle names, it is difficult to carry out in-depth research into the influence of a third, fourth or even fifth middle name.

The Heredity Number

As its name indicates, the Heredity Number is the sum of the biological mother's birth surname and the biological father's birth surname. In order to obtain this number, you need to be absolutely certain of the names given to the biological parents at birth.

Heredity Number = Biological mother's birth surname + Biological father's birth surname

Pamela's mother was given the surname Brown at birth and Pamela was registered with the surname Vellin, which was her biological father's birth surname (it seems that this is not always the case). The addition of Brown and Vellin results in a Heredity Number 11 obtained from the number 74.

```
              BROWN VELLIN
Heredity:     29655 453395
              27 +   29              =56 → 5+6=11
                or
          2+9+6+5+5+4+5+3+3+9+5=56 → 5+6=11
```

The Heredity number tells us about family, the home, childhood, the childhood house and then later, the adult home. It is the attic, treasures, the past, roots, animals, the mother and fertility.

This is the fourth House in astrology.

Furthermore, the Heredity Number always describes the familial context of the childhood even if the native's father and/or mother are not his biological parents. Therefore, only the biological parents' birth surnames are to be taken into account, whether or not these two people were responsible for the native's education.

Consequently, if the biological father's birth surname is unknown then it is not possible to calculate the Heredity number. It is still possible, however, to deduce its value by adding all possible numbers (1 to 9, 11 and 22) to the fadic sum of all of the letters in the mother's birth surname and seeing which result gives the most accurate interpretation.

Heredidy	1	2	3	4	5	6	7	8	9	11	22
See page	131	145	157	172	184	199	213	226	240	255	263

The Active Number

The method of calculating this number and its application are unique to the Maia method and we have Michel's intuition to thank for it. This hypothesis was validated through in-depth study.

The Active number corresponds to the reduced sum (with the exception of 11 and 22) of all first and middle names declared at birth even if there are more than three!

The Active number is a very personal component of the native's energy and is even more intense if it is also found in other parameters of the chart. Simply put, it reflects the native's way of acting and reacting.

For example, if a person has an Active number 3 which is also present in his Maturity number and first middle name, then this energy is multiplied in the native's associations and socioprofessional potential. This is the same as astrologists finding a planetary cluster in a sign or a house.

In the example of Pamela, the sum of her first and middle names, Pamela, Natalie and Scarlet, is:

```
         PAMELA NATALIE SCARLET
Active:  714531 5121395 1319352
          21  +   26   +   24              =71 → 7+1=8
                       Or
7+1+4+5+3+1+5+1+2+1+3+9+5+1+3+1+9+3+5+2=71 → 7+1=8
```

The 8's expression is intensified in Pamela because it reinforces the vibrations of the 8 already present in her Expression and Aspiration numbers. This woman must really know what she wants. It is certain that she will do anything to achieve her goals, using whatever means necessary.

Active	1	2	3	4	5	6	7	8	9	11	22
See page	131	145	157	172	184	199	213	227	241	256	263

The planes of Expression

In the same way that astrological signs relate to an element (fire, earth, air and water) and a character (cardinal, fixed and mutable), each letter belongs to two categories. It is creative, mobile or stable and intellectual, physical, emotional or intuitive:

	MENTAL analysis, logic, deduction...	PHYSICAL sense of organization, strength...	EMOTIONAL emotion, sensitivity...	INTUITIVE feelings, perception of others/events...
CREATIVE creativity, impulse...	A	E	O R I Z	K
DUAL gain, need to change, hesitation...	H J N P	W	B S T X	F Q U Y
BALANCED discernment, sense of tradition...	G L	D M		C V

This table makes it very easy to pinpoint certain characteristics relating to creativity, intellect and physicality, etc.

By cross-referencing we can see, for example, if a person's changeable character is due to overly high emotions or if it is a response to the subject's intuitions. Logically, you can see from the table that no letter can contain both emotional and stable characteristics.

The following in particular should be taken into account:

The number of creative letters in addition to the numbers of the second middle name.

The number of emotional letters in addition to the numbers of the first middle name.

The number of physical letters that refer to very precise aspects of existence.

In our example, Pamela possesses:

11 mental letters	12 Creative letters
5 physical letters	8 dual letters
8 emotional letters	5 balanced letters
1 intuitive letter	

Repartitioning this information in a table shows us the nature of her expression:

	MENTAL analysis, logic, deduction...	PHYSICAL sense of organization, strength...	EMOTIONAL emotion, sensitivity...	INTUITIVE feelings, perception of others/events...
CREATIVE creativity, impulse...	AAAAA	EEE	IORR	
DUAL gain, need to change, hesitation...	NNP	W	BSTT	
BALANCED discernment, sense of tradition...	LLL	M		C

We can see straightaway that Pamela is gifted with a powerful creative mind and high ideals. Her difficulty stems more from her changeable emotional states which can sometimes make her feel unbalanced. She is very impatient. She could learn to channel her energy into all types of artistic and/or sporting activities which require movement.

Planes of Expression	1	2	3	4	5	6	7	8	9	11	22
See pages	139	152 to 153	164 to 165	177 to 178	191 to 192	205 to 206	219 to 220	233 to 234	247 to 249	256 to 257	264

The Inclusion

This number is obtained by entering into a table the quantity of letters worth each of the values from 1 to 9. The letter K worth 11 is added to the letters worth 2 and the letter V worth 22 is added to

the letters worth 4. Here are the results for Pamela Natalie Scarlet
Brown.

PAMELA NATALIE SCARLET BROWN
714531 5121395 1319352 29655

6 letters worth 1:	AAAASA	(see pages 133 to 139)
3 letters worth 2:	TTB	(see pages 146 to 152)
4 letters worth 3:	LLCL	(see pages 158 to 164)
1 letter worth 4:	M	(see pages 173 to 177)
6 letters worth 5:	ENEEWN	(see pages 186 to 191)
1 letter worth 6:	O	(see pages 200 to 205)
1 letter worth 7:	P	(see pages 214 to 219)
0 letter worth 8:		(see pages 228 to 232)
3 letters worth 9:	IRR	(see pages 241 to 247)

1	2	3	4	5	6	7	8	9
6	3	4	1	6	1	1	0	3

Another way of presenting these results consists of placing
them in a grid containing 9 boxes:

6	3	4
1	6	1
1	0	3

Each box contains the number of letters with the value of
that box; this number is called the modulator. In our example the
modulator of box 6 is 1. This means that Pamela only has one letter
in her name worth 6 (the O in Brown), whereas she has 6 letters
worth 1.

These values are very important because they determine
additional character traits. The boxes are also associated with areas
and people related to the native.

Box	Letters in English alphabet	Meaning
1	A J S	refers to the model, the father, authority, superiors, the conscious, the ego and social issues, etc.
2	B K T	refers to the mother, women, a partner, desires, dreams, intuition, moods, sensitivity, memory, childhood, the unconscious, the masses, popularity and nourishment, etc.
3	C L U	refers to siblings, children, primary school, training, writing, creativity, legality, contracts and foreign countries, etc.
4	D M V	refers to familial authority, being cherished by loved ones, roots, good education, work techniques, choices, honor, work ethic and stubbornness, etc.
5	E N W	refers to liberty and the respect of others, writing, groups, changes, sexuality, lovers, one's own children, movement and excess, etc.
6	F O X	refers to love, promises, union, marriage, responsibilities, affinities, selectivity, the arts, aestheticism and justice, etc.
7	G P Y	refers to beliefs, faith, mental capacities, originality, doubt, revolt and drugs, etc.
8	H Q Z	refers to personal evolution, knowledge, money, insurance, inheritance, death, ambition, power and courage, etc.
9	I R	refers to ideals, political activism, fraternity, the collective, dreams, sacrifices, travel, foreign countries, knowledge, higher education, grandparents, brothers-in-law, sisters-in-law, uncles and aunts, etc.

Different schools of thought have different opinions as to what value a modulator must be in order to reflect an excess or an absence in the personality. It is highly likely that this difference of opinion originates in a failure to take the mother's birth surname into account. Because of this, each person has tried to adjust their interpretation of the inclusion chart so that it would "fit" better to a numerological chart in which certain elements were missing.

Some people consider a number as missing when the number of letters with that value is lower than a percentage of the total letters. This percentage changes in accordance with the frequency of letters used in a language. For example, the number of letters with a value of 5 is high in English because the E, N and even W are frequent. This means that even if a native has two letters worth 5 then that value would be considered missing.

Other people have arbitrarily decided that 1 is missing when there are less than 3 letters with that value. These mental acrobatics are always justified using arbitrary considerations that change according to a person's personal preference. The interpretation of numbers can seem very random and lacking in common sense.

However, we can say that a number is really missing when no letter has that value. That seems logical, does it not? Consequently, 1 is a missing number when there is no A, J or S in the mother's birth surname or the subject's own first and middle names. 2 is missing if the letters B, K and T are all absent, and so on.

In the same way, more than 9 letters with the same value reveals an excess because beyond 9 there are no longer any single-digit numbers with their own energy but combinations of numbers trying to find a balance.

That said, in no way is having a higher number of letters with a certain value an indication that that chart is superior to another which has fewer letters of that value.

For example, 7 letters worth 9 is not "superior" to 3 letters worth 9. It simply casts a different light on the chart.

Finally, the inclusion number reveals nuances of personality aspects which allow us to, for example, differentiate between two people with the same Aspiration, Potential and Expression numbers.

Furthermore, the aim of the inclusion is to find the frequency of letters with the same value. For example, you cannot ignore 7 letters worth 1 in an inclusion chart where the other modulators in the squares 2, 3, 4, 5, 6, 7, 8 and 9 do not exceed 3. If that is the case then it is no longer a question of quantity but of disproportion. Statistical studies have shown that a number appearing a disproportionate number of times must be somehow taken into account because it will dominate and break the balance of the other forces present. The box in the inclusion chart that corresponds to the highest number of letters of a certain value contains the **intensity number**. The more disproportionate it is, the more that number intensifies a component of the personality. If, additionally, this intensity number is also in excess because it is higher than 9, then a non-negotiable part of the interpretation must be dedicated to this aspect.

If you find yourself with more than one intensity number, apply a hierarchy based on the rarity of certain letters. The following order should be applied: 8, 7, 4, 2, 6, 3, 1, 9 and then 5.

Pamela possesses 6 letters worth 1 (AAAASA). She also has 6 letters worth 5 (ENEEWN) but as letters worth 1 are a little less frequent than those worth 5 in the Anglo-Saxon world, 1 must be taken as her Intensity number.

Intensity	1	2	3	4	5	6	7	8	9
See page	132	145	158	172	185	199	214	227	241

Missing number or karmic number

An absence of letters in an inclusion chart reflects areas of existence that are either underexplored or contain karma. A clear distinction must be made between the native who has explored a particular area in an inappropriate way (karmic number) and the native who has never explored it (missing number).

Missing number: there is no letter of this value nor is it the Aspiration, Potential, Expression, Active or Heredity number.

This means that the native has not yet explored the specific area relating to the number in question. Therefore inexperience prevails and creates imbalance. The native has a learning curve before him. First contact with a situation is never easy and many mistakes may be made. However, as he gains experience, and because life never stops throwing the same situations our way, the individual will familiarize himself with those energies (in particular during the personal years corresponding to that missing number).

Karmic number: there is no letter with this value but this number can be found in the Aspiration, Potential or Expression number or in the Active or Heredity number.

This means that the native has clearly explored the areas associated with the number in question in his previous lives but in a disorganized way and/or by causing damage to others and so this is now a source of imbalance in his current life. There is no doubt that this attitude needs to be changed and that the destiny chosen by him will give him a second chance and an opportunity to evolve.

Hence when analyzing a karmic number you must look for its presence in:

- The Aspiration Number: the being has really decided to explore and master the areas associated with this number in which he made mistakes in previous lives.
- The Potential Number: the being has the full potential to express the qualities indicated by this missing number. Its presence reveals that in another life the native used his skills inappropriately in the associated areas.
- The Expression Number: the being has a sort of tailored-made personality that makes it easy for him to correct the errors and mistakes that he accumulated in his previous lives and which are related to the area indicated by the number. However he still loves to express that energy for better or for worse.
- The Life Path: the being has completely changed his road map in order to move in the direction of the areas of existence that he has not yet explored. He prioritizes investment in the sectors related to the number in question.
- The Maturity Number: the being wants to be confronted on the socioprofessional front in the areas indicated by the missing number.
- The Heredity Number: the being is trying to resolve a problem related to this missing number but frequently ends up sharing this problem with family members (more often than not from the mother's side).

The core elements which contain the missing or karmic numbers, especially those on the planes of expression, can refine and highlight the causes of difficulty. For example, a missing 8 for a person whose name contains 8 physical letters indicates, amongst other things, an important life transformation. This transformation could lead to a friend or family member's death and/or illness. This sort of ordeal is often a difficult experience and it can help the native's ability to transcend. One way or another he will end up acquiring a more acute understanding of the other's behavior and intentions.

Other additional elements

Using the mother's birth surname and the native's first name, you can find other elements which shed light on different aspects of the personality, e.g. the first vowels, the first letters, last letters and, the middle number, if there is one. It is crucial to take the value and symbolism of the corresponding letter as described in chapter III into account.

The number behind the initials (first name and maternal surname) indicates the way in which we will reveal the character defined by the Expression number. The position of the initial letter is probably the most influential because it is written with a capital letter. As we saw earlier, the original Latin alphabet only comprised upper case letters.

The Balance number obtained from all of the initials (all first and middle names + maternal surname) reveals how we will react in the face of our own questioning.

The total number of letters considered in the inclusion chart tends to reveal a constant that will be present throughout the individual's existence, even in difficult times, thereby highlighting the unique quality of the chart. For a further understanding of this, refer to the number or sub-number described later on in this work. In the example of Pamela, the first and middle names and the maternal surname contain a total of 25 letters.

Other secondary elements

- The Duty number is calculated in the same way as the first realization (day + month of birth). It reflects the main work that must be accomplished in the native's life.
- The Initiation number shows us how we approach spirituality. It is the fadic sum of: Aspiration + Expression + Life Path + Day of birth.
- The Subconscious Number describes our essential requirements although they are not always clearly formulated. If there are no missing numbers then this element has a value of 9, otherwise the total number of missing numbers (not their value) must be subtracted from 9. In the example of Pamela, it has a value of 8 (9 – 1 because she only has one missing number).
- The Eccentricity number describes how we react when faced with a major difficulty. It is calculated by reducing the sum of the first name + the day of birth.

The apparent personality

It will not have escaped anybody's attention that a dichotomy exists between the image that we display in public and our true personality. Without necessarily wanting to hide our true identity, we cannot display in public our deepest thoughts, our secret desires, our fantasies, our feelings of guilt, our weaknesses or our pain.

However, while numerology reveals our true nature, it does not skip over the apparent personality that we prefer to display to others. The numerological analysis of the different names and nicknames that we may adopt over the course of our existence constantly redefines how we present ourselves in public.

It must be noted that some of society's transformations have taken place at the level of name change which is a much more flexible process nowadays. Indeed, the legislation now allows brides to choose which marital surname they wish to take in accordance with their aspirations. The presence of the feminine is becoming more and more marked.

Therefore it is useful to calculate the Aspiration, the Potential and the Expression numbers using the native's current surname (his patronymic) combined with his usual first name or even his nickname if that is more commonly used. In this way, we obtain new parameters to describe the social personality of the subject.

The difference between true nature and social personality is easily seen in the outward image of a public figure. This image corresponds to a numerological chart based on his patronymic and current first name. Yet deeper analysis using the Maia method shows us who he really is and what drives him.

This is why, from childhood, the birth surname, if different from the mother's birth surname, must also be taken into account. An analysis of this birth surname along with the assumed first name will precisely describe children in a social situation, e.g. at school.

This means that it is necessary to recalculate each time a person changes his name. This makes sense since a patronymic is usually modified following a social transformation (marriage, legitimization, etc.). Furthermore, the vibrations emitted by this new numerological configuration are always more or less in harmony with the essential parameters of the chart. The native's true nature may no longer fit with the face he needs to project. Three new elements relating to the native's more apparent and social aspect need to be taken into account without, however, emphasizing too much these vibrations. The birth numbers are always the most influential. Sometimes the same numbers are obtained in which case it goes without saying that the subject's personality can be qualified as whole.

```
                PAMELA          SMITH
All letters 714531          14928
            7+1+4+5+3+1 +  1+4+9+2+8        =45→4+5=9
Patrimony:  21/3        +      24/6  →  21+24=45→4+5=9
```

```
              PAMELA           SMITH
   Vowels    -1-5-1            --9--
              1+5+1      +       9                =16→1+6=7
Ideality:      7         +       9         →    7+9=16→1+6=7


              PAMELA           SMITH
Consonants    7-4-3-     +      14-28
              7+4+3      +      1+4+2+8              =29→2+9=11
Structure:    14/5       +      15/6      →  14+15=29→2+9=11
```

The Ideality Number

This number corresponds to the fadic sum of all of the vowels in the native's assumed first name, or nickname if the latter is more frequently used, and of his current surname. It reveals the person's social aspirations and indicates his ideals.

In the example of Pamela:

```
              PAMELA           SMITH
   Vowels    -1-5-1            --9--
              1+5+1      +       9              =16 → 1+6=7
Ideality:      7         +       9       → 7+9=16 → 1+6=7
```

The Structure Number

This number is the fadic sum of all of the consonants in the native's assumed first name, or nickname if the latter is more widely used, and of his current surname. It refers to the potential projected by the native but also of the skills acquired in this existence.

In our example:

```
              PAMELA           SMITH
Consonants    7-4-3-     +      14-28
              7+4+3      +      1+4+2+8          =29→2+9=11
Structure:    14/5       +      15/6      →14+15=29→2+9=11
```

The Patrimony Number

This is the Expression obtained from the native's assumed first name (or nickname) and current surname. It often describes the type of personality we assume the person has upon first meeting.

For Pamela we obtain:

```
           PAMELA          SMITH
All letters 714531          14928
        7+1+4+5+3+1  +  1+4+9+2+8        =45→4+5=9
Patrimony:  21/3       +     24/6   →21+24=45→4+5=9
```

Elements linked to the date of birth

The Life Path

Core element of the chart, the Life Path is the fadic sum of the sole numbers present in the date of birth. No matter the format of the date. In this book, we use the usual written US form.

The Life Path shows us the path that we have chosen to privilege in this incarnation. It expresses the subject's mechanisms and true archetypes. While it is more or less easy to transform a personality (Aspiration, Potential and Expression), it is difficult to change the intrinsic fundamentals present in your Life Path. Furthermore, you can change your name during your life and this would affect your apparent personality but it is obvious that in no lifetime can you change your date of birth.

There are three methods of calculating the sub-numbers hidden in this date. It is highly advisable to research them all because they all contain key information on the native's path.

First method: simple addition of each figure

```
10/16/1965
1+0+1+6+1+9+6+5=29 → 2+9=11
```

The numerologist Dan Millman suggests that the obtained sum should only be reduced once. In the example of Pamela, that would give us 29/11.

Second method: by adding the day, month and year of birth in column.

```
    1 0
+   1 6
+ 1 9 6 5
-----------
  1 9 9 1
```

1991 → 1+9+9+1=20 → **2**

For Pamela, this method of calculation does not reveal the Master number 11 but produces a 2 from sub-number 20, which must be taken into account during interpretation.

Third method: adding the fadic sums of the day, month and year but conserving the Master Numbers.

```
1+0=1 (reduced month)
1+6=7 (reduced day)
1+9+6+5=21 → 2+1 → 3 (reduced year)
```

```
1+7+3=11 Life Path
```

In the example of Pamela, we obtain 11 again.

These different methods of calculation reveal that Pamela has a Life Path colored by the Master Number 11 and by the number 2 as well as by two sub-numbers (29 and 20). All of these results must be taken into account if we are to correctly determine her Life Path.

Life Path	1	2	3	4	5	6	7	8	9	11	22
See page	130	143	155	170	182	197	211	224	238	253	261

The Birthday

This number contains additional information on the True Self revealed by the Life Path. It informs us about specific aspects of the subject's nature which are mainly expressed during the second life cycle; this cycle is precisely equal to the reduction of the birthday.

Pamela was born on the 16th day and so will aim to deepen her knowledge in her preferred area, more than likely one that resounds with knowledge already gained during her past lives. She is capable of acting (1) whilst also assuming her responsibilities (6), however, she must temper a form of rigidity that may lead her to following her path without considering the potential risks.

The Life Cycles

The cycles define 3 distinct periods in a person's existence. They shed light on the way in which his destiny is going to unfold. Independently from the life's realization that we shall look at a little later, they reveal the atmosphere and nuances present in the Life Cycle. These cycles add detail by indicating the place and context in which a subject's destiny will be fulfilled. They describe hazards and unexpected and unforeseen events on the native's chosen road map. It is important to consider the personal years which correspond to the same number (for example, a personal year 3 during a life cycle 3 intensifies it).

These cycles are calculated using the three elements that comprise our date of birth: the day, the month and the year.

- The **First Cycle**, or Formative Cycle, is obtained by reducing the birth month to a single digit (with the exception of 11). This corresponds to the periods of childhood, adolescence and the beginnings of our working life.
  For Pamela this is a number 1 cycle.
  October $10 \rightarrow 1 + 0 = 1$

- The **Second Cycle**, or Productive Cycle, is obtained by reducing the birth day to a single-digit (with the exception of 11 and 22). It corresponds to working life and often to life as a parent.

  Pamela was born on the 16th of the month and so her second cycle is worth 7 as reduced from 16. Note the importance of the birth day's sub-number if the date occurs after the 9th of the month. For example, 7 could come from either a 16 or a 25; this would alter the meaning of the 7.

  $16^{th} \rightarrow 1 + 6 = 7$

- The **Third Cycle**, or the Harvest Cycle, is obtained by reducing the year of birth down to one figure (or an 11 or 22). It often corresponds to a more peaceful life such as retirement and times in our life when we are more available for new activities. These times can be favourable when there has been a good harvest over the preceding cycles.

  Pamela will be in a third cycle 3.

  $1965 \rightarrow 1 + 9 + 6 + 5 = 21/3$

Cycles	1	2	3	4	5	6	7	8	9	11	22
See pages	140	153	166	179	193	207	220 to 221	234 to 235	249 to 250	257 to 258	264

Note: the date on which we enter into the second or third cycle depends on our Life Path. According to Florence Campbell we must take into account astrology's *progressed* lunar cycle, which lasts for 28 years and 4 months. As for the second life cycle, it starts in the personal year 1 closest to the 28-years-and-4-month cycle. As indicated in the table below, the second cycle starts at 27 years old for people with a life path 1 as this is the closest to the 28-years-and -4-months. The same rule applies for the third cycle.

The following table indicates the date of entry into each subsequent cycle, according to each life path.

If the Life Path is worth	Cycle 2 begins at	Cycle 3 begins at
1	27 y.o.	54 y.o.
2 or 11	26 y.o.	53 y.o.
3	25 y.o.	52 y.o.
4 or 22	24 y.o.	60 y.o.
5	32 y.o.	59 y.o.
6	31 y.o.	58 y.o.
7	30 y.o.	57 y.o.
8	29 y.o.	56 y.o.
9	28 y.o.	55 y.o.

The Pinnacles

There are 4 of these and they define the way in which the subject journeys along his Life Path. A pinnacle 1 corresponds to a period of taking initiative whereas a pinnacle 7 describes a calm life, marked by reflection and research, etc. They do not, therefore, define the character but rather the style of action undertaken. They also shed light on available opportunities.

Do not forget that this potential occurs within a given context (life cycle) which describes the framework in which it applies. It is also important to take the corresponding personal years into account.

The age at which the native passes from the first to the second pinnacle is equal to 36 years minus the single-digit life path number. However, if a master number 11 or 22 appears on the life path then you may want to consider subtracting 11 or 22 from 36 if the result corresponds with the person's evolution.

The third pinnacle starts 9 years after the second and the final one begins 9 years after the third.

The pinnacles are calculated using the <u>non-reduced</u> day, month and year of birth, bearing in mind that any result displaying a master number 11 or 22 is not reduced:

- **First Pinnacle**: Birth Month + Birth Day
  For Pamela
  $10 + 16 = 26$
  $\mathbf{26} \rightarrow \mathbf{2+6 = 8}$

- **Second Pinnacle**: Birth Day + Birth Year
  For Pamela
  $16 + 1965 = 1981 \rightarrow 1+9+8+1 = 19$
  19 $\rightarrow 1+9 = 10$
  $10 \rightarrow 1+0 = $ **1**

- **Third Pinnacle**: First Pinnacle + Second Pinnacle
  For Pamela
  $8 + 1 = $ **9**

  If you want to refine the calculation, you can also add the non reduced First Pinnacle and Second Pinnacle to get the sub-number[6], an additional element for further analysis.
  For Pamela we take the respective sub-numbers 26 (first Pinnacle) + 19 (second Pinnacle) into account.
  $26 + 19 = $ **45** (45 is the sub-number of 9)

- **Fourth Pinnacle** = Birth Month + Birth Year
  $10 + 1965 = 1975$
  $1975 \rightarrow 1+9+7+5 = $ **22**
  Remember: never reduce 22 because it is a master number, as 11.

Pinnacles	1	2	3	4	5	6	7	8	9	11	22
See pages	140	153 to 154	166 to 167	179 to 180	193 to 194	207 to 208	221 to 222	235	250	258 to 259	265

The Challenges

Challenges are calculated using the three pieces of information present in our date of birth and they are part of our destiny. They shed light on behaviors which can hinder our evolution if we are not aware of them.

---

[6] See below Chapter VI for the interpretation of sub-numbers

Thanks to the ability of our computer software to search through a substantial number of charts, we have been able to correct mistakes, and not insignificant ones, in the calculation of challenges. Other methods of calculating them have often raised problems e.g. most methods prevent the challenges 9, 11 and 22 from being revealed and yet these challenges exist!

In order to calculate the three life challenges, you must use the non-reduced day, month and year of birth, without which some results would be meaningless.

- First minor challenge = Absolute value of (day of birth – month of birth).

  This relates to the period from birth to around 40 years of age, or more precisely, until the end of the first half of the second life cycle because the calculations are done using the day (cycle 2) and the month (cycle 1).

  For Pamela, her first minor challenge is worth 6. This is calculated as follows: her day of birth 16 – her month of birth 10 = 6

  If you get a negative value, the result is the absolute value. October 7th → 7 – 10 = -3 → 3.

- Second minor challenge = Year of birth - Day of birth.

  Its influence starts to be felt at around 40 years of age, or more precisely, from the beginning of the second half of the second life cycle because the calculations are done using the day (cycle 2) and the year (cycle 3).

  For Pamela, her second minor challenge is worth 5 and is calculated as follows: her year of birth 1965 - her day of birth 16 = 1949 → 1 + 9 + 4 + 9 = 23 → 2 + 3 = 5. Note the sub-number 23 which will give us more information about the nature of the challenge 5 (see below for the interpretation of sub-numbers).

- Major life challenge = Year of birth - Month of birth. It is the most important of the three. It is applicable throughout a person's entire life and is felt most intensely during cycle 1 (month of birth) and cycle 3 (year of birth).

For Pamela, this main challenge is worth 2 and is calculated as follows: her year of birth 1965 – her month of birth 10 = 1955 → 1 + 9 + 5 + 5 = 20 → 2 + 0 = 2. Yet again, we find the sub-number 20.

By calculating the challenges in this way, it is possible to obtain the result 0 for the first minor challenge. If that happens then there is simply no first minor challenge.

Any challenge situated in a current personal year, cycle and/or potential, has additional power.

Challenges	1	2	3	4	5	6	7	8	9	11	22
See page	139	153	166	178	193	207	220	234	249	257	264

Core elements shared by mother's birth surname, native's first and middle names and the date of birth

The Maturity Number

Although this number is an important element in the native's expression, it is also a way of differentiating between two numerological charts for people with the same first, middle and last names or with the same date of birth. It also expresses the essence of all of the data taken into account in the construction of a numerological profile.

It is calculated by adding Expression Number + the Life Path, then by reducing the total to a single digit, unless it is a master number (11 or 22). The value obtained corresponds to the combination of the expression of the native's personality and his destiny, which is itself linked to the subject's true nature.

Just like the 10th House in astrology, the Maturity Number defines everything related to personal accomplishment and evolution, e.g. professional ambition, career, social success, reputation, honors, time, grandparents, etc. It is more influential when the native has reached certain… maturity, as its name suggests. Therefore it is difficult to say exactly when this influence will be felt; it all depends on the native's ability to achieve wisdom.

In practice, this number often becomes important when the subject is around 40.

Pamela's Maturity Number is:
Expression Number 8 + Life Path 11 = 19
$19 = 1+9 = 10 \rightarrow 1+0 = \mathbf{1}$

Simply put, this clearly shows that sooner or later Pamela will decide to live her life as she wants, notably once she has resolved her problems vis-à-vis authority.

Maturity	1	2	3	4	5	6	7	8	9	11	22
See page	132	145	157	172	185	199	214	227	241	256	264

The Karmic Debts

These debts were only partly covered by Florence Campbell and Kevin Q. Avery. In fact, these numbers correspond to karmic debts which are all double-digit numbers starting with a 1, not only 13, 14, 16 and 19. There is one exception: 11, in which the 1 does not directly hide the other 1 but rather reinforces its expression. In any case, 11 will be discussed separately as it is a Master Number.

The presence of sub-numbers 12 to 19 in the chart's core elements indicates the native's karma, or more specifically his karmic debt. In a way they are the ego's debts and they are incurred when the number 1 quashes the energy of its neighboring number.

In practice, each of us will pay back the majority of our debts. In order to do this, it is important to define which are the most pressing by noting the number of times they appear and on which of the chart's core numbers (Life Path, Expression, Potential, Aspiration, Maturity, Active or Heredity). Debts that emerge within the Apparent Personality numbers (assumed first name and patronymic) are less influential.

Karmic Debt 12

You have a debt relating to the fact that you have given your word to another (spouse, associate, partner), depriving it of its expression. In any such past life, you find it difficult to bear criticism or remarks, while being able to use this weapon yourself. You tend to see flaws (supposedly) in your partners instead of their qualities. Your obsessive fears could hamper your life, and they are still evident today, including the need for evidence on everything.

Today you need to understand your partner (who is often the same soul once known) and let them their rightful place by treating them equally. However, difficulties of expression, inability to make your voice heard by your partner and your associates in general, may well arise.

Karmic Debt 13

You have a debt to pay in terms of your work. Yet it is past, you could not answer this before certain tasks, you do not wish to assume. Suddenly, you are asked to work with rigor, consistency and thoroughness. Otherwise, there is a risk of conflict relating to all your commitments. It is at this price, that you will come to the end of this karma. In some cases, this may indicate a fear of death and all matters pertaining thereto. Today, you have now a lingering feeling of guilt and the feeling of owing something to somebody else.

Karmic Debt 14

You have chosen to review the way you used to assume your sensuality. This debt reflects anything that refers to physical abuse suffered and/or committed in other lives. It speaks of behaviors in connection with a frenzy to exalt your senses that led to excess. You were not able to contain the impulses that flowed from them and you were able to take advantage of certain situations.

Today, it is likely that you feel bad about yourself. You have chosen a safeguard before incarnating yourself; while you want to live a free and unfettered life, you find yourself limited by physical disability, confinement or any other constraint that does not give you total freedom in your field of action.

Karmic Debt 15

In the past you had a craving for excitement and love. Only in your past lives, you had no limits, no restraint in your conquests, and you had difficulty controlling your instincts. Easy pleasures followed another, to the point of disregarding the wishes of others. This almost obsessive desire in terms of love and your senses made you forget trivial circumstances and daily responsibilities.

Today, the temptation is there but life does not allow you to transfer as easily. Responsibilities are to be assumed. Your life is punctuated by events and somehow you no longer call the shots. Rather you appear to be led by the nose in love at work. Besides, your love life is not what you had in mind. Some relationships are impossible while others put you more in a state of submission. However, it is through your reliability and your ability to fulfill your obligations that you will find real satisfaction. It is in this way that you open the most beautiful doors.

Karmic Debt 16

In a distant past, you betrayed the trust that was placed in you. Your tumultuous love life, your secret loves, your excess of authority and your handling of your emotional relationships has caused hurt. Partners were violated and could not fully express their potential. Sometimes, the relationship was even illegitimate.

Today, it is likely you have found a former love and that finally, you're looking to experience that love in a positive way, although it may also lead to a separation or even a betrayal. In all cases, a deep reflection on these events will allow for the awareness of the emotional and spiritual needs of the other. Moreover, this debt represents a tendency for introspection, withdrawal and confrontation of your inhibitions. The paths you take to change are often surprising, even disconcerting, to your friends who think they know you and eventually they see you in a different light.

Karmic Debt 17

In the past, an imperious desire to govern, to impose, to bring about a spiritual diktat and to increase material goods has distracted you from your original faith. The lack of respect for the values of love, sharing, selflessness led you to exaggerations sometimes to the point of causing death in the name of a religion. Always with a strong will, a firmness in principles, an ability to control your life like that of others, in this life you risk finding yourself in dead ends, unable to manage your life as you want to and the obligation to take into account the will of others.

You have still kept a lot of creativity, resources, extraordinary stamina, a heightened sense of reality. Your eagerness for life will serve you well to overcome all sorts of restrictions that you have created through your lack of true spirituality. Also, you are advised to value friends, to provide protection and providence. To help you, you can count on influential people, protectors, awakeners. And if you can overcome your uncompromising nature and regain your faith, you'll get everything a fulfilled life can bring.

Karmic Debt 18

In one or more past lives, you used your abilities to initiate, control, direct, to accumulate wealth for your own benefit. You also used your strength and your power to gratify your sexual instincts, with scant regard for the lives of others. You are looking to integrate all kinds of community to better enjoy it. In fact, you trampled on the ideals of humanism and duty towards your neighbor.

To rectify this somehow, you've chosen, before you incarnated, to find it necessary to again use your knowledge and abilities to serve the greatest number. If you forget, many obstacles related to your past abuses may be in your way. Emotional flashback, non-recognition by your loved ones or your peers may be your lot. You need to show kindness in your heart by opening yourself up, for example to charitable actions or just by giving a little of your time to the needy. Since you still have a great capacity to proceed, you should use it in the best way to move away from strictly selfish goals. Finally, by putting yourself at the top of the worst-off people in order to help them, you reach a level of satisfaction much higher than that obtained previously when you thought only of satisfying your own needs.

Karmic Debt 19

Long ago, you held power (social, spiritual, physical etc). With this superiority over a group, you benefited. Today, you must use this power to conduct, to lead, to light the way for those in need. But to show that authority in your social life, it will be necessary to face setbacks, material losses, and in some cases, to follow a real journey of initiation.

If this debt is the most difficult to live with, it is also the most beautiful promise of renewal if you show you can succeed without prejudice towards others and gather your strengths by avoiding loosing focus. Whatever your level of influence, you will have the opportunity to use your resources for the good of many, by developing all types of actions whose purpose is to allow others to gain confidence in their own value so they regain their own esteem and in turn become capable of undertaking tasks.

To summarize...

- There are 4 core elements: the Aspiration number (Soul Urge → vowels), the Potential number (the being's potential → consonants), the Expression number (way in which he expresses Aspiration and Potential) and the Life Path (road map and true nature closely intermingled). All 4 of these elements are contained in the Maturity Number.
- You should always consider the sub-number behind a core number.

- Find the numbers absent from the inclusion table (missing/karmic numbers), the excessive modulators (> 9) and the most frequent modulator in the square (Intensity).
- See if any number appears in more than one core number and interpret these unique associations.
- Take into account any sub-number or number on a core element that corresponds to a challenge, a missing/karmic number or a karmic debt.

CHAPTER VI

Interpreting core numbers

"I do not believe in human freedom in the philosophical sense of the word. Everybody acts not only under external compulsion, but must be intrinsic to adapt."

(*Albert Einstein*)

If there is one pitfall to be avoided in numerology, it is systematically applying generalities to any and every subject. Beginners interpret numbers as though the rules are set in stone and try to make the accepted interpretations apply to all those carrying the number in question, without considering any nuances. This is the same as ignoring interactions between numbers when it is vital to take them into account. Furthermore, this is one of the main difficulties I experienced when creating my numerological software. I wanted the interpretations to be as personal as possible but I have always known that there is no way a computer program can refine a reading in the same way as a practiced numerologist. How do you incorporate intuition or global vision into computer code? In the end, it was only when I multiplied the number of conditions that the latest version of the software was finally able to generate extremely pertinent readings.

You should not, therefore, take the following definitions too literally, but try to add the finishing touches yourself. Keep in mind that there are all sorts of markers in the chart which can tone down, vary or even (in rare cases) contradict information conveyed by the core number. For example, 1 letter with a value of 1 in the inclusion table indicates the importance of the father or the person having fulfilled this role in the subject's life. The modulator 1 tells us that the native identifies with that person in a big way. A woman will look for a man who will in some way incarnate this fatherly, teacher-like ideal, but if she only has one letter worth 7 then there may be a context of revolt or estrangement from that father. Hence all information must be nuanced or confirmed by the other numbers in the chart. Additionally, the indications given do not take into account any possible missing numbers or challenges, which would significantly modify the interpretation.

Furthermore, it is totally normal to be able to broadly recognize ourselves in every interpretation of a core number. We can all see some of our qualities reflected in an Expression 1, an Expression 2, and so on. The difference lies in the intensity! This means that whichever analysis stands out the most is the most accurate. This variability could be taken into account to create protocols to evaluate the accuracy of numerology.

Some people make the error of not distinguishing between the different sectors of existence on which a number can act. For example, the value of the Maturity number tells us which qualities an individual will use in his social potential. It is easier for a person with an Expression 1 to succeed with a Maturity 1. On the other hand, an Expression 2 with a Maturity 1 describes socioprofessional success requiring more adaptation and effort.

For more detailed information, particularly in relation to interaction mechanisms, I cannot recommend my bedside table book, *L'art d'interpréter la numérologie* (The art of numerological interpretation) by Françoise Daviet, highly enough. I have been able to verify the accuracy of her analysis year after year. For information on the Life Path, Dan Millman's book, *The Life You Were Born To Live*, is essential reading.

I would also like to thank Michel for his proofreading and precisions on the correspondence between numbers and signs of the Zodiac.

To conclude, three fundamental rules must be respected if you want to construct a pertinent numerological profile:

- Any number found in a core element is nuanced by the sub-number it came from, if any. Particular attention should be paid to the presence or absence of a karmic debt 12, 13, 14, 15, 16, 17, 18 or 19.
- Any number found in a core element is nuanced if it corresponds to a challenge and/or a missing/karmic number.
- Any number found in a core element necessarily relates to identical numbers found in other elements of the same chart. This shows us in which specific area the revealed information shall be put into action. This is particularly true for the boxes of the inclusion chart (inclusion).

Once again, let us not forget the important differences between the core elements

True self and destiny = Life Path
The strength of the personality = Expression Number
The self and the strength of the soul = Aspiration Number
The means available = Potential Number

When number 1 acts

Life Path 1: Reaching success by yourself is your way to go. Your itinerary will cost you some efforts, but it eventually leads to your project's individual achievement. It is sometimes accompanied by unpredictable changes.

In case of karma 1, you will live like a fighter. You may overcome many obstacles. It will be necessary to meet your own goals by yourself, without any help from others. You will be asked to prove voluntary and persevering.

Tip: moderate by interpreting all the sub numbers revealed by the 3 ways of calculating the life path (see Chapter V).

Expression 1: You are voluntary, ambitious and exercise authority. You have confidence in yourself and you will have the opportunity to express your potential. Passion is the fuel that keeps your engine going. You know how to organize, guide, direct and take the initiative. That's why you will blossom in a business where you will assume that role or an independent business.

Tip: see all sub-numbers behind this 1. Do not forget that Expression is also the reduced sum of the Aspiration and Potential numbers. This can reveal another sub-number. For example, Aspiration 7 + Potential 3 gives 10, sub-number of the Expression 1.

Aspiration 1: Your deep desire is to move forward by demonstrating effectiveness. You are known for your originality. You can count on certain people to succeed. You feel comfortable when the game is changing around you, even when it may seem unfavorable. You can then courageously put forward your aspiration to change the situation and find the recognition you seek.

Potential 1: You want to invest in major projects, be a person who decides and succeeds, sometimes ignoring your emotional life. You love beautiful things, have a taste for a comfortable lifestyle, sensitive to your home, your wallet may suffer. Now you must also show economy because you may go missing. You have the means to earn your financial independence on your own. Your efforts allow you to be, bearing in mind that you need professional independence to give the best of yourself. This also applies if you play sports.

First Name 1: Your father has been playing second fiddle. You benefit from a certain freedom in your socioprofessional activity, even if the presence of hierarchy is likely. You need to be very powerful, so, you tend to over exert yourself, to exceed your physical abilities in your daily activities in particular.

1st Middle Name 1: You are unique in many ways. You idealize your partner. Your ego can be the source of difficulties in your relationships by leading you to experience a form of solitude.

2nd Middle Name 1: You are a player and a live wire. Independent pioneer, you have the desire to explore your ideas in a fun way. You often initiate new projects. Blessed with initiative, an independent character, you constantly push the limits; do satisfying yourself with knowledge, or anything too conventional. You are the perfect explorer, but also eternally dissatisfied when you cannot do things in perspective between what is established, and what remains to be discovered. The protection of influential people favors your success.

Heredity 1: Your family (often large under this aspect) is marked by love for his children and a genuine desire to ensure offspring and perpetuate the family name. As a child, you liked to play and/or to play sports. You have a form of edgy emotional susceptibility that comes from your early youth. The father figure is probably an authoritarian but benevolent. From your family home, you have inherited will, leadership and a form of partisanship that makes you want to protect your clan. Finally, later in life, you want to be in charge of a small group (family, friends ...) Due to a strong and protective mother, you will have a somewhat similar behavior in adulthood with your own family and will try to recreate this safe environment.

Active 1: You know to get out of situations presented to you when the going is good. You also appear to be someone who is innovative and bold.

Example: an Aspiration 6 colored by an Active number 1 provides information on the continued commitment of the native with regard to their family.

Maturity 1: More of a leader or liberal than subordinate, you will be more and more willing to take responsibility for yourself and to not owe anything to anyone, even if a man often plays an important role in your socioprofessional progress. Often controversial situations with established authority, whatever it may be, will arise. Courageous and hardworking, dynamic, with exceptional professional skills, you will advance your ideas and projects, with the need to be recognized by many. However, this will overcome a reserved nature bordering on timidity in certain circumstances. This may be accompanied by a desire to distance yourself from an oppressive social or family environment, in favor of a monastic, marginal or solitary life in a quiet and natural environment. You'll still have a little competition, you know, the kind that you enjoy without necessarily seeking direct confrontation.

Intensity 1: You have strong opinions on many subjects. You display a lot of ambition, courage and vitality. You're able to put yourself out to meet your goals whilst appearing agitated. You also have a tendency to make everything about you.

Karma 1 (no letter 1): First of all, it is obvious that you don't trust yourself enough. Taking initiatives, committing yourself frightens you. Learn how to stand up for yourself. In fact, all that is connected to the symbolic image of the father. Your identification with him, or the person in this role, took place while he was away, barely present, if not downright absent for whatever reasons (abandonment, escape into drugs, alcohol, gambling, professional life leading him to never be there etc). Sometimes, the father himself has suffered from a form of depreciation and in turn this could affect you. Suddenly, you are often in situations of dependence on another, under influence, malleable. You must learn to assert yourself, not to rest on the decisions of others.

1 letter worth 1: A strong influence from your father or the person playing this role is surely the source of your masculine ideal. This relationship with your father tends to energize you. You take him as an example but in spite of the admiration that you feel for him you can very well go against him. This is one of the ways that allow you to assert yourself. Responsible, you want to succeed socially, to surpass yourself. You are blessed with a strong, determined and enterprising character and your athletic nature means you are drawn to competition. You are consistent, you know what you want, and you are imposing. You are not unduly frightened by difficulties, on the contrary, they stimulate you, oblige you to surpass yourself. Insensitive to others' weaknesses, like your own, you do not like people who whine. You like to impose your law in all areas, you tend to force others, including in love, where your eagerness is sometimes a little too obvious. Proud, a little dictator, your sensitivity and your hypersensitive ego can sometimes lead you to violent reactions. This aspect also indicates the possibility of loss or lack of a brother. You will need to be vigilant vis-à-vis all that affects the head, the heart and blood circulation. Beware of accidents that there may be many of.

2 letters worth 1: You will overcome an emotional knot linked to the image of your father, arising from either too strong a presence of the latter or simply from his absence whether voluntary or not The way you see men and the image you create is tainted by your mother's or even your grandmother's personality, if by chance, the latter held the role of the mother This image leaves you with a permanent mark, which may cause a mixture of genres deforming the male archetype. In this case, the feminine takes the place of the masculine. A form of maternal dependency sets in. If you are a man, you look to be recognized and valued by women. You are looking for a comfortable life and do not accept in any way that everything related to mediocrity takes over your life. You are blessed with a good memory and you have an intuitive mind. Above all, you prefer your brilliant inspirations. You favor anything that is innovative for your benefit but especially for the benefit of others. You are a productive and selfless person that does not systematically seek to impose your natural authority. You need to learn not to let yourself get overwhelmed by a certain amount of concern about the vicissitudes of life, which tend to make you nervous. You like to make yourself useful without asking for anything in return, you are easily relegated to the sidelines. You're afraid of being discredited in the eyes of your loved ones, which often requires you to do too much. Contact with the public is encouraged, despite some shyness. You know how to make yourself appreciated and you have tact but you will still need to control your excessive emotionality.

3 letters worth 1: In many ways, your father, or the man holding this role, displays a desire to keep his juvenile nature; he likes to be taken care of. It is possible that the paternal role is assumed by a family elder. If you are a woman, you tend to meet partners who are younger than you, just like the state of mind of your father and/or your brothers, if you have any. The perception you have of your father may be that of a person who has an opinion on everything, despite a rather immature side. You have an entrepreneurial spirit; you value your ideas which are often new and original. Despite a brilliant mind, you are not immune to being oversensitive. You are sensitive to words spoken, to the turn of phrase and to the image and impact of the family name you bear. A rivalry with a brother or sister cannot be ruled out. You tend to start things but rarely finish what you start. You are adaptable, have the gift of the gab and are able to get out of difficult situations, thanks to your great abilities. Your playfulness and your competitive spirit naturally lead you to take on many challenges. That said your narcissistic side can make you hard and extremely sensitive. You are often too sure of your qualities and your capabilities, which sometimes cause insensitivity to the fortunes of others. You are also skilled in commerce.

4 letters worth 1: Your father appears as a real head of the family with firm principles. He may have tended to favor one child, especially if it was a son. This preferential context vis-à-vis your brothers and sisters initially bothered. If you are a woman, you could show masculine qualities to please a father who was expecting a son rather than a daughter. If you are a boy, you can be marked by your father's excessive harshness, which, paradoxically, will not prevent you from adopting the same behavior later. You are a pragmatist, focusing primarily on that which is objective. Your nature is often a little too down to earth, which makes you a person who has very strong views, even bordering on stubbornness. Being very insensitive to everything related to the subjective, when you show an interest in so-called esoteric areas, they must be tangible and efficient - magnetism, for example. You're serious and solid and common sense prevails over everything else. Perhaps because of an education that was a little too strict, you have developed a pronounced sense of responsibility, and moreover you tend to want to do too much. You will relieve yourself of the burden of education, which due to an inferiority complex, always pushes you prove your skills. You do not always feel comfortable with the unexpected and new because your mind is sometimes too slow to understand. You need to get to know a subject before you give an opinion on it. It is possible that your mind is a little misogynistic and resents female authority. Your desire to create a family is strong, and of course anything related to material acquisitions is one of your primary concerns.

5 letters worth 1: Your father is voluble, rather a hedonist who is fond of his independence and freedom. You are special, innovative and sometimes very parochial. In some ways, it is very difficult for you to rely on yourself. If you are a man, unless there are contrary aspects in your numerology chart, you will seek to resemble this father; above all by copying this form of freedom and independence that characterizes him so much. If you are a woman, you will have a tendency to meet paternalistic men. You are driven by a thirst for discoveries and new experiences that shape your original mind and you hate being compared to anyone. You like to travel. Acting more on impulse, you like to tackle multiple projects simultaneously. Impatient, not very persevering, you tend to start but you don't always finish. You need to be surrounded by people and to get recognition from those that get involved in your projects, but it doesn't stop you from bothering more than one of them! You seem to see your horizon darken if life no longer gives you the excitement you need. You can be counted on to think outside the box. A real maverick! You are also capable and responsive as well as revolutionary or rebellious etc. And not always loyal. Anything related to communication is encouraged as well as anything that can lead to some social progress. Your spontaneous and direct nature sometimes shocks and you can be somewhat naive and you tend not to adequately protect yourself. Not all truths are always good to say, or else you have to put the shapes. You keep a young character and this is your true nature.

6 letters worth 1: Your father, or the person holding this role, tends to show a strong presence and to act responsibly in such a way that he is recognized as someone who is useful to others. If you have a karma of 6, that is to say that you do not have the letters F, O or X, this aspect may suggest a father who is not involved for one reason or another (absent, unknown, little involvement etc). Anyway, the paternal imprint will be at the root of your charming side. You are constantly seeking recognition of your abilities. Your mind is rather sociable, you are an aesthetic who seeks to surround themselves with beautiful things and to create a harmonious life in accordance with your aspirations. You tend to focus above all on what you love, leaving aside anything that you find vulgar or that is not to your taste. You also need to feel useful and sometimes indispensable. Anything related to the social, the medical, the legal and even the psychological is very encouraged. You will need to work hard to take care of your financial life and to assert your views. Conflicts with authority are to be feared. You will quickly surround yourself with leaders who, directly or indirectly, will help you in your professional life. You are a protector, you can give much to others but you are also very demanding and expect the same consideration in return. You like to pass over everything you do even on your best day, which might cause you problems when you do not feel at your best, especially in love.

7 letters worth 1: Your father is an intellectual who is rather critical and responsive, if not disgusted, vis-à-vis all that it appears unnecessary and mundane. If you are a woman, you find the image of this father among your partners. If you are a man, it is this image that you take as an example in order to affirm your mental strength. You should be careful not to give in to the temptation to adopt this form of paternalistic authoritarianism. A tendency towards a certain paranoia may develop during your life. Your rather curious nature forces you to push the boundaries, whatever they may be. You spend a lot of time reflecting and fine tuning your strategies because you are demanding and a perfectionist. You like to expand intellectually and you have a great need to be recognized as a cultured being. You will seek to get past the image that you have created of your father, as if you had a challenge ahead. You must learn to calm yourself down, not to yield to some nervousness which leads you straight to burnout. Contacts with the foreign may be frequent and despite your fears, sometimes unspoken, your destiny has some good surprises in store for you. You will seek to keep the direction of your business even if you surround yourself with employees. You need to be part of a group of elitists. You are very idealistic and you can easily think that you have a mission to fulfill. In love, in friendship, as in the workplace, you need to meet people that you think are exceptional.

8 letters worth 1: Your father may be very present, which can give you the feeling that he is too imposing and he is overly authoritarian. It may be that you suffered some form of jealousy vis-à-vis his male offspring, of course, if you're a boy. This has perhaps had the effect of overshadowing your own development. Whether you're a son or daughter, you will tend to copy this model, despite some mistakes, allowing you to assert yourself in life. You'll have to overcome possible inhibitions caused by this omnipotent paternal presence. You have an urge to control everything that happens around you and you want to know about things in depth. You do not give in to your first impulses easily and you do not show your emotions unnecessarily. Your nature is rather reserved, almost impenetrable. You are blessed with great powers of concentration, an unusual strength of character, there is not much that scares you or puts you off, and you rather love adversity. Your ability to bounce back in all sorts of situations is matched only by your taste for all that is mysterious and unfathomable. That's why you can have a great attraction to the occult or anything related to the meanderings of the brain. Provided you do not forget your ambitions, your financial and material successes are your main concerns. You are blessed with a strong magnetism that leaves no one indifferent and above all you know how to use it to achieve your goals. Your sex drive is strong. Be careful not to resort to revenge when you feel betrayed.

9 letters worth 1: Your father, sometimes with too much empathy for his family, has not always been able to affirm a strong presence. This feeling has led to a tendency to cause you to withdraw into yourself and to remove yourself. It is possible that because of his lack of personality, a distance caused by his various activities and his different interests, he has left you with the image of him being difficult to define. This distance may also result from difficult tests that life sometimes throws up (diseases, accidents). Ultimately, in no way does this model allows you to get an accurate picture of the paternal role, much less does it give you an example. To overcome this lack of paternal consistency, you, throughout your life, try to pinpoint the essence of your partners. You have a rather dreamy nature focusing on subjective worlds. Your extreme sensitivity can be a real handicap to your achievement. Like a sheet of blotting paper, you absorb the energies around you and you easily layer over them. Your imagination is boundless and you tend to invent worlds and lives. You must learn to be more rational, more accurate and not to get carried away like a wisp of straw in your emotional and sensory tornados. Anything related to charity and the humanitarian domain is favored, and more generally, anything that allows you to help your peers. You like to romanticize your life and you prefer adventure and escape through reading. You should be wary of falling into excessive responsiveness vis-à-vis the restraints that life imposes on us, which can lead you straight to self-destruction. Do not try to automatically flee that which bothers and annoys you. You must keep in mind that it is necessary and essential to form your own opinion through your own experiences. Do not seek to endorse, systematically, the responsibility for anything that does not work well.

More than 9 letters worth 1: See above for the interpretation of the reduction of this number.

Example: If you have 12 letters at a value of 1, you get a 3 by adding 1 + 2. Refer to this value, that is to say 3 letters at a value of 1. Remember to also take into account the 1 and 2 which makes up your 12 because they also refer to sub numbers. You must, therefore, interpret them by taking into account the definition of these two figures from the definition of the sub numbers given below. Remember, this mainly concerns the father and the husband if you are a woman.

1 Mental letter: You are quick to respond when faced with situations where reasoning is required. Your mental activity is lively, alert; often underpinned by the need to confront yourself, to prove yourself. A man (a father, a partner etc) can represent both an example and a challenge through these intellectual abilities.

1 Emotional letter: You enjoy the company of others after one round of observation. You communicate your feelings in an almost instinctive manner. You react immediately. You are not always able to filter things out, to step back... in fact, your reactions are often too abrupt.

1 Intuitive letter: Your gut instincts are quick and sudden. They are inspiring and you make good use of them to organize yourself and act in society. In fact, you often know what you want.

1 Physical letter: There will be solitary moments in your journey which will help you to move forward. Your willingness to assert yourself, to set yourself up to live through the challenges to come. The context often focuses on issues related to physical health.

1 Creative letter: your creativity is expressed within groups. You are independent in your choices for your leisure and sport.

1 Balanced letter: The attachment to your father and/or one man in particular is very strong. Similarly, you ensure that your efforts bring you greater stability.

1 Dual letter: You're able to question in relation to education received and your roots.

Challenge 1: You must demonstrate your ability to make a decision and stick to it, avoiding making your loved ones responsible for your failures. It will affirm a determination and a measured willingness by counting on yourself first, in the face of adversity. Conversely, there may be a lack of confidence in your ability to take the initiative, to identify yourself. Find the balance between inaction and agitation, being fair and avoiding authoritarianism. Any excess would lead to a megalomania and/or paranoia complex.

First Cycle 1: It is a powerful training cycle that promises great opportunities for development. As a child, you are dynamic and sometimes arrogant. You look to take initiatives early, to take over in all situations. In this regard parents and educators should temper your passions and teach you to analyze a situation before you commit. A man, often the father, has a strong influence on you.

Second Cycle 1: The environment leads you to assert your personality. You have the power to decide, to choose your direction. And given that your chart is very positive. It is a context conducive to professional success. You gain in autonomy.

Third Cycle 1: The time for rest, complete sedentary is not is not straight away because here you are still very involved. This is sometimes the reward for the efforts you put in during the previous cycle whether it be gains or recognition. In all cases, new commitments, responsibilities fall to you. Alertness remains important.

First Pinnacle 1: You highlight strong intellectual capabilities when it comes to moving forward, to developing and fulfilling projects. As a child, you are quite quickly left to your own devices. Whatever your history with him, the father occupies a prominent place in your development.

Second or Third Pinnacle 1: Renewal in terms of ideas and activities. Your lifestyle may change thanks to your initiatives. Professional projects are favored as well as the affirmation of your abilities. The advice is to stay measured in your endeavors.

Fourth Pinnacle 1: Finally, you continue to show real vitality. You still have the need to undertake, to succeed. Often, you still retain an activity but probably in a new direction.

Sub-numbers of 1

10: Indicates ups and downs. Fulfillment, setback and renewal. Opportunity to start afresh without losing dynamism. Act as leader of men, blessed with concentration, a rational mind to assert its success. Ruthless in the pursuit of your objectives. Confers authority. Too often.

Note: all other sub-numbers reduced to 1 are also sub-numbers of 10 (19 → 1+9=10, 28 → 2+8=10 etc).

19 (see also its meaning as a karmic debt): Can highlight difficulties in terms of reputation, honor, authority. Specifies identification with a figure of excessive or failing authority stresses the need for a woman to balance her polarity, leads to separations... Can also lead to a rebirth, a new class once the debt is erased.

28: Contributes to the taking of new initiatives. Sometimes some relationships linked to authority may cause a nervous instability, become less efficient, especially if there is external pressure. Cause of melancholy, ups and downs, frustration, loneliness during certain periods, but also indicates an ability to exercise determination to change the course of things. Galvanizes loved ones, looks for a form of perfection in their success (28 is the second perfect number, sum of the positive divisors excluding the number itself.)

37: Promotes socioprofessional success after a change, gives the taste for independence, makes it original, protects sentimental life.

46: Promotes a harmonious social life, makes seductive, increases sexual needs. By trying too hard to please and respect the established rules, you can sometimes be influenced and deviate from your primary objectives.

55: The *sine qua non* condition of success obligatorily includes the perseverance and tenacious pursuit of his objectives. Predisposed to contacts with the foreign, gives impetus, makes things fun.

64: Does not favor business because the social action is predominant. Predisposed to professional changes, sometimes obliged to reposition themselves, to question themselves, to act on new foundations.

73: Gives a taste for independence. Prefers to work alone if possible so as to put forward their vision, freedom, vitality. Productive and intuitive which doesn't prevent a form of mysticism and inner wisdom, with the feeling of being slightly above the melee. Often leads to difficult management in terms of the world of business.

82: Increases willingness and the ability to take the initiative, even to direct a project. Emotional life, associations can become unstable. Sometimes refusing to join one or many unions.

91: Fosters all forms of creativity in the socioprofessional area, marking a tenancy towards eccentricity in the area concerned. Made extravagant.

When number 2 occurs...

Life Path 2: This itinerary will push you towards others. Similarly, you will achieve your goals thanks to the help of other persons. Getting together and collaborating will prove important throughout your life.

In case of karma 2, you will be prone to undergo events, more than to create them. It is possible that marriage and associations may burden you. You must react!

Note: 20 is the only two digits sub-number of 2. All others sub-numbers give 11 (29, 38, 47...) and should never been reduced to 2. So moderate by interpreting all the sub-numbers revealed by the 3 ways of calculating the life path (see Chapter V). In case there is another sub-number different from 20, you got a Life Path 11/2.

Expression 2: Living in harmony is your reason for being. To do this, you avoid conflict and use diplomacy. You are accommodating, considerate. You easily agree to be subordinate to others when you return a mark of respect for your attitude. You let others know that you are available. You would like to share this accommodating nature. You are on the quest for the perfect partner until this goal is reached.

Tip: this expression is very rare. Most of the time, they are sub-numbers (19, 38, 47...) which give an Expression 11. However the sum of the Aspiration and Potential numbers may give a 2 like Aspiration 9 and Potential 11 (9 + 11 = 20). In this case, Expression is 11/2.

Aspiration 2: Your deep desire is to vibrate the fraternal spirit animates you. You want to show that you are a diplomat and indulgent, that you want to live in community and / or surrounded by friends Meetings (often female) will all you to achieve this desire to act for others and to be associated. Your imagination, your intuition, too. You need loving recognition. You have the need to not be too vague, you want to stay in your place. You are not necessarily looking for fame and fortune but simply benevolent emotional and material security. Your mother's role in your life is preponderant.

Potential 2: You practice your listening potential, your sensitivity, your imagination, your sophistication, your creativity to obtain a concrete social result. Attached to some material aspects, for your safety, of the family assets transferred or acquired through your union, you act so as to preserve your assets. Your attraction to nature, your ability to feed and/or decorate can be stepping stones to your achievement.

First Name 2: You are a perfect organizer, helpful (sometimes excessively), obsessed with everything concerning the family and private life. Idealistic when it comes to choosing your partners and the quality of life (especially family), your obsession is not finding in your partners and colleagues the qualities that you expect from them. You often attract people to you and enjoy a certain popularity. Attracted by psychology, medical care, you can be a good educator or advisor within the family organization. Your mind is hyperactive.

1st Middle Name 2: You are emotionally dependant. In the quest for the ideal love, you can show yourself to be subject to the willingness of your partners in order to not hurt them, hence indecision, dissatisfactions resulting from your failure. Faithful in generally, you need to be wary of your prejudices in relation to your partners. You often follow traditional and conformist principles of life. An artist to the core, poet, very attached to childhood, you have developed a very specific link with your mother. Your spouse may appear immature in some ways.

2nd Middle Name 2: Sometimes childish, capricious, hypersensitive, too interested in yourself, you look to be surrounded within a group, often exclusively. You like to explore but in a limited and familiar context. You love the game. Very attached to your mother, you keep this need to be indulged. Amazing in your reactions, you appear nice, friendly and good-natured. You can be a very good trader in a well-established shop environment. Your feminist is exacerbated.

Heredity 2: Your mother has a male side, maybe this comes from her authoritarian ways. The parental home is attached to its roots, the concept of family in his home. He likes to perpetuate the traditions (cooking, job well done ...) The impression is strong and can lead you to, as an adult, want to start a family in the broadest sense of the term. You need a house, which combines elegance and comfort. You carry an interest in real estate acquisitions and a form of gentrification does not displease you. On the other hand, this family spirit of association, cooperation, is dominate and represents a model to follow.

Active 2: You usually act calm and collected, taking care that your actions do not invite too much criticism.

Example: an Expression 1 nuanced by an Active number 2 reveals a number of forms of ambivalence with regard to the native when it comes to deciding. The action, yes, but often under the influence of emotions.

Maturity 2: More collaborative than leader, you can stay in the shadows and allow the ascension of another. Your tendency to do a lot in your activity, even to sacrifice yourself, will be noticed otherwise you will feel resentment. Shy when it comes to asserting your individuality, you will blossom over time by expressing your sensitivity.

Intensity 2: You show attention, dedication to others. You've undoubtedly a sense of cooperation and friendship. Your strong sensitivity often leads you to be overwhelmed by your emotions. You also have a strong sense of aesthetics.

Karma 2 (no letter 2): You are hyper sensitive. You are stubborn and adamant : learn how to control your emotions. You will be easier to live with, at home, or at work. In fact, all that is connected to the karmic origin of the link to your mother. The nature of this relationship is that you lack the presence of a mother in the entire maternal sense of the term. As a result, this lack, this legitimate and unfulfilled expectation from the child in you, leads you to want to be unconditionally loved. Perhaps you don't perceive that it is a source of difficulty for others. As a result, this appropriation attempt degenerates into conflict. A break-up often ensues and depression too if you're not careful. Therefore it is best to identify that which belongs to your dreams, your projections of reality from the other which has its own history. Listening qualities should be developed to ease the effects of this influence.

1 letter worth 2: The perception you have of your mother has done more to benefit your head than your heart. It is his masculine side that has obscured the signs of affection that you expect. You still have the image of an insensitive mother, who did not display much of her feminine nature, but that does not stop you idealizing her in any way. If you are a woman, you will seek approval from your spouse to meet his expectations, while striving to be like him. If you are a man, you will be attracted to a woman with a masculine spirit who is able to assert herself. You are subject to strong emotions that you find it difficult to control, that you shake strongly, especially as you often use them as a weapon. These emotions can lead you to show excessive authority. You have an ability to roll with the punches and pick yourself up again. Caution is advised particularly in your associative relationships, whatever they are, because your tendency to impose your views may cause you problems. You're ready to fight tooth and nail for your family, your home, your spouse or your offspring. If you have children, they will surely be difficult to raise. You have a very original way of removing yourself from anything that is not part of your ideal world. You look to get rid of anything that can hurt you, anything that interferes with the smooth running of your life. You're an original creator who knows how to surround themselves with beautiful things, refusing mediocrity. You know how to defend your values and your personal interests which are often the same as those of the people around you. Sooner or later you will enjoy a certain popularity, but within a smaller group. You're very sensitive to feminine relationships.

2 letters worth 2: Your hypersensitivity is largely due to resentment, heart ailments, emotional difficulties and the incessant complaints from your mother. Your subconscious is still marked by the impact that you had on the expression of the maternal psyche. You will probably find it difficult to get rid of it, especially if the weight of the existential irritancy of your mother still weighs down on you. If, in her home environment, she has not found the recognition that she so badly needs, she will be inclined to keep repeating: "With everything I've done for you... ». A transfer occurs when you impose a certain emotional responsibility, even guilt. If you are a woman, it will cause the urge to attach great importance to your role as a mother. You will seek to fulfill a need for recognition and emotional security very early on. By developing some empathy you will easily be able to anticipate all situations and the motivations of those around you. If you are a man you seek above all to preserve the harmony in your marriage. In case of conflict, you will not be sheltered from disturbances because your emotional balance is very, even too, dependent on that of your partner. You are blessed with good listening skills. Blessed with a childlike, poet's and dreamer's mind, you also have an artistic side (often music). You can also be fussy, moody and demanding. You are sometimes too focused on the opinions of those around you. Loyal to your friends and your family (yours or one you've blended into), you like to create a calm atmosphere that mainly benefits those around you. Above all, you appreciate anything you find in your familiar environment. You often ask for advice, but paradoxically, you do not always take any notice of it. This means you use it to reassure yourself with regard to what you do, just to get an opinion. You also encounter difficulties when it comes to making choices. You love children and animals. Often a slave to your obligations, your family/professional circle, you need to empower yourself. Your sexuality can sometimes be twofold or ambiguous. You are a charmer and charming but sooner or later you must stop believing in fairy tales.

3 letters worth 2: Your mother, or the person holding this role, retains a youthful, open, dynamic mind with some ability to charm her audience. She often tends to use, even abusive speech, her words often lacking depth. The irony is that she does not have, herself, very good listening skills. She often seeks to be supported by those around her, oddly lacking autonomy. In your case, you tend to express your feelings in a way that is too intellectual. Communication with your partner can often be tense, just like the communication you had with your mother. Nevertheless, in your various activities, you'll enjoy a certain popularity. If you are a man, you have an attraction to "adolescent" women with more focus on fun than commitment. Having said that, your character is accompanied by a form of immaturity in your emotional relationships. You will have several homes, with the risk of you having really difficulty settling in one place. If you have brothers and sisters, your relationships with them are very odd. In your home environment, you'll probably find yourself surrounded by twins. You have a creative imagination and you know how to link your fine sensory perception to your deep thinking. You are inspired. Sociable and communicative, you know how to charm your audience, you need to talk.

4 letters worth 2: Your mother, who was very influenced by a disrupted education, has certainly found it difficult to find her place within the family structure. It's likely that above all she has sought security for her and her family. She is surely seen as a bit too traditional, set in the way she sees things, in education. You yourself, you will undoubtedly be influenced by the maternal influence and you will have a clear tendency to bring attention to your associations. This recognition mechanism also leads you to be very sensitive to your social position, wanting to conform to the current standard, surely one that your mother adopted in her time. You are looking to find your place in the sun but you should note that you do not always give yourself the means to achieve it because often the prisoner in the shackles of education. Above all, you are rational, you prefer everything that is constructive and well-established, in the image of your education. You have a real ability to focus on your goals but you must be careful not to lock yourself in a world that is a bit too closed off and frozen. Anything that is foreign to your usual mode of operation can cause you anxiety. You really do not like being pushed around and you need to rely constantly on your bearings. You tend to focus on experience rather than theory, despite strong opinions that you are happy to discuss all day long. You are slow to launch yourself into action, but once you get going, not much can stop your momentum. You are a "diesel" engine! You have a sense of organization and discipline. You may not by fundamentally resentful but let's just say you have a good memory. You like to be surrounded, especially by children, but paradoxically, solitude does not scare you. You can have a "surly" side which hinders your spontaneous expression.

5 letters worth 2: Your mother must have been perceived as someone very committed to her freedom of action and to her autonomy. This need for movement may have caused instability in a real loving relationship, as in yours. Energetic and progressive, you often control those around you. Very attached to your friends and your family when you want to do something, you tend to overemphasize their opinions. In fact, you like novelties but they must also be shared and appreciated by your colleagues. Your friendliness means you will accept just about anyone, even freeloaders! You may be affected by interference both literally and figuratively. Original in your creations, paradoxically, you need peace and quiet to concretize what you think. It's likely that you have to suffer your family's disloyalty and you find yourself in a state of permanent doubt, leading to very difficult choices. You will probably experience many moves as well as numerous events which are both sudden and unexpected. You have sacrosanct principles but you do not often respect them often in your own commitments. You are sometimes selfish but you still keep a family spirit. You risk facing many family problems which are often inextricable. You are blessed with a fertile imagination, you have a certain gift of observation that allows you to know with whom you are dealing. You love what is new and you like to enjoy it. You have a fantastic spirit, you love humor, sometimes caustic, and you do not leave anyone indifferent. You will keep a young character, sometimes careless, careful not to overemphasize the lie when you want something or someone.

6 letters worth 2 *(uncommon)*: Your mother (or the person holding this role) has certainly been very involved with her family responsibilities. Therefore she has a very strong sense of duty and she has a great interest in her offspring. It is possible that you feel suffocated because you feel that you were too overprotected by a mother trying to control everything. You will surely experience great difficulty in cutting the umbilical cord, which will consequently give special attention to the love that your family can testify to. You particularly appreciate being pampered. Your main desire, bordering on an obsession, is to find harmony, peace and tranquility. You look to make your world intimately pleasant, which can cause existential anxiety. You end up not making a choice for fear of losing your privileges and for fear of not being able to enjoy life as you wish. This indecision can lead you to adopt a lax attitude and to not be too violent. You prefer the voluntary, allowing you to dilute your responsibilities. You can turn to the art world and the world of craftsmanship, which will help motivate you and give you confidence in your abilities. You need to feel that you are loved and appreciated, which sometimes hampers your work when you feel that these conditions are not met. Your changing moods are very harmful in the nature of your relationships, often bringing a sense of insecurity to your loved ones. You need to feel safe in your emotional life, but it is essential that you do not systematically bear the weight of your discomfort with life on others. You must ignore the memories you are feel negative.

7 letters worth 2 *(uncommon)*: Your mother is perceived as difficult to define, even secret. She has a deep, hardly palpable nature. This reservation does not stop her from expressing her disapproval. Influenced by your mother's curious nature, you will be naturally attracted to knowledge, study and thought. In your relationship with your partner, it is essential that you can retain, even a little bit, a minimum of independence. You believe in the virtues of friendship that are essential in your eyes despite some reservations in expressing your feelings. You will seek above all, to create a lifestyle for yourself that meets your expectations, even if it is a long way from normal social context. Living in isolation, in seclusion with others who share your views or your idealistic view of life, does not frighten you in the slightest. However, you should move away slightly from this form of seclusion, withdrawal, where you like to escape to. Your ideal, often kept secret, is above all based on a life devoted to your family, even if does make you a bit of slave.

8 letters worth 2 *(rare)*: Your mother could be very possessive and uncompromising, not really knowing how to show affection. This attitude causes you real difficulty to free yourself from the burden of this dominating, even castrating maternal presence. Unconsciously or not, you'll tend to find a partner with whom you can reproduce this exclusive relationship, tinged with domination/submission issues. Your attitude towards life is very ambiguous because you are looking for signs of tenderness, and at the same time you do not want to show what you take for weakness Your apparent rudeness is the weapon you use to try to block out your overly-strong emotions. You're still a kind soul, ready to help others, and it is through actions that we can really see who you are. It is obvious that you will try, by any means possible, to preserve a secret garden, which few people can enter. You have the ability to collect all kinds of energy, even occult, that may disturb you, without you really being aware of it. You must learn to control them.

9 letters worth 2 *(rare)*: Your mother is sensitive, responsive and blessed with a certain empathy that can become daydreaming. Her lack of realism sometimes leads to her being trapped by the attention people give to her and the desire for her loved ones to fulfill all her expectations. She is characterized by a form of submission, often causing an exaggerated withdrawal into herself when things do not go as she wishes. It is quite possible that this situation has caused you a difficult choice between your dreams and sense of reality. You will be marked by high expectations emotionally. You should be careful not to systematically exaggerate the consequences of difficult situations you encounter in your life. Your empathy will be so strong that you will have difficulty not getting overwhelmed by the emotions of those around you. You like to focus on others but you should not systematically make it a vocation. You learn not to run away when you encounter too many difficulties.

More than 9 letters worth 2 *(rare)*: See above for the interpretation of the reduction of this number.
Example: If you have 13 letters at a value of 2, you get a 4 by adding 1 + 3. Refer to this value, that is to say 4 letters at a value of 2. Remember to also take into account the 1 and 3 which makes up your 13 because they also refer to sub numbers. You must, therefore, interpret them by taking into account the definition of these two figures from the

definition of the sub numbers given below. Remember, this concerns mainly the mother but also the wife if you are a man.

2 Mental letters: You are able to amass knowledge. However, you need others as you share the outset to be able to teach on your turn. Your learning styles are rather academic. There is the teacher and the student. Your studies will lead you to free yourself from emotional family ties. A partner can greatly increase your mental capacities by rewarding you.

2 Emotional letters: You like sharing your feelings with your loved ones. You are particularly sensitive to the point that it is very easy to affect you emotionally. You experience sensations intensely. You need to be recognized.

2 Intuitive letters: You are intuitive compared to people close to you. These forebodings are deep and mostly unfounded. However, you find it hard to talk about them. You keep them to yourself, free from judgment and criticism. They serve your relationships. They allow you to perceive people and then you adapt to them. In fact, you are also a genuinely good listener because you feel beyond the words which cannot be said. You also listen to your dreams. Learn to decipher what they are saying.

2 Physical letters: Over time, you become more introverted, you dare to ask less spontaneously. Repressed emotions will likely be among the causes. It is possible that sooner or later you will feel the effects of your disaffection, being cut-off from your roots. Your development requires some difficulties with your mother to be resolved. Your interest in esoteric sciences, psychology and personal development will help you. Otherwise, you need a good dose of encouragement to begin a physical discipline. Physical exercise okay, but if someone takes the time to explain why and how. A permanent lack of confidence often slows you down when you consider a sport. Ultimately, you put more energy into others than you do yourself.

2 Creative letters: Your creativity is driven by the elements and nature with which you like to relax. You're the inspiration.

2 Balanced letters: The attachment to your mother and/or a particular woman is powerful. Similarly, you want to fix yourself, to get involved over time. The association must be a stability factor.

2 Dual letters: You have a karmic connection with your mother. Restrictions on your freedom have long accompanied you throughout your education. It is your married life that will free you.

Challenge 2: You must demonstrate the ability to partner and collaborate without entering into servitude, if not you may appear paradoxically submissive and aggressive. You have to have confidence so that your partnerships work. You will also discover what great opportunities lie behind situations that at first appear synonymous with addiction in your eyes. If you encounter this challenge, you will become a brilliant partner, an ideal partner both at work and in love.

First Cycle 2: It is often a sign of marriage, cohabitation before the end of the cycle. As a child, the influence of the mother or a woman is important. You are sensitive, often dreamy, and your growth depends heavily on the family climate, tenderness received or not. You need stable and protective markings around you. Later, you might plunge back into the memories of that time.

Second Cycle 2: The environment is predisposed to exercise restraint, to cooperate, to remain attentive to the needs of others. Orientation towards an activity with which you feel in tune is born. Again, it is a question of cooperation, alliance. This configuration implies the importance of a public or customer.

Third Cycle 2: Life tends to become calmer. Your concerns are with the family (spouse, children etc). You cultivate the art of being patient, attentive and available. You avoid agitation. It is the prospect of more friendly times in a context in which you can express your feelings.

First Pinnacle 2: To begin, you are under the authority of your mother mainly or in any case of a woman. This influence will develop your sensitivity and could lead you to an early marriage. Events will help you to better open up to others by teaching you tolerance and listening skills. Your childhood is marked by the importance of peers and/or loved ones.

Second or Third Pinnacle 2: Success thanks to the efforts provided with rigor and method. A new activity may require perseverance, courage and righteousness. Stability is at stake. The family home often monopolizes your attention. Your commitment is needed in this area.

Fourth Pinnacle 2: Finally, you move towards associational activities, or at least, you are trying to maintain good relationships with others (usually the spouse). Creating with your own hands, unleashing your creativity, getting in contact with nature, all this suits you. This is a rather quiet, peaceful, relaxing period. Focused on the family, you want peace, surrounded by those to whom you open yourself up, because somewhere, they are themselves also part of your core family.

Sub-numbers of 2

2 only has 20 as two digits direct sub-number. Beyond that, we get sub-numbers of 11 (29, 38, 47 etc).

11: *It has the status of a master number. In any case, it is not reduced to 2! See below for the interpretations.*

20: Confers a desire to be just and fair in the fields of meanings where it is found. Leads to success and satisfaction. Highlights the emotional life, the importance of partnerships. Grant support and protection in the engaged action. Also highlights a sensitive and vulnerable native to criticism in the field concerned. Dismisses emotions that cause problems by sometimes making you fearful and weak when it comes to addressing a challenge.

When number 3 links...

Life Path 3: You will live a happy destiny, full of contacts and communication. You will meet very few obstacles. Your creative spirit will be able to express itself. You will meet some real success.

In case of Karma 3, you will have the feeling that destiny keeps putting you in situations where it is necessary to communicate and to express yourself, even if if you do not necessarily enjoy it. Nevertheless, it will be necessary to be determined enough to express what you think.

Tip: moderate by interpreting all the sub-numbers revealed by the 3 ways of calculating the life path (see Chapter V).

Expression 3: What a charming personality! Generous, accommodating, attentive, you are a good friend. You know how to set the mood, and if necessary, round the corners and pick up the pieces. Socially, you tend to want to please; you even go along with anything to the point that you sometimes forget about yourself. This needs to get out of the way. Your interests take you to explore many different areas. You are even more dynamic when someone supports your initiatives. Effective, practical, you know how to get to the essentials. Sooner or later, you express your creativity. Socially ambitious, your relationship will lead you to contacts with people of different nationalities.

Tip: see all sub-numbers behind this 3. Do not forget that Expression is also the reduced sum of the Aspiration and Potential numbers. This can reveal another sub-number. For example, Aspiration 5 + Potential 7 gives 12, sub-number of the Expression 3.

Aspiration 3: Your deep desire is to build relationships, communicate and create while maintaining independence. In most cases, thanks to your friendly relations you open yourself to greater knowledge and understanding certain aspects of life. Contact with children is preferred. It is possible that you deal with it sooner or later, in addition to those you may already have. Socially, as in childhood, you need to be recognized by the father figure. It is essential you maintain a deep communication with him.

Potential 3: You like to connect, share and create. You have nice capabilities in expressing yourself. Never at a loss when it comes to finding ideas for developing your relationships, you know how to animate situations. Your creativity is expressed through a manual technique. Enjoyer of life, you spend without counting and in this area, you will need to be alert as there are people who want to play with your expansive personality, since it is well known that every flatterer lives at the expense of those who listen. That said, this potential allows you, even in the case of temporary difficulties, to not miss out financially. I must say that your ability to learn when you are interested promises social success through education.

First Name 3: An all-rounder, your activity is frenzied. Capable of mastering several work techniques, you do not take the time to breathe and you become short of breath more than one. Very creative self-taught, skillful, you can arouse enmities and jealousies in your socioprofessional circle. You love animals but very selectively.

1st Middle Name 3: Your critical and perfectionist mindset towards yourself and others, particularly your associates (spouse, partners etc) is formidable. Quick-witted, able to understand the ins and outs of a given situation, however, you have difficulties sticking to an idea due to your tendency to have several irons in the fire. So this causes difficult choices in terms of your partners and makes your relationships with your siblings difficult. You are capable of eloquence while having a contradictive mind. Your Cartesian mind needs evidence, you look to analyze too much, to dissect, to debate, to be involved in controversy. Paradoxically, you like to seek the advice of your family without necessarily listening to them. A kindred spirit characterizes you in your marriage and your associations. A child at heart, loving to go out, you need a partner in your image, while wanting, this is your ambiguity, keep your independence. You like to find a reciprocity in your partners.

2nd Middle Name 3: Curious, playful, passionate, inventive, constantly on the go, you like to share your interests. You tend to easily question conventions, standards and everything that is established, but with some amateurism. Your desire to move, to get about, you have a taste for travel, meetings, exchanges, new experiences. This does not prevent you from keeping a critical mind and taking a step back in all circumstances. Your "warrior" side allows you to easily find support from influential people (search for a father figure). You need to prove to those around you that your ideas which appear extravagant have a very tangible reality. You have a love of music. You find recognition through your offspring through your children's ability to pursue studies as well as a satisfaction in being idealized by them. That said you are not always easy to follow.

Heredity 3: The parental home in which you grew up was sensitive to appointments, diplomas, to the sound of a name. Even though you are attached to your youth, you enjoy living life in its simplicity. Your family problems are connected to communication, issues connected to the expression of individual identity and the lack of maturity of some of the family members. Rivalries with your sibling have often occupied your time and your mind.

Active 3: You often act with real spirit. You like to get involved in actions where the joy of life is present. The relational guides your actions.

Example: A Realization 7 qualified by an Active number 3 indicates that the pursuit of knowledge is accompanied by the need to get in contact with others, making friends who are often of interest because of their knowledge and skills.

Maturity 3: Your social achievement and personal development will overcome the recognition of your need to be socially recognized and rewarded. You quickly learn to take advantage of challenges presented to you and to use your address book. You will also be appreciated for the way you express yourself with warmth and enthusiasm. So it is up to you to give yourself the means to do so. Anything related to communication, coordination, representation, creation is in your favor. The age of maturity will be marked by a change in your career with opportunities to seize.

Intensity 3: You have an expressive, inspired and imaginative personality. You prefer an intense relational life. You love words and all types of expression. Your nature sometimes makes you impatient and extravagant.

Karma 3 (no letter 3): You find it difficult to say things, to express yourself, to communicate. Your thoughts don't seem clear. Any form of art could enable you to communicate more easily. This difficult communication with your loved ones can lead you to feel resentment. A problem also lies in relation to your image, even your sexuality. You should not cut yourself off from others or conversely spread yourself too thin with thousands of activities. You must find the resources to be less closed off, accepting of others, even if they do not meet your expectations, and to accept yourself. To remain too mysterious, not to release your emotions, to live only in the dream, you could close the door to some interesting relationships.

1 letter worth 3: You often show a vindictive mind and aggressive, even critical speech. Above all, you look to prove you're the one who calls the shots. You like challenges. Conflicts do not frighten you too much, adversity frightens you even less. You are very responsive when you feel your action is being impeded. You need to talk intellectually but you rarely take into account views opposed to your own. Despite everything, you have a pleasant and sociable nature and you are good with people. You are very comfortable when it comes to stating your comments and thoughts but you have real difficulty recognizing your mistakes and weaknesses. You are driven by a competitive, sporting spirit. Organizer, outstanding host and skeptical by nature, you seek to guide others, to shape and to rationalize. Perhaps a karmic reunion with your siblings or children with them eventually taking a prominent place in your life. It is also possible that family disagreements with them need to be overcome. Beware of injury at the time of travelling or untimely actions. You have a certain ability to remember anything that is useful to you during conversations or exchanges, in order to reuse it at an appropriate time. Your nature is twofold which means that that you are very unpredictable. This may surprise people, but not you, because you always know where you want to direct your energies. You feel smart and you insist that this be known. A few teachers on the sidelines, easily give you good and bad points. You like to be surrounded, but above all you do not like to waste your precious freedom of action.

2 letters worth 3: You're looking for a soul mate, your male or female double. An aesthetic at heart, you have a genuine desire to beautify your life and you are looking primarily to have friendly and harmonious relationships with your loved ones. Your personality is fun and boasts a certain kindness. You can be very critical with respect to anything that does not fit your vision of beauty because sometimes you are very selfish and very temperamental. With your maternal mind, you have a certain popularity with respect to your family, even an audience when you reach a certain maturity. You are embarrassed by anything that you see as vulgar and dirty. It should be noted that a possible excessive presence of the mother (or lack thereof) may hinder your socioprofessional path. By emancipating yourself, you find the power to assert yourself in order to avoid remaining stuck with this maternal issue, like that of others. You like to receive, achieve, look after and help. You easily weave a special relationship with children and the feminine world as well as the animal world. You do not see any downside to being a subordinate, especially if your interests are safeguarded. You have a lot of imagination and you are blessed with great inspirations and lightning intuition. You do not always know what, in you, stems from the intellect or the anemic. Consequently, everything that relates to the world of psychology and/or the esoteric attracts you. You'll be surrounded by more women than men. All the same, beware of people you consider as friends, who you need, because your incredulous nature does not always sort the wheat from the chaff.

3 letters worth 3: You have a sharp, quick and analytical mind. You like frequent travel. An outstanding organizer, you are blessed with a concise mind which tends to seek perfection, because you find it hard to bear the vulgar. You can also be obsessed with details or that which you consider to be unfair. You must be careful not to become completely indifferent to your surroundings. You are attracted to the world of writers, singers and dancers and you have a juvenile character. You attach great importance to everything related to hygiene, cleanliness and perfection. You have a compelling need to talk, sometimes too often to mask an anxious, schizophrenic nature. You need to be careful not to be overwhelmed by obsessions, which may be due to difficult relationships with siblings. This habit that you have of comparing everything and wanting to follow a model that is not yours, inhibits your true profound nature and your primary expression. Learn to relax and to express your individuality. Avoid, whenever possible, constantly referring to a model. Do not take others' comments at face value. You have a real need to grow by asserting yourself through your own beliefs, while keeping, of course, your legendary impulsive spirit. It is possible that you experienced a negative kind of competition between you and your brothers and sisters. You are a kind of adolescent in search of a guide who could help you develop yourself, but it is especially important that you feel you have control over yourself. You have many strings to your bow, and you don't hesitate to use the ones you like best at a particular time. Be careful not to be too capricious or you risk losing a sense of who you are.

4 letters worth 3: You attach great importance to your words because you want to be taken seriously. You alternate between periods of silence, withdrawal and on some occasions, a surprising pomposity. You chew your goals over long term. What you see as gaps in your abilities or your curriculum, you will overcome by an excess of work. You are constantly looking to organize your business methodically, and to do this, you do not hesitate to surround yourself with competent people you need to succeed. Your too strong presence, your strong character, your abilities and your stubbornness may overshadow those around you. It should be noted that your stubbornness can sometimes lead you into unfavorable situations or even dead ends. Sudden changes of occupation are to be feared, sometimes resulting from legal or lawful setbacks. You have a real ability to create and design whilst cleverly hiding your goals. Your relationships with your siblings can sometimes be very ambiguous, there may be jealousies that need to be overcome. It is also noteworthy that the over-presence of your father, or conversely his complete absence, may have had the effect of creating a lack of confidence in you. A vague feeling of guilt can make you put your faults on your family. As already stated, you have a real talent for conceptualizing and implementing your ideas. You may be attracted by the artistic and craft world. You have the abilities to pragmatically research, manage, plan and teach. You do not hesitate to assert, even impose, that which you hold true. You are definitely a trustworthy and loyal person.

5 letters worth 3: What distinguishes you most is your independent, bright and fast mind. You like the new and exploring new horizons and you have an avant-garde character. You are not insensitive to the exploration and discovery of the world of sexuality. Your lack of patience is often characterized by a lack of concentration on the words of others, and you only seem to hear the beginning of your contacts' sentences without waiting for the end, believing you have understood everything. Therefore, you are often annoyed by the slowness of understanding or performance of those around you. You must learn to calm down, to avoid being too capricious in your body as well as your head because you may experience high occupational instability, often arising from a chaotic school curriculum, despite your infinite skills. You like holidays and travelling. You like to be guided without being dominated. You are an ardent defender of freedom, especially your own. Anything related to close relationships with your brothers and sisters and cousins is special. You have a competitive mind and you love challenges, which there are sometimes too many of. You need to temper this tendency that you have to continually redesign the world in your head. You will keep this youthful and impulsive mind that distinguishes you so much. You're a joker and you often have fun through others. You may be attracted by the world of entertainment (singer, dancer etc). You have an easy and quick repartee. Learn to moderate your expressions and do not attempt to explain everything. Your schooling may have been thwarted. You shouldn't always sweep over things, otherwise you'll tend to appear as being indifferent or superficial. You're insatiable, you want to know everything and you have to admit that you don't resist much.

6 letters worth 3: You have an analytical mind which is highly developed. Your mind is sharp, precise and psychoanalytical. You have a unique way of seeing the world like a camera taking photos. You have difficulty finding your place in relation to the extremes, between that which affects the rational and that which affects the metaphysical. You are intuitive without really being aware of it. You have real talent for communicating and organizing. You must learn to free your mind of unnecessary thoughts, by living more in the concrete rather than in your psyche. You enjoy travel and toing. You will surely be attracted by the medical and/or social world. You need recognition for services rendered. You attach great importance to being surrounded by intelligent and influential people. Your creative mind often takes a back seat because your desire for perfection blocks part of your spontaneity. You like being well presented and you also love being around people who are well presented. You know how to communicate and show your warmth and you choose those with whom you can have an intelligent discussion. Anything related to writing is encouraged as well as everything that helps you understand the intricacies of the brain.

7 letters worth 3: You are driven by a natural curiosity and you're very good at teaching, communicating and passing things on. You have a great capacity for research. You are attracted by everything related to training (yours and that of others). You are sometimes disconcerting because you easily alternate between silence and pomposity. Your ambivalent nature forces you to constantly choose between conformity and originality. You're an elitist who seeks to surround themselves with people in line with your aspirations. Often absorbed by your ideas and your goals, you tend to forget your loved ones. The latter will not fail to remind you or even blame you. You are attracted by faraway destinations. You are blessed with a sporty and competitive mind. You have everything you need to fight for and put a lot of yourself into your projects, which sometimes leads you to face problems with the law and/or hierarchy. You may also have an admiration for a brother or a person you consider as such. You are animated by a deep faith, but you still need hard evidence and certainties. You like to broaden your fields of expertise and your knowledge. Education is preferred as is everything that relates to journalism and speech. You are often weighed down by your convictions and your beliefs, and to convince others, you can become a great presenter. Be careful not to be too caustic vis-à-vis what you dislike, especially when you feel challenged. Sudden changes in academic and vocational pathways are to be feared. You are very attached to the basic education of your offspring. You can be passionate about good books.

8 letters worth 3: As a doctor, a psychiatrist, or a psychologist you need to constantly explore the conscience. In the eyes of others, you appear to be a mysterious person who is difficult to determine and sound out. Your relationships and your meetings are often unconventional and can be done in very specific contexts. You sometimes have difficult relationships with siblings, relationships which may be marked by separations, losses or profound changes. Your schooling has been very disrupted, which requires you to make progress on the ground, as they say. A reorientation of your thinking may occur following a major event and/or a significant encounter of an initiator, master genre. Your daredevil spirit can be a solid support in times of adversity and your fighting spirit pushes you not to accept defeat. You will need to be vigilant with regard to your excesses, too much self-confidence, which sometimes leads you to suffer numerous accidents, especially in your daily journeys. You are too naive and too credulous but when it comes to those who have cheated you, you have a sharp tongue. You have a powerful magnetism that leaves no one indifferent, but which may upset some. You have a wit that is instinctive, baffling and curious to say the least. Your relationship to money is often difficult, especially early in your life, it becomes better managed with time. Dating with strangers may be quite easy to do. Sooner or later anything related to death will attract you.

9 letters worth 3: You are a passionate being blessed with a gentle way of life, harmony and wellbeing. You look primarily to reconcile and to reunite. You have a tendency to be too determined to free yourself from the constraints of life. In fact, you're looking for a kind of earthly paradise. Your strong tendency to oscillate between reason and faith makes you appear as someone who is fickle and unsure of themselves. Studies are not favored in the first instance but a real motivation triggered by a loved one or life circumstances may lead you to pursue them further. You like to organize, but do not impose anything. Your dreamy side leads you, naturally, to establish some form of distance between you and your environment, but without completely overshadow yourself because you want to share your beliefs and the faith that motivates you. You can be an aesthetic, very sensitive to moods and to fragrances. You are especially uncomfortable in places that you do not like and in places that have bad vibrations. Your mind is more mystical than others and you prefer these "magical" places, sometimes to withdraw into yourself. You are helpful especially with respect to your brothers and sisters however, this can become sacrifice. You rely on your feelings and your intuition a lot. You are helpful to perfection, but you must be careful not to become exploitable and/or especially not to systematically flee that which bothers you. It is in the domain of business, whatever that may be, that you must be most be vigilant in your commitments, especially with regard to the signing of contracts. If you are attracted to physical activities, you do not seek to push them to extremes in any way, not being obsessed by the spirit of competition. You sometimes appear older than your years.

More than 9 letters worth 3: See above for the interpretation of the reduction of this number.
Example: If you have 14 letters at a value of 3, you get a 5 by adding 1 + 4. Refer to this value, that is to say 5 letters at a value of 3. Remember to also take into account the 1 and 2 which makes up your 14 because they also refer to sub numbers. You must, therefore, interpret them by taking into account the definition of these two figures from the definition of the sub numbers given below. Remember, this concerns mainly studies, siblings and creativity etc.

3 Mental letters: You like to reason and talk nonsense for fun and it sometimes comes across as a type of provocation. You like to acquire knowledge through multiple channels. For you, communication methods should be varied, surprising and imaginative. And you like to share this knowledge in the same way. The risk is getting involved in a lot of projects and joining a lot of schools of thought to the point of not being able to focus enough to follow through. Your mind is attracted by intellectual and artistic activities.

3 Emotional letters: You are sensitive to public reaction around you. Others' opinions are important and determine how you behave in society. More often than not, you are on edge.

3 Intuitive letters: You have a real gift for guessing, feeling and perceiving. However, you interfere with your imagination a lot which is equally important. In fact, your intuitions are sometimes misleading. Similarly, your desire to please pushes you to annoy, sometimes too much, which you have felt. Nevertheless, you are sensitive and you see those who seek your status.

3 Physical letters: Constraints arose in relation to studies. Where appropriate, brothers and sisters will be involved in some of your difficulties and trials. Over time, people will envy you; others will not be able to resist plotting behind your back (sometimes it will be the same people). You'll have to be cautious in your relationships. Otherwise you need to act originally and inventively every day. So as to be able to communicate any physical intoxication brought about by this expenditure. Sexual activities and innovative and imaginative sports are your cup of tea. On the other hand, you don't like disciplines which are too square, too restrictive.

3 Creative letters: Your creativity can be expressed in the practice of aerial sports where movement is present. You like to combine entertainment and education.

3 Balanced letters: You like your relationships to be sustainable. For you, communicating is a stabilizing factor. Your tastes are safe. You creativity is expressed if you feel real security around you.

3 Dual letters: You will gradually detach yourself from futile things to better discern and go deeper. For this, it is possible that siblings play a role and betrayals and mockery may also startle you.

Challenge 3: You will learn to create while making yourself heard and understood. It will be about finding the right words to say or write how you feel. This challenge requires you to get involved in a group, to expand your social circle. And when you communicate, when you express yourself, care must be taken not to remain on the surface of things and be tolerant towards the ideas you do not share.

First Cycle 3: The context allows you to highlight your communicative personality. Very young, you like to have fun and indulge in artistic activities, at the risk of not following school properly. It is possible that you lived as a boarder. Otherwise, you have a sense of contact and friendship. Animation, the art, the relational, the trade with an audience, an accustomed clientele are in your strings and suit you well during this cycle.

Second Cycle 3: Your occupation is marked by a form of social success, well-being, and "joie de vivre". Your fulfillment is through contact with others. Your creativity is high. You are inspired. You have to put it into practice. It is a great cycle also marked by support.

Third Cycle 3: It's a good time to live happily, surrounded by loved ones, always on the lookout for rewarding outings, friendly parties. Travel is likely. In this regard, there is a real possibility of meeting with an audience in terms of your artistic or literary achievements.

First Pinnacle 3: To begin, you will develop your creativity. You are an expressive child, sometimes good at art. If present, siblings play an important role in your evolution as well as the meeting of some teachers and educators that mark you. You made many friends through your sense of touch. You can use your charming and playful side. You can also show interest and ability for sport and/or artistic activities (drama, music in particular).

Second or Third Pinnacle 3: Now you find opportunities for expansion and openness. New interests emerge. You express yourself, communicate and expand your creativity. The aspect indicates a protection in terms of your studies, the acquisition of new knowledge. Commercial activities are favored. You are listening but also seek to convince.

Fourth Pinnacle 3: Finally, rather harmonious relationships and achievements are on the programmed, either through a pleasant retirement or in a still active social context. Opportunities arise to travel, to expand your relational circle and/or to simply have a good time. If you participate in an art, you can do so in satisfactory conditions.

Sub-numbers of 3

12 (see also its meaning as a karmic debt): Develops creativity. Individualist and unconventional mind. Fickleness. Prefers their own interests to those of the group. Marks a certain mistrust in relation to a loved one from your family circle imposing their way of seeing or is jealous (the significant indicates who it is). Need to be heard, to come out in the open, not be confined to second fiddle, while reviewing their way of expressing themselves. Guilt in terms of their commitments. Rivalries. Remoteness of relatives.

21: Takes a step back whilst having fun in life. Ability to take advantage of opportunities and protections that present themselves. Intuition. Luck. Harmony. Tenacity that leads them to success, as well as to expressing all their creative potential. Able to give from time to time. Loves to please. Tendency to scattering.

30: In connection with communication and creativity in the area concerned. Developed sense of humor, joviality but also superficiality. Characterized by a tendency to be flexible, talkative, very free in their words, active, generous. Predisposed to resentment when the subject has difficulty expressing their emotions. Indicates good aptitude for writing and expressing their point of view. Must take opinions of others into consideration as well as their own. Inclined towards a form of laziness.

39: Leads them to see life more favorably following difficult events. Tendency towards emotional scattering. Ability to achieve their objectives.
Note: Sub-number of 12 (3 + 9).

48: Makes them capable of planning, anticipating, developing. Able to assert themselves, to communicate, to develop but predisposed to frustration. Increases a form of dependency *vis à vis* the partner in emotional terms. Difficulty in expressing their uniqueness. Exposed to power relationships, pressures that can block a situation at times.
Note: sub-number of 12 (4 + 8).

57: Makes the mind happy, intelligent, creative, inventive in the area concerned. Brings wisdom. Has a flair for business and allows the expansion of their activities. Does not always take the time to make themselves understood. Concerns relating to everything about the law. Problems linked to a form of isolation, loneliness. Needs to stay cautious. When things go wrong, rebellious spirit. Headstrong.
Note: sub-number of 12 (5 + 7).

66: Refers to loyalty, feelings, affection, service, the aesthetic sense, to generosity in the field concerned. Increases listening qualities but also the need to receive approval from others. Quick to seek out and enjoy love intensely.
Note: sub-number of 12 (6 + 6).

75: Favors analysis. Ease in communicating and expressing themselves with the body. Sensitive, emotional. More often than not confers charm and magnetism, spontaneous and ambition. Need to get away from it all as soon as concerns arise in their life. Recognition of their qualities. Success thanks to originality. Material and/or social success.
Note: sub-number of 12 (7 + 5).

84: Develops a more visionary than practical side.
Note: sub-number of 12 (8 + 4).

93: Has a good dose of creativity. May have difficulties when they commit.
Note: sub-number of 12 (9 + 3).

When number 4 stabilizes...

Life Path 4: Success will be the fruit of your efforts and your regularity. You will improve slowly but surely.

In case of karma 4, if it is difficult indeed to carry something out without being righteous and perseverant in your efforts, it is necessary to make the apprenticeship of patience. Why do you always want everything immediately?

Tip: moderate by interpreting all the sub numbers revealed by the 3 ways of calculating the life path (see Chapter V).

Expression 4: You are naturally prudent. Efficient and hardworking, you're comfortable in concrete situations. You need to have the upper hand so that no detail escapes you. Others like you because you are a trustworthy person. The sense of duty and honor makes sense to you. You do not always take the initiative because you need to feel safe before you commit. You like seeking advice and often, it is relatives who encourage you to push forward. But when you decided, your effectiveness is formidable. Remaining measured, success is virtually assured, although you may have to wait.

Tip: see all sub-numbers behind this 4. Do not forget that Expression is also the reduced sum of the Aspiration and Potential numbers. This can reveal another sub-number. For example, Aspiration 6 + Potential 7 gives 13, sub-number of the Expression 4.

Aspiration 4: Your deep desire is to patiently build a job that gives you a stable situation. You have mental resources, you try to assert your social skills. You pay special attention to the social field. You have a sense of the collective, of a group. Without denying what is already there, you want to change things deeply. Persevering, you constantly impel your projects. Friendship plays an important role. Friends can even help you develop socially.

Potential 4: You gradually succeed because you are a worker, organized and patient. Others can count on you. You know how to show integrity and respect the rules of the game. Everything is a matter of time and the day will come when you highlight your skills in an activity that suits you. You're not always comfortable with material issues. You are afraid to fail and so you deploy your efforts to feel financially secure. Despite some delays and obstacles, you will reach your goals.

First Name 4: Capable of a lot of effort every day, you have an undeniable sense of duty and responsibility. Workaholic, serious and irreproachable, you are however, barely able to challenge yourself. Stubborn, you still believe you are right even if you are the sole defender of this truth. In fact, you have difficulties taking others' beliefs into account when they do not correspond to your values.

1st Middle Name 4: Faithful, reliable, inflexible, even intransigent in your emotional relationships, you are a solid person on whom people can rely in case of difficulties. You like constructive, sustainable relationships, established on well-structured bases. You are able to commit in the long term. Meeting a partner who will enable you to meet your need for structure, a house, a good place for you and also...a family. You favor everything related to nature and animals. You also have a particular interest in anything related to food and care given to the body (aestheticism, massage, etc). Your commitment to ancestors, to the lineage and to the family name is real. Your natural reserve often masks your deep feelings, lest they expose you and destabilize you.

2nd Middle Name 4: Sports team coach, conductor, politician, project manager, anyway, you have the will to impose your innovative ideas whilst being respective of the established order and structures of the moment. You are characterized by an attraction to luxury and beautiful things. You are attached to others' success, with the need to pass your achievements on to your offspring. You look at others' difficulties with your eyes open. You know how to find innovative solutions and have the ability to participate in creations at large. However there is a risk of confrontation with authority. In the end, you give little importance to leisure. Family problems may be a hindrance to your projects.

Heredity 4: You find that the parental home in which you grew up was too sensitive to appointments, diplomas and the sound of names. Your family enjoys life and has left a mark on how you communicate and on your identity. A form of immaturity generated situations of misunderstanding or even rejection, and in response you probably chose an outlet through art (music, dance, theater ...). This aspect indicates that your life is punctuated by frequent moves, often leading you to be hosted by the brothers and sisters and/or friends. Your ability to find support is directly proportional to your ability to get out of your reservation and/or accept others in the way they voice their opinions. Your handyman side allows you to improve your daily life or that of others. You have the ambition to eventually acquire a property that meets your needs.

Active 4: You act with determination.
Example: an Aspiration 5 with an Active number 4 gives us a native with a practical inventiveness. Their curiosity is pragmatic. They not only observe and discover, but they also test it and see how it can help.

Maturity 4: You will gradually realize that your choices significantly affect your quality of life. When you persevere, when you give the necessary time to a task, when you stay focused on your goals, you succeed in your socioprofessional projects. By being aware of your values, of what you need to do to improve yourself, you will succeed and could even enjoy honors and power attached to certain positions and responsibilities. In addition, your activity will often be characterized by a significant workload.

Intensity 4: You demonstrate concentration and have a love of work well done, and the sense of values, even of the established order. However you may seem stubborn and appear to lack openness in certain situations.

Karma 4 (no letter 4): Learn to be clearer and simpler, instead of making everything complicated. You are almost too tidy. In fact, you manage your difficulty in situating yourself in relation to time. If any situation displeases you or you want to pay immediately by devoting as little time as possible, or you constantly push the deadline. You must find the right tempo. Meanwhile, you attach importance to your roots, to your history. As such you will seek to build a home.

1 letter worth 4: You like to commit and get involved and create strong and sustainable projects. You make sure you surround yourself with competent people and you rely on established structures. Obstinate, tenacious, not losing your grip easily, you can be an authoritarian leader, but you are also a trusted and loyal person with a sense of responsibility. You have a real ability to adapt even when a situation is upsetting your natural reserve. You have a propensity to be part of an elite. You do not like the vulgar. You pass your knowledge on in a practical way. You need to realize things concretely and this, qualitatively. You are definitely a parent who is able to provide help and support to your offspring. You may find yourself in conflict with authority of any kind, and especially your family. Looking constantly to control everything, you find it hard to ignore your mind. You want your arguments to be based on the solid, because you really cannot stand the idea that you may be found out. You have built a barricade that allows you to keep intruders away and above all protect you from questions relating to your natural authority. You want respect and you cannot stand anyone doubting you. Blessed with a strong sexuality, you can also, if you're a man, be a little misogynistic.

2 letters worth 4: Above all, you are a methodical worker, a model of its kind, working to ensure the success of your family and especially to provide them with some protection. To do this you rely on family values a long-term union and a solid education. You are blessed with great sensitivity, combined with an instinct that lets you easily capture your environment in order to understand it better. In addition, your interests will be focused on anything related to trade and food, with this need to live in a stable environment as well as good financial and emotional security. You have certain abilities in the field of manual creation. In trying too hard to seek peace and tranquility, you must be careful not to annoy authoritarian people, whether with your partner or in your workplace. It is by delegating too much and/or giving undeserved trust to some loved ones, and this, to escape the harshness of life, you might get cheated. When you suffer an absence of harmony for too long that you accept in silence you suddenly decide to break free , without warning, and surprise everyone around you. You attach great importance to the world of childhood, and you really like to make a cozy nest. Your special relationship with your mother (sometimes your grandmother) can lead to a dependence.

3 letters worth 4: You are often obsessed with your achievements, resulting in a compelling desire to find all sorts of ways to secure yourself physically and financially. You are an aesthetic and you have many creative talents. An effective worker, you need to concretize your ideas and to see them in a tangible form. Above all, you are a pragmatist who has their feet firmly on the ground liking to stay very close to nature. The fact remains that you can also be very possessive. You tend to focus on what is timeless because you're more conservative. You are a realist and a constructor and you love the simple life. You have a rather sensual nature. You can become very pessimistic when you do not get what you want, your sky becomes darkened, sometimes leading to a somber mood, lacking joy and folklore, both for you and your family. You attach great importance to university qualifications, hence an overwhelming desire to continue studies that you deem necessary in order to succeed professionally. Your family will surely influence the direction you take in your path. Everything related to the fields of technology is encouraged.

4 letters worth 4: Your mind is essentially Cartesian and logical. You have a rather solitary nature which sometimes leads you to withdraw into yourself. You are a true workaholic, persevering, honest and direct in all matters affecting family and socioprofessional relationships. A follower of a stable environment, you can easily stress if you feel too rushed by and/in your work, or simply, if your environment places too much pressure on you. You are very attached to your house, to your family and to your worldly goods. You can be very possessive, sometimes too stubborn, too serious and lacking imagination. You will encounter people who will challenge your views, which will effectively bring you more flexibility and teach you to put things into perspective. You sometimes have a marked tendency to exaggerate the difficulties you encounter, to paint a black picture of your life. You use this exacerbated pessimism as a defense, because deep inside you, you are almost certain that the outcome of the problems will never be worse than you can imagine. You have a deep respect for elders, traditions and your ancestors (father, grandfather). You want to perpetuate these family traditions, especially if they relate to an occupation. You will also organize your life so that your own offspring carry the torch and continue what has been acquired. You may be attracted by crafts.

5 letters worth 4: You like renewal but you know how to keep a cool head. You are sensitive to the advances of modern life but you will not be cluttered with useless gadgets. Torn between new and old experiences, you commit yourself cautiously, but you'll have to experience sudden, sometimes dramatic changes. Paradoxically, these are the dramatic shifts that will give you the opportunity to overcome your misgivings with regard to anything to do with the unexpected and the ability to cope with the overly rapid movement of life. You can be very possessive with your friends, co-workers and relatives. You like rushing others but do not like others rushing you. Your words, combined with the original tone of your voice, play a big role in how you express yourself and may offend some. You have a reserved front because you are not as closed off as it seems, you must simply learn to get to know yourself. You are a trustworthy person. You like to see what you imagine become a reality. You will remain very close to nature. A form of insecurity may inhabit you, especially if you have not quickly found a secure contact point. You rely more on the results of your own experiences, often numerous, that on any advice from your loved ones. You possess an intelligence that is practical more than anything else. You can be stubborn and determined, but you also know how to calculate risks when you embark on new adventures.

6 letters worth 4: *(uncommon)* You tend to focus on anything related to viable and sustainable relationships. You are blessed with a real willingness to commit to secure relationships in order to build a stable life with each other. You are aware of your familial and social responsibilities and pay special attention to the education of children. You think it is important to stick to your commitments and you are very respectful of the spoken word. You organize and plan leaving little room for something like that. In trying too hard to be perfect, voluntarily or not, you may find yourself at odds with your sacrosanct principles of life and the constraints that they impose on you. You are loyal, honest and straightforward, but sometimes cold and distant. You will learn to temper your critical mind a little, to deal with that which doesn't meet your initial objectives. You may also be very irritable or extremely jealous and envious in your search for unattainable beauty. You are eager to harmonize your life, but sometimes you have great difficulties with regard to the strategic choice allowing you to achieve it. You are very emotional, you try to hide it and you can sink into excessive sentimentality. When you cannot get what you want, you feel abandoned, leaving you with a bitter aftertaste. The difficulties encountered in your career give you this impression that you have failed to choose the right path, even the sense of failing to fulfill your responsibilities.

7 letters worth 4: *(rare)* Your idealization of your prospects and your goals occurs primarily through work and family values, thus accessing a life where these values are exemplary in your eyes. You willingly get involved in trade union or political organizations that represent, for you, an extended family. You also focus on what others succeed at in their own activities and you are ready to help if necessary. Anything related to education and training is accessible to you, provided that all of this is surrounded by the rational and the technical. Above all, you are a pragmatist. It is in the field of work that you find your true potential. You have a strong tendency to require a lot of others and to impose the rules that you impose on yourself on them. You're a loner who only likes to be surrounded by people who share your views and/or your approach.

8 letters worth 4: *(rare)* You tend to keep your goals secret and you find it difficult to discuss the strategies you want to use. You like to secure yourself through the acquisition of material and financial goods. Your true nature is instinctive, so you can easily find all kinds of opportunities required for your socioprofessional development. You have an ability to create from elements that others define as impalpable. You are blessed with a great tenacity and great strength in the face of adversity. You might be subject to profound transformations, perhaps family and/or professional catastrophes, which will force you to start from scratch. You may experience alternations between constructive and destructive periods. Your sexuality can be overwhelming.

9 letters worth 4: *(rare)* You appear as a slightly mystical character, in search of calm and peace, preferring remote places, far from what you consider to be stressful. You are flexible enough to adapt your projects to life circumstances. It's your need for rest and tranquility which prevents you from fighting against adversity head on preferring to deal with the circumstances. You like to mull your goals over. You are blessed with a certain empathy, you are very aware of what your loved ones expect of you, but you rarely express it. This ability to perceive your friends is not absolutely synonymous with what others may perceive of you, because you appear intangible and difficult to define. Providence often guides your steps. You will learn to be violent, especially with regard to some of the excesses caused by food and drink etc.

More than 9 letters worth 4 *(rare)*: See above for the interpretation of the reduction of this number.
Example: If you have 12 letters at a value of 4, you get a 3 by adding 1 + 2. Refer to this value, that is to say 3 letters at a value of 4. Remember to also take into account the 1 and 2 which makes up your 12 because they also refer to sub numbers. You must, therefore, interpret them by taking into account the definition of these two figures from the definition of the sub numbers given below. Remember that this applies primarily to will, work, relationships with family and roots etc.

4 Mental letters: You do not believe in chance. For you, everything must result from a method, a plan. You like to show that each effect has its cause with an acute sense of regularity to achieve your goals.

4 Emotional letters: You relegate your emotions to the background behind your sense of obligation and duty. You are however, sensitive, considerate and present when required, as long as you remember to remove your mask.

4 Intuitive letters: What an odd situation that one! On the one hand, you are able to perceive, to guess, to probe, and on the other, you refute these predispositions. Cruel dilemma. Especially since the messages, the meanings of these intuitions remain equivocal. However, use this potential financially where your inspirations are usually based.

4 Physical letters: A deep spiritual awareness will be a result of tests and/or difficulties experienced by your loved ones. Through their suffering, you will re-evaluate your existence. Issues regarding death and the circumstances of your birth call to you. Return work on yourself (rebirthing, regression etc) can lead you to detach yourself from these prenatal impressions. Otherwise, you like activities that leave a lot of room for concentration, method and regularity. You need to excel yourself to accomplish a physical exercise activity. You need regular physical activity; otherwise, you feel something is missing.

4 Creative letters: Your creativity is measured by the time you have to spend to refine your work.

4 Balanced letters: You are attached to the fact that your work, it seems so obvious, will provide you with security and stability. That's why you're capable of all efforts to achieve this serenity. Similarly, the home must be a place of comfort, the place where your values make sense.

4 Dual letters: You'll step back thanks to work, concerted efforts and your commitment to your family.

Challenge 4: You must demonstrate the ability to sustain the effort needed to realize your projects and focus on a practical approach to life. It is by acquiring the perseverance and serious qualities that you overcome all restrictions. Your independence and your freedom will not be possible if you persist in being so unhelpful. You need to get rid of a type of psycho rigidity. Routine does not necessarily come with boredom; you will discover motivations, excitement in an altogether ordinary life. This challenge requires certain overly strict educational modes to be overcome in order to not get overwhelmed by emotions that are often linked to your childhood memories which you want to escape from.

First Cycle 4: The context allows you to learn a physical activity rather young. Reflection is encouraged and allows you to adapt to the reality of your environment. The family background may seem stuffy or restrictive. Soon, you feel a need for stability.

Second Cycle 4: Professional activity is more than necessary and offers less room for relaxation, leisure trips. Everything pushes you resolutely towards the concrete. You are logical. The mind is rational, methodical and allows you to be very responsible in what you do. You also have a strong tendency to be wary of ideas that aren't yours.

Third Cycle 4: Often you choose to pursue an activity until the end. This course may tire you prematurely but it is also the means that you have chosen to fully assure you. Retirement must allow you to master new areas or to deepen those that you already know.

First Pinnacle 4: To begin, you are a persevering child, a worker. You look to enter professional life quickly. You learn to be patient and constructive. However, since childhood, you may feel a little hampered by the family atmosphere. The educational method suits you through force and hinders your freedom of action.

Second or Third Pinnacle 4: You meet success thanks to the efforts provided with rigor and method. A new activity may require perseverance, courage and righteousness. Stability is at stake. The family home often monopolizes your attention. Your commitment is needed in this area.

Fourth Pinnacle 4: Finally, time is not for idleness. Besides what do you want? There is a real opportunity to combine the pleasure of living and in a place close to nature (country). By your very nature, you prefer that which links you to the earth and earthly foods.

Sub-numbers of 4

13 (see also its meaning as a karmic debt): Guilt complex. Leads to a desire to be irreproachable in their actions and commitments so as to facilitate their integration. Need to feel safe and supported. Doubt, fear of not mastering events which lead them to adopt a rigid stance.

22: It has master number status. See below for the interpretations.

31: Increases the ability to adapt to all situations. Gives the possibility to succeed in their businesses but often at the expense of being overworked. Sensitivity to anything that allows their efficiency to be improved. Opposition to any authority judged to be dishonest.

40: Develops the need to be recognized for their actions and to control events. In case of problems, has a tendency to put responsibility onto others. Does not easily practice introspection.

49: Is timid but does not look to others. Protector, mediator. Pursues a goal, a noble cause. Spontaneous, organized, sometimes with difficulty communicating. Holds back socioprofessional development at one point. Although often an unexpected event can lead to a favorable twist of fate..
Note: sub-number of 13 (4 + 9).

58: Allows fulfillment to be found by fighting thanks to a voluntary, spontaneous, fast mind. Enables them to work hard to succeed. Develops the insight to know what is interesting or not in a situation. Indicates dogmatism, flexibility and change in the context where it is found. Makes them inwardly strong, by giving the feeling of continually experiencing dramas, by fighting alone

against the whole world. Restrictions.
Note: sub-number of 13 (5 + 8).

67: Gives a sense of analysis and inventiveness. In connection with the healing and wisdom. Leaving the modest world for spheres without excluding the possibility of material and financial ease thanks to a circle of friends sharing the same interests.
Note: sub-number of 13 (6 + 7).

76: Gives solid management qualities. Makes them able to put their ideas into practice. Sometimes locked into their beliefs to the point of becoming dogmatic. Uncompromising, determined, able to resist and to fight for their ideas and comfort in the long term. The expected gains do not always come about. Possibility of professional confrontations.
Note: sub-number of 13 (7 + 6).

85: Reveals a masculine nature in many circumstances. Often stubborn.
Note: sub-number of 13 (8 + 5).

94: Confers a certain humanism when coupled with a practical sense. Ill at ease with changes, moves. Has a tendency to want things to stay as they are.
Note: sub-number of 13 (9 + 4).

When number 5 is released...

Life Path 5: Your way of life causes frequent transformations. You crave travel, adventure, sport... Believe me, you won't be disappointed!

In case of karma 5, this itinerary asks you to adapt yourself to brutal changes of situations in all spheres of your existence. Be vigilant because this itinerary also includes risks of accident.

Tip: moderate by interpreting all the sub numbers revealed by the 3 ways of calculating the life path (see Chapter V).

Expression 5: Even a little rebellious against the standards and the routine, you are mobile, available and ready for the challenges. This needs to get out of the way or else you will quickly feel cramped. In some ways, you are the opposite of a homebody after all. This mindset is a valuable asset when you feel that nothing goes your way. You then find the resources to bounce back, you accept the events as they come and know how to adapt. You will finally have the hindsight, the ability to not take yourself seriously to cope. To thrive, you need different activities. Especially beyond the narrow framework of a single perspective. And especially not to be hindered in your movements. You claim a space of freedom better than others. You are able to challenge, especially as you know how to listen and build on the advice given to you. Your ingenuity, agility, your manual dexterity and your ability to solve problems will help you achieve your goals. You will change your line of business during your life because you aspire to learn new techniques.

Tip: see all sub-numbers behind this 5. Do not forget that Expression is also the reduced sum of the Aspiration and Potential numbers. This can reveal another sub-number. For example, Aspiration 6 + Potential 8 gives 14, sub-number of the Expression 5.

Aspiration 5: Your deep desire is to experiment, discover, grow and advance in other areas of your choice. Open to all possibilities, your sense of innovation, your ability to observe, your constant curiosity will naturally lead you to find solutions and to push the limits. It is within groups and associations whose purpose is to improve the human condition that you blossom the most. Your acute awareness of the world and phenomena can lead you to improve the ordinary. On the spiritual level, if you so desire, you might even consider helping others through esoteric disciplines that you know how to control and even by adding your relevant two cents. At home, there is a continuing need to combine work and pleasure. Contacts will be rich and varied, your relationships will be made in all possible ways. Convincing, you know to join your cause, and in fact, friends help you move your projects and you do the same for theirs. You also have a tendency to get carried away abruptly. Over time, it will be necessary to curb your excesses anger. An overlooked problem of children will affect you.

Potential 5: You lead a life that must be rich, varied and marked by success. Your donations and your creativity to communicate and present an idea, a project and / or product are outstanding. Your energy, your spontaneity are great but sometimes lead you to exhaustion, to give everything you have. You do not like routine, preferring various activities and situations. During your journey, adaptations, new directions, sometimes returning to education are to be expected (you do not dislike this). Earned money comes from different sources (often because of activities that change over time).

First Name 5: Keen observer, you develop your knowledge through your listening skills in particular. You are equally comfortable intellectually and manually. Your freedom of action is however, often thwarted due to the unexpected and social obligations. Capable of self-mockery, blessed with real humor, you look for activities that give you real pleasure and offer the possibility for you to express yourself in a playful way.

1st Middle Name 5: Attached to having many friends, relationships, buddies, you can sometimes become a slave by dint of wanting to please too much. You need to be fascinated by language, to captivate your relationships. With a juvenile character, you seek advice and approval from your loved ones without really listening to the advice given. Your vane side makes it difficult to have a life together, because you are often shared between your partner and your friends. You have difficulty distinguishing great love from deep friendship. You may also indulge in some adventures. If you have children, you know to treat them as equals. You can also exhibit a taste for the theatre and/or show a theatrical attitude with your partners.

2nd **Middle Name 5**: With an open mind, your creativity is marked by originality. You look to free yourself of all limitations. You quickly feel a deep dissatisfaction when you feel dependant from your environment. Your taste for discovery goes well with your independence of mind. But beware of utopias! Thanks to your intellectual abilities, you like to take charge by mixing business and pleasure. Your interest in new technologies or parallel sciences, never departs from your constant concern for rationality. If you are a woman, you have a clarity and an acute awareness of those around you. You tend to focus on your children, by learning a lot through them, sometimes to the point of questioning yourself.

Heredity 5: You have inherited a taste for action and the adaptability of your ancestors. Your family is characterized by a mixture of cultural and/or opening to the world. The love of children is present as well as the pleasure of organizing friendly receptions, lectures, experiments. The presence of foreign cultures and/or travel impresses you. This infiltration may lead to you to move to another country. Transformations and unexpected events are part of this first period of life. You change and frequently change your place of residence, sometimes living among brothers and sisters if any, unless it is you who are hosting them. Love stories may also involve travel and the need to change housing, a bit like the story of your own parents. It is possible however that these frequent changes from childhood involve some form of instability. A pervasive sense of injustice may arise even at this time.

Active 5: More often than not you act with enthusiasm, looking to experience new and rewarding situations.

Example: a Realization 8 amplified by an Active number 5 accentuates the native's capacity to convey their ideas and innovative projects with determination and enthusiasm.

Maturity 5: Your social situation will improve due to your ability to adapt. Over time you will learn to modulate your reactions, to change your behavior, not to get carried away by your impulsivity faced with the forbidden, to an arbitrary authority and everything that limits. You can then take advantage of the opportunities that will arise. Your eagerness to learn, to develop your skills, combined with your ability to produce the necessary efforts will help you succeed in your chosen field. In the end, it will be the radical transformations and changes in your activities that will lead you to guide yourself in the direction of your appetencies. The influence of a partner (associate, spouse .etc) will not be unconnected to this development.

Intensity 5: You like change and adventure. Fascinated by the discovery of the world in general, you show interest in many areas. Able to seize opportunities that present themselves, adaptable, you are also sensitive to the pleasures of the senses. You often appear nervous and impulsive.

Karma 5 (no letter 5): You prove to be too possessive, too dependent on things and people around you. A slight change in sight, and you become a nervous wreck.   In fact, you have a dilemma. On the one hand, you attach great importance to your independence, your freedom as you like to show yourself, highlighting your abilities. Far from the stage and in the forefront somehow. Seeking to escape certain situations, this does not prevent you from being critical *vis à vis* the freedoms that your peers offer. You fear change, new things and prefer to avoid anything that might upset the established balance. Your irritability and your lack of flexibility will be tested at times by your children if you have any. Your journey will also be marked by the need to integrate yourself into a social environment different from its culture, its characteristics. Moves, frequent and/or sudden changes of place can make your adaptation problematic. Your roadmap predestines you to deal with changes, namely anticipating them rather than rejecting them. To discover that they are not blows of fate but opportunities to grow.

1 letter worth 5: Particularly attached to your sacrosanct freedom of action, you end up having too much confidence in yourself, which tends to complicate your relationships with others. You like to be surrounded, but you don't want to lose your leadership. You are a humanist and focused on others as soon as they recognize your worth and your values. You look to lead your loved ones in your projects as in your utopias. You are blessed with a certain charisma and your presence is very noticeable. It goes without saying that you often have bright ideas and that you want to be indispensable by trying to make yourself useful. You have a love for children that you tend to take as friends. You are attached to the fact that they must experience their own lives. Your constant quest for love is hard to achieve because it must be that of total love, namely the body, heart and mind. You have a pronounced taste for travel and new technologies. Above all, you need to learn patience, which is not really one of your first virtues, and to not exhaust yourself by taking on too many projects simultaneously. You are very touchy and choleric but also excitable and playful. You must be careful not to sound too flippant and superficial. You could say that you're a hustler, but you do not always measure the impact that your very fast stances have on others. You are overly dependent on "I like" and "I don't like".

2 letters worth 5: You have a tendency to mix deep friendship and love because you cannot always tell the difference between the two. You like to receive and to be taken care of. You have a predisposition to be surrounded by a large, sometimes blended, family. You are attracted by novelty, but you sometimes clutter your life up with useless gadgets. You have a gift for local business (shop). You know how to receive, collect and get comfortable, but you must be careful not to invite everyone into your house. Altruistic at heart, you're blessed with a community spirit. You are very sensitive, but sometimes appear too casual, especially when you consider others as yourself. You do not always know the difference between your own personality and that of those around you. Your love relationships can be very ambiguous because you tend to find your mother included in your love life. One way or another, she ends up being too present. You also have a hard time attaching yourself emotionally because of your indecision and your determination to combine life together and independently. You have a real artistic taste that you will express sooner or later and it will probably be the source of great inspirations for you. You enjoy modern means of communication (telephone and internet etc). You are a great defender of the widow and the orphan.

3 letters worth 5: You are blessed with a quick and elusive wit. Constantly looking for new things, you have real problems focusing on a single goal because you can be too impatient. You love being surrounded by friends and creating/building with them. Your rebellious and revolutionary spirit tires some people out. Dreamy, utopian, you love travel, and/or anything that can get you out of what you consider as monotony in a company that you often find too conformist for your taste. You have original ideas and you do not especially like being compared to others. You're almost always looking for challenges. You are passionate about new sciences and adventures. You have an interest in the metaphysical and the esoteric, as long as it is objective. You tend to talk too much. You must be careful not to become superficial, even overrated. By summarizing things, you end up losing touch with your profound human nature and forgetting that of others. You have many strings to your bow, you know how to get involved in multiple projects, but be careful not to spread yourself too thinly. You are a teenager who will not grow up. It is clear that you must learn to control your nervousness and be patient.

4 letters worth 5: Your taste for new technologies must be combined with the practical side they can bring to your life. They have to be functional and effective. You connect pragmatism and novelty. You present a certain obstinacy with regard to your goals. You need to be reassured about the quality of your relationships. You are altruistic but you are still looking to preserve your assets - not too much than needed. You are very attracted to the aesthetic and beauty. You may have talents as a magnetizer and an ability to pass an energy through your hands. While having great respect for your parents, you feel the need to free yourself of your educational background. You are constantly looking to improve your quality of life, quality of housing, food and new energies. You have a tendency to blend your work and family life, which is not always easy, because you're often forced to move frequently for your business. Your income may come from different activities. You are very loyal friend. You are particularly heavy when you always look to be right. You also risk suffering the jealousies of those around you. While being open and friendly, you are sometimes distant and elusive. You can be very unforgiving when you feel betrayed and closed when you feel invaded. You may have a great love for the animal world. You are very respectful of the culture of your ancestors. You may date people who you have a very big age gap with.

5 letters worth 5: A real will-o'-the-wisp, you constantly look for adventure. You are a loyal friend, an everyday friend but your superficiality sometimes/often makes you appear shallow. You like seeking new horizons and new technological advances. You really do not like what you see as boundaries, you want to remove them, and this, in every field, literally and figuratively. Instinctive, fast and blessed with a brilliant mind, you are constantly searching for immediate gratification, often refusing daily life that you find hard to grasp and a monotonous life that does not really inspire you. Note that this hectic life does not allow you to have much better financial protection, especially early in your life. You have a young character and you're more inclined to go Club Med than to live in conformity. Inventive at will, you are a techie. Direct and straightforward, your sincerity can play tricks on you, especially since you tend to be a little too sarcastic. You are still generous, altruistic and in short, human! Loving breakneck speed, watch out for accidents. You're attracted to things that fly and glide, in short, everything that frees you of weightlessness. It is your lack of patience that can lead to difficult experiences.

6 letters worth 5: You possess deep analytical skills and an ability to get involved in various areas requiring a great expertise. Your intelligence is above average and you know perfectly how to use it. You tend to select friends based on their quality. You like to be clean and neat and you attach great importance to your appearance as well as that of people around you. Your naive side sometimes open you up to others a little too much, you must be careful not to reveal too much of yourself and not to over expose yourself. Your love for IT and modernity more generally, must always, in your eyes, be accompanied by efficiency. Your listening skills with regard to your fellow creatures is remarkable because you're blessed with a sharpness that allows you to easily deconstruct what you are exposed to. You should still be wary of your sweeping assertions that seem real to you, and to your loved ones, towards those who sometimes show a little too much confidence. Before presenting your ideas, you must make up your own duly substantiated and proven opinion. The love of an animal or a life companion (horse, dog, cat etc.) can play a big role in your life. Throughout your life, you will move many times for a variety of reasons, but often for good reasons. You have a facility to turn to social groups. You will seek, of course, to surround yourself with competent people who are able to help you achieve your goals. You are very attached to experiencing a kind of harmony in your relationships with others and you are blessed with a great capacity to overcome antagonism. You must be careful not to spread yourself too thinly over various activities, which may lead to you sometimes being too exploitable and at the mercy of others. You have a sharp eye that allows you to see incorrect details and rectify them. Frank as gold, you have an undeniable talent for everything that relates to oral expression. While maintaining a certain independence of mind and body, you will easily develop a significant relational fabric. You need sexual experiences, but it should be noted that these can easily lead to disappointment in love because you have great difficulty in finding the ideal partner. It must be said that you set the bar high and that often your love is borrowing from your cerebral type.

7 letters worth 5: You're the perfect idealist who needs to feel commissioned in what they undertake. You are especially attracted by ambitious, even non-standard projects. One of your main shortcomings is the fact that you have difficulty accepting authority and any form of social hierarchy. You love you create and you do it by yourself. Blessed with great knowledge, you have a keen intelligence and you can be very insightful with great curiosity. You like to get involved avant-garde activities and to explore new horizons. You'll get a taste for the exotic and different cultures. You look for a form of elitism in your relationships and friendships. You will be able to get involved in group actions, provided they preserve your sacrosanct independence. You'll probably have to recreate your knowledge and you will enjoy your offspring. You know how to show yourself to be nice, magnetic, attractive, but you try, sometimes a little too hard, to show your individualism. Your excessive and uncompromising side causes anger in you that distances you from others and plunges you into long periods of solitude. You are very idealistic in love. You have an aptitude for psychology. You are the lawyer of lost causes, sensitive to minorities, revolutionary in spirit, innate or in spite.

8 letters worth 5: Experimenter and explorer of the unfathomable, you appreciate all kinds of relationships from very different backgrounds, while remaining very vigilant. You release a certain magnetism, in addition, you have a talent for clairvoyance, the occult in general, and interest in the medical world. You prefer to keep quiet about what you do. You are sometimes too naive, and you sometimes give you too much, which can work to your advantage. With experience, sooner or later, you'll end up learning that you need to preserve yourself and to keep a secret garden. You are a lover of the night, a night owl attracted by unconventional evenings, which may, perhaps, gratify your unusual sexual life. It may be that you have secret children and that, sooner or later, you will end up discovering some family secrets. You're a fighter with a pronounced instinct for survival and at the very least, we can say that you do not have cold feet. You will experience what are called symbolic deaths. You will find yourself faced with strange situations and you're one of those people who can disappear from one day to the next without warning. You are able to understand your world and the people around you with a simple glance. This ability stems from a deep intuition combined with detailed and precise analysis.

9 letters worth 5: You tend to flee a certain reality, to throw yourself into dreams that are sometimes unrealistic. You have a sensitive ability to discern unusual worlds and to make sense solutions in an original way. Your ability to put new ideas forward highlights this intimate relationship that you maintain between the unfathomable and tangible reality. You're also in search of artificial paradises and/or large spaces. You have an absolute need to be on a mission and to feel you have a deep impact on those around you. You have an undeniable ease to get in touch with all sorts of people from different backgrounds but who share a similar modus operandi. You also find it particularly easy to be part of a group. You must be careful not to show yourself to be too elitist. You enjoy sharing your enthusiasm with your loved ones. You will also learn to channel your aspirations, and above all, not to let yourself be overwhelmed by a kind of fatalism that too easily leads you to accept that hand that fate deals you. You have a taste for the exotic and you do not get too locked into a predetermined structure which is too burdensome or too rigid (like that of the family). Your love relationships can be difficult with some people who are too absorbed in their daily lives. You attach great importance to know-how and knowledge, even if you sometimes tend to overshoot your goals. You will learn to deepen the areas you are studying. You want to be unique, perhaps even within your family.

More than 9 letters worth 5: See above for the interpretation of the reduction of this number.
Example: If you have 16 letters at a value of 5, you get a 7 by adding 1 + 6. Refer to this value, that is to say 7 letters at a value of 5. Remember to also take into account the 1 and 6 which makes up your 16 because they also refer to sub numbers. You must, therefore, interpret them by taking into account the definition of these two figures from the definition of the sub numbers given below. Remember, this concerns mainly that which affects freedom, sexuality, groups and children etc.

5 Mental letters: You enjoy new ingenious ways of thinking and are open to other methods. You learn through a mobile spirit which is adaptable to different learning styles. For these reasons, you are a perpetual student (often talkative). You steer clear of flawless and heavy speech, unchanging knowledge of our ancestors. You feel as though you must address knowledge with excitement through the prism of emotion. That's why your mind is sometimes at its lowest ebb as soon as disappointments and upsets arise.

5 Emotional letters: You like people who are not too intrusive. You like to experience your emotions intensely. Sensual pleasures are at the forefront because you look for sensations. You are also likely to appear unstable at times.

5 Intuitive letters: There is always that voice in your head that tells you what course to take, which path to follow, what decision to make. Your highly developed intuition serves your keen sense of observation. You can trust that potential. It is alive and well. This is not the fruit of your imagination even if this does not exclude some interference. You are able to feel the needs of younger people (child, adolescent). Expand your magnetizer abilities.

5 Physical letters: You will experience one or several secret liaisons to make you realize that you must change your behavior. You can exert yourself to the point of not sleeping enough. Your impatience and impulsiveness may play tricks on you. Falls and spectacular accidents will be your lot unless you find greater inner peace and relax from time to time. If not daily, you like to discover the forms of intoxication and fulfillment that can save your physical body. In fact you like experimenting and love to listen. However, be careful not to overdo it by always pushing the boundaries ever further. Learn to be calm and level-headed without denying this great thirst for physical adventure. For you, the body is and must remain free of all movement.

5 Creative letters: Your creativity is drawn to the source of your experiences. You love to innovate, create while you feel free.

5 Balanced letters: You are curiously attached to the fact that it is the variety of situations, the exploration of new experiences that will stabilize, reassure you. That calm happens and so you're less reassured.

5 Dual letters: You take a step back when you get to take off the masks and show yourself as you really are. It is also possible that the malicious attitude of some loved ones triggers something in you.

Challenge 5: You should channel your sensuality, your thirst for discovery, your insatiable appetite. You will learn to be measured, balanced, in a word to rediscover whilst remaining cautious. Again, it is accepting the opportunities that life offers, even if they do not always live up to your aspirations. For all that, the quest for freedom and independence should not obstruct the aspirations of others or prevent you from listening to them. You will need to overcome a tenacious desire to do only what you like, by dealing with your environment. You will also need to show your friendship towards those whom you consider friends more intensely and learn to be thankful for services rendered.

First Cycle 5: Childhood is experienced with a sense of freedom. Often sexuality is discovered early. Change is often at gatherings, moves are numerous. You need to develop, to be recognized. If your parents don't support you enough, you indulge in all kinds of experiences, and feel a lot of nervousness, even anxiety.

Second Cycle 5: The environment is conducive to change, to many adventures, to desires, to the willingness to explore new areas. You enjoy a real autonomy of action to reach out to new activities. Channel this need for movement to get the most out of it and avoid risks inherent to head butts.

Third Cycle 5: The environment provides the means for various activities. Life is active and full of discoveries and travels of all kinds. A bit of monotony is planned. Through these new experiences, there is the possibility of spiritual opening.

First Pinnacle 5: You quickly show a taste for change, variety. As a child, you have a thirst for discoveries, journeys. Periods of intense happiness contrast with some binding changes that you need to cope with by adapting to new circumstances (moving, changing schools etc). You like to confront yourself to the outside. You are looking to achieve to become free. Sexuality may be discovered early.

Second or Third Pinnacle 5: You find job or family changes to which you must adapt. By being open, listening to others, you'll enjoy significant advantages. The challenge is not to be too individualistic. Travel and relocations are likely, as well as the need to change course or adapt to a new socioprofessional order. There is a dynamism in relation to your contacts, exchanges of all kinds, facilitation, education etc.

Fourth Pinnacle 5: Finally, it is a good time to travel, explore, and change your mind. The experiences are varied and good humor ensured. Tone and alertness are preserved through good spirits.

Sub-numbers of 5

14 (see also its meaning as a karmic debt): Describes good intentions as well as great availability, but also the risk of letting themselves be manipulated by others due to their difficulty in saying no. Many events will have the effect of reducing the native to their basic needs. Strong sensuality. Feeling of being different, feeling of not having been understood.

23: Develops curiosity and the ability to adapt. Need to experiment which leads to recognition. Talent. Success. Leads to sympathies, favor the benign influence of protecting people in the family circle. Increases sensuality. Sometimes lacks realism. The imagination can play tricks.

32: Characterizes alternations between unexpected success and disappointments. Duality between both, courage, the strong mind, willingness and hesitations, the feeling of not being capable (complex from studies and family), even dependence on someone. Succeeds if they find the courage to challenge themselves and move forward. Predominance of emotions, sensitivity. Tendency to not take the time to breathe, to live at a hundred miles an hour.

194

41: Develops a need to focus their mind on specific objectives to avoid any scattering. A tendency to lead several projects simultaneously. Socioprofessional success. Need for freedom, new experiences, new horizons often in response to family and/or socioprofessional responsibilities and obligations. Often indicates that the action becomes agitation and harms.

50: Increases creativity and the need to experiment. Strong potential to succeed thanks to their originality, their openness, their spontaneity. Charm, gaiety, marked extroversion encouraging contacts and support. Moves. Compared with the foreign. Refers to sexuality, magnetism, the need to communicate. Endeared to risk taking. Sometimes emphasizes an addiction.

59: Refers to anxiety leading to over the top reactions *vis à vis* the mental state and imagination. Sometimes made to set goals which are not always realistic. Difficulties and disappointments are to be expected.
Note: sub-number of 14 (5 + 9).

68: Sometimes reveals a lack of continuity in efforts and a changing attitude. Earnings are favored to oblige the native to face up to the need for healthy financial management, leading them to value their heritage. Refers to introspection, dedication, sensitivity and fidelity. Develops a sense of humor. Makes listening and respect for others necessary.
Note: sub-number of 14 (6 + 8).

77: Increases the need for independence. Inclined to look in depth, to analyze without leaving anything to chance. The sense of alertness serves as a basis for knowledge. Predisposes to taking a critical and specific view of things and beings. Gives a need to control, to master, not to give in to excesses that seem attractive. Represents the spiritual wisdom gained through introspection and research. Knowledge is intuitive. Makes original expression possible. Language is clear, precise. The mind is bright, demonstrative and needs to be challenged. Likes to lead others when it comes to change and transformation. Sometimes acts are contrary to thinking and the mood is also fluctuating.

Note: sub-number of 14 (7 + 7).

86: Confers a form of indulgence, may lead to no longer assuming their responsibilities. Makes them look at themselves.
Note: sub-number of 14 (8 + 6).

95: Door to an idealized humanism. Gives the need for change, travel. Sometimes pushed to take their dreams for realities.
Note: sub-number of 14 (9 + 5).

When number 6 occurs...

Life Path 6: You should be able to tell right from wrong. Of course you will have responsibilities to stand up for. Be positive and ambitious, and you will succeed.

In case of karma 6, your hesitations can sometimes drive you to make the wrong choice, to have to face up some responsibilities you are not made for. Make your choices according to who you are, otherwise the burden might be heavy to carry.

Tip: moderate by interpreting all the sub numbers revealed by the 3 ways of calculating the life path (see Chapter V).

Expression 6: Your actions and thoughts are very often at each other. You shine when your environment meets your criteria and needs (safety, approval and affection from friends and relatives). You are accommodating and attentive and this makes you a great confidant. Driven by an ideal of beauty, you can create a certain aesthetic sense. You also like to highlight yourself. But sometimes you hesitate. You do not easily make a decision. Trying too hard to spare others, you tend to forget about yourself. That said, your dedication commands respect at work and in your emotional relationships. You sometimes seem to be overly possessive.

Tip: see all sub-numbers behind this 6. Do not forget that Expression is also the reduced sum of the Aspiration and Potential numbers. This can reveal another sub-number. For example, Aspiration 22 + Potential 2 gives 24, sub-number of the Expression 6.

Aspiration 6: Your deep desire is to live responsibly and in balance with your relatives. You are appreciated for your kindness and availability. You look for people who share your values. You are more affectionate and dialogue more than your partner in this quest (the same aspiration number 6 for example). Your relationship will be stronger no matter the risks in your life. In this aspect, it is often your friends who make you meet this person. Very sensitive to gestures and attentions of another, you also know how to give the best of yourself. That said, a form of naivety characterizes you and you think that people can't imagine what you want. Truly, you need to approve your action in the eyes of others. More than others, you need to be valued.

Potential 6: You seek harmony in all things. You have taste and have a particular interest in all that is aesthetic. You enjoy giving and receiving presents. Imaginative, able with your hands, not lacking practicality, you love objects and know how to make them. You will succeed in artisan, social or medical activities, everything that rotates around human relations interests you. Besides, you have to make decisions on new employment opportunities in your life because it is likely that you change your orientation.

First Name 6: You present yourself well, are on your own. Serious and responsible worker in the quest for recognition for your daily work, you look to be valued to the point of becoming a slave to the services you need to get there. You are particularly at ease with colleagues who share your modus operandi. You easily combine work and health. Nevertheless, you remain dependant on the socioprofessional climate that for you, is predominant in your balance.

1st Middle Name 6: With this great need for love, tenderness, you idealize marriage and your partner. You want to have a marital and/or community life, harmonious and structured. Capable of taking care of others, of relieving them, you easily take responsibility for that which is wrong with others, with a tendency to meddle your partner's affairs. Critical of anything that does not correspond to your established precepts, your perfectionism may also lead to you becoming indecisive in terms of choices with an uncertain outcome. The importance that you give to your principles of life can lead to a form of frigidity and/or rigidity if your associations are not consistent with your aspirations. Ultimately, you are blocked as soon as conflicts and rivalries arise. You are not really a humanist, driven by values. Aesthetic, you love to surround yourself with beautiful things.

2nd Middle Name 6: In search for an ideal love, attached to the affection from your father if you are a woman, you need to experience intense and passionate loves which, despite everything, end quickly due to your critical mind. You like the presence of charismatic partners, influential in love and work. You will easily find support. You like to combine fun and work with an ability to protect children, to educate and assist them. Your taste for dance, outings, relationships make you an excellent choice. However, you must avoid an excessive selectivity due to your desire to move towards what is beautiful and shining. Your ability for achievement is great.

Heredity 6: Your parental home attaches great importance and attention to his house. Your mother takes a large share of family burdens and responsibilities, despite the fluctuating of events. You love to fix, beautify, decorate. The sense of service is also present in relation to the relatives of the family circle. Bequests and grants from family can be expected. This is important to you since you inherited this sense of responsibility and family from your ancestors. In love some partners show a significant age difference.

Active 6: You act with the desire to maintain harmony with your surroundings and your environment. More often than not your actions must allow you to obtain the consent of others.

Example: Aspiration 2 is particularly amplified with an Active number 6. The desire to avoid conflict is so obvious sometimes to the point where it leads to compromises.

Maturity 6: You will blossom when you put your heart into it and when your efforts at work are (finally) acknowledged. You will overcome your indecision in order to facilitate your success and finally get real stability in your activity. Deeply influenced by the relationship with your mother, this will be your opportunity to consider how your attitudes and your behavior enable you to receive this affection that you expect in return or not. To achieve this, life will give you good reason to change your priorities.

Intensity 6: You are always willing when it comes to taking responsibility in agreement with a profound sense of justice. You are able to harmonize, to pacify your environment, which does not prevent you from staying firm when it comes to the ideals you defend. Stubbornness and the idea when nothing is going to characterize you better.

Karma 6 (no letter 6): By nature, you don't look for responsibilities. On the contrary, you'd rather avoid them. Nevertheless, at work as well as at home, you will have to face up to them, for your own achievement. You will take a major step forward as soon as you prove to be easier. In fact, you have to accept the imperfection of beings and the world, not to want to stick with your ideals at any price. It is necessary to show yourself to be less demanding with your loved ones. Sensitive to beauty, aesthetics in all its forms, you tend to want everything to be perfect, getting stuck on the slightest detail. Some things put you off and others will attract you, each time in excess. You may confuse service and servitude. Not really comfortable with your image, you cannot stop looking to improve yourself, but curiously, too many compliments in your favor make you suspicious. Take a position, having to arbitrate in situations that are not made by you will be forced passages to be aware of the responsibility inherent in any trial. You're spending too much time waiting for others, too dependent on their eyes, and in this sense, it is desirable to empower yourself from this supervision that only you impose on yourself. It is likely that a type of castration is at the root of this state.

1 letter worth 6: A true defender of the widow and the orphan, you have a very clear tendency to systematically take up the case for people who suffer and for overlooked minorities. You want to be the one who provides care for others, the one who possesses the skills and the know-how in terms of how to be most effective in this area. A critical, but still accommodating, mind, you do not like to expose injustices. You should avoid being overly critical, try to be more tolerant with respect to what you consider as faults in others. Dedicated to the extreme, you must learn not to feel too sorry for yourself because it is because you think you are the only person able to solve all the problems you are faced with. You may be recognized for a very great capacity for organization. A lack of recognition on the part of those to whom you want to show yourself to be helpful, sometimes overly, leads you to show you a cold, distant, frigid and pinched side. You have a great sense of sacrifice that can lead you to protect or over-protect your offspring, your spouse and to do too much in your profession. Be careful not to lock yourself in deep resentments. You build throughout your life thanks to what you bring to those around you. A good body/soul doctor.

2 letters worth 6: You love your home and you need to be surrounded by your own (family) as well as loved ones. You give special importance to your home that you know how to decorate. You are attached to domestic life and to children. You have an interest in the medical field, and more broadly fin any activity that can assist, advise and help people. You have undeniable artistic tastes and you really like to show yourself at your best. Your commitment in love and at work is undeniable. Pragmatic, serious, loving to plan and organize your lives, but often anxious and intransigent, you encounter situations that paradoxically lead you to indecision. A form of selfishness can characterize you when you are looking to protect your safe world and you may even fall into a childish mode of operation. You're convinced by your well-established strong life principles. Above all, you need to abstain or avoid falling into words and sentences in the style of "It should be like this, it must be like that ....". If your partner cannot satisfy your need for stability and/or harmony, blockages can occur and lead you to a form of frigidity and to a cold and reserved attitude. Otherwise, you will enjoy an emotional development and a beautiful sensuality. You still need a strong presence at your side.

3 letters worth 6: Dedicated, determined and loyal, you love organization, especially if it meets your expectations. Full of life principles, you are looking primarily to display a good education. You have a pronounced taste for detail and perfection, which has a bearing on your quest for ideal love, which may consequently be difficult to achieve. A good listener, you're a good confidant and you like to be ready to help those in need. You are blessed with a sociable spirit, sometimes a little too conventional, what tends to make you] too worried. Faithful in friendship as in love, you're the perfect partner. You prefer anything that is practical, you cannot stand mess and hate chaos even more. Sometimes too routine and/or too attached to the letter, you end up lacking cheerfulness. You're good for the couch with a shrink (if you do not get yourself). You're a telepath who receives all kinds of information, you will learn how to sort this out in a way that suits you best. You have a keen sense of observation and you can be very insightful. You love being surrounded by brilliant people.

4 letters worth 6 *(uncommon):* You place great value on your commitments with your partners. You like to organize, plan and arrange your daily life. You're able to invest in long term projects in a calm and thoughtful way. You are easily able to combine work and family life, even if you only rarely display your true feelings. You invest a lot in everything related to your success, which often takes on a social character, and that of your children. You are a pragmatist who enjoys working with materials (wood and earth etc). Pragmatic with your feet firmly on the ground, you enjoy having possessions. You are seeking peace, tranquility, you do not like the vulgar, you're a conservative, sometimes a little too reserved. You're not without some authority, you want some responsibility. You must beware of falling into a form of pushiness, and especially not to become intolerant. It is your stubbornness that can be the most damaging. Depending on the theme, some emotional difficulties may cause financial or material loss, even a loss of prestige.

5 letters worth 6 *(uncommon):* Above all, your mind is critical, it tends to exaggerate events resulting from adverse winds, which sometimes makes you particularly worried. You tend to choose your relationships based on your prejudices. Your difficulty in making decisions could lead you to live a bigamist life, even if, paradoxically, you judge this to be contrary to your life principles. A paradox! Dedicated to those who suffer, you continually seek to show yourself in a good light in others eyes by helping people. You must learn not to be a slave and to stop complaining about your troubles for the sole reason of being more valued. You love adventure and change, provided that your excessive mind finds it suitable and/or your associates (work, friends, and spouses) think the same. Above all, you are a trusted person who is a good listener. One thing is sure, you hate being rushed and/or invaded by others, but yourself, you do not hesitate to do so. You must learn to choose your relationships and to not always criticize everything that you dislike. You like to feel useful and provide assistance to those in need. You're a charmer who knows how to express themselves perfectly.

6 letters worth 6 (*rare*): You are a perfectionist in the purist form, blessed with a desire to organize everything according to your predetermined criteria. Dedicated to the extreme if the request for assistance occurs within a framework that matches your preconceptions, you can be completely absent and unattainable if these conditions are not met. The fact remains that despite everything, you can still be very present for others. You are looking for a partnership in love and work with loyal and reliable people, which sometimes cause difficulty in finding this ideal partner. You have a great desire to live in a pleasant, harmonious, clean and healthy environment. You are attracted by all that is beautiful. Sometimes you become so obsessed with attention to detail that you become immune to criticism. Anything related to psychological analysis, the medical and beauty is particularly favored. You are attached to good parenting and you can sometimes be a bit too moralistic and uncompromising. You must learn to keep quiet and not to be overly critical if the events or behaviors of those around you displease you. Be careful not to be too emotionally dependent on an emotional or invasive professional relationship. Your life principles can cause you to want to do too much with the result being that you wear yourself out by taking on too many tasks. Learn to relax.

7 letters worth 6 (*rare*): You tend to project your ideals and your quest for perfection in your close relationships because you like to see them concretized in and through them. Refined and an aesthetic, you continually give your opinion on everything and anything, and above all on what you do not deem to be tasteful. You have an attraction for education, training, hygiene and everything related to writing (executive secretary or notary clerk etc), psychology and the arts. You often act theatrically, enjoying being recognized for your dedication which is sometimes pushed to extremes. Your need for protection or overprotection may lead you to take out all kinds of insurance or to work in organizations that deal with this. Sensitive to the suffering of others, especially if it affects people or minorities living on the other side of the world, you like charity. You need structures and organizations to develop yourself fully and to feel useful. You like to feel like you have a mission and you have even an inquisitive mind. You are curious about everything and you have a vital need to be reassured about the love people have for you, especially that from your loved one. You want perfection. Sensitive to expression, you appreciate the profound exchanges with those you are close to. Children may move away from home.

8 letters worth 6 *(rare):* A doctor of something, you are able to thoroughly analyze the moods of your contemporaries. Sensitive to organization and perfection, you have a trained eye to see and understand the modus operandi of others. A bit of a gossip, you perceive depth while having the ability to analyze what you feel. You must also learn to moderate your wit that can be hurtful. Your taste for secrecy allows you to organize your life as you wish. You may be attracted by all sorts of diverse areas, focusing particularly on anything related to the occult (or that which is hidden, for example, research etc). A special adaptability in work and in life in general allows you to be the right person for the job, especially if the difficulty is great. Your craving for romantic exchanges and experiences of any kind will surely lead you to surround yourself with strange people. You will also need to overcome your habit of ending or giving up on, sometimes forcefully, that which does not suit you. Secret loves or children. You may be blessed with a strong magnetism that leaves no-one in your family circle indifferent. A sense of mystery emanates from you. Despite your intelligence, you can be very naive.

9 letters worth 6 *(rare):* Inspired and fussy, sometimes you can sometimes be a little giddy, you should try to create order in your life and in your head. You need experiences that take into account the different hazards that life imposes on you. You look primarily to get a place in the sun. Your investment in romantic and professional relationships and friendships is conditioned by the benefits you can get from them. You are easily absorbed into your dreams and your utopias. Everything related to the arts is especially favored. You need to feel you're useful to something or someone. You will learn to express your true feelings, and not to hide behind an image that allows you to preserve your tranquility, to be very precise in your goals and your wishes rather than bearing the brunt and criticizing that which doesn't suit you. A poet in your spare time, without a doubt you will write down on paper what you tend to hide. The field of the mind combined with a deep spirituality is familiar. You have a tendency to deploy a wealth of energy to finish tasks quickly in order to enjoy sweet rest periods. You often invest in the education of children to continue what you failed to do yourself. You really need to be reassured about your many talents and your great abilities. Charity performed a long way from your country may be an objective. Perfect host.

More than 9 letters worth 6 *(rare)*: See above for the interpretation of the reduction of this number.
Example: If you have 12 letters at a value of 6, you get a 3 by adding 1 + 2. Refer to this value, that is to say 3 letters at a value of 6. Remember to also take into account the 1 and 2 which makes up your 12 because they also refer to sub numbers. You must, therefore, interpret them by taking into account the definition of these two figures from the definition of the sub numbers given below. Remember, this concerns mainly love, marriage, sexuality, choosing and the relationship between what is fair and what is beautiful…

6 Mental letters: You want to benefit from the knowledge that your close friends and family have. For you, the beauty of knowledge is that it is transmitted to the heart of the family unit. For this reason, you want to be noticed by your partner. With this person, intellectual exchanges are frequent. There is emulation. You like to win in this way. Social and medical issues and issues concerning health and psychology interest you in particular. You have respect for tradition and you know how to listen and pass on cultural heritage. The parent/child relationship is predominant. For you, knowledge is pre-eminently human, to serve your close friends and family. Your indecisiveness torments you. Making choices concerning different main interests arises from your youth.

6 Emotional letters: You are hypersensitive. You want to surround your family with a deep and true affection but are always afraid of being misunderstood. Family is your main focus of attention. You try to find fulfillment through harmonious and balanced sensations. Love should not be a source of conflict.

6 Intuitive letters: You have great talent for feeling, perceiving and guessing (often compared with your partner). You avoid conflict thanks to this predisposition to see the future clearly. If you make the choice to use this potential for humanist purposes, you will develop these perceptions further. In some cases, we can speak of mediumship. The graphics, the photo, and the image you are talking about.

6 Physical letters: You enjoy being involved in complex emotional relationships. Sometimes hidden love, the secrecy surrounding your liaisons may leave a deep impression and have a significant impact on your life. Often you will need to get away from the loved one, the relationship may become impossible. You will, however, be sensitive to many marks of attention. If not daily, you like above all to please and give. You have difficulty with your body if you cannot shape it to your ideal. All exercises are a pretext to search for the aesthetic, plastic beauty.

6 Creative letters: Your creativity is expressed through various arts. You are adaptable and show belief in your creations.

6 Balanced letters: You are fond of giving meaning to your relationships, your advice. Love is not an empty word and thanks to it, you know that security and stability are at the end of the road.

6 Dual letters: You take a step back following your own quest, unless you are the subject of an investigation. In all cases, a karmic partner will help this transformation.

Challenge 6: You have an interest in not wanting too much from others, especially yours and show yourself to be more tolerant particularly with respect to those who do not see things your way. Your desire to live in a harmonious world, perfect, can indeed lead to you being very critical and sometimes you think you are more devoted than others. It will not hide your own weaknesses, be fair and learn not to make systematic comparisons between service provided and service provided. Besides, before you commit, it is important that you measure the inherent obligations and responsibilities. Realistic, methodical, structured but flexible, here's the challenge.

First Cycle 6: The family context in its broadest sense (parents, grandparents, uncles etc) is fulfilling overall, but it also leads you to assume responsibilities earlier. You're attached to your family and have a great need to be loved and understood. But the weight of certain obligations weighs on you and you would be better handled carefully. Once an adult, you are probably looking to find a friendly and caring profession, emphasizing the quest for a harmonious emotional life.

Second Cycle 6: The environment is quite favorable in terms of your family and social involvement. Responsibility and stability characterize this period. If you are willing to assume certain obligations, you will reap great joy. By showing yourself to be conciliatory and willing your emotional life will be harmonious. Your socioprofessional commitments are marked by your willingness to assist, to arrange which will be appreciated.

Third Cycle 6: You benefit from a more nurturing and comforting environment. In all cases, a sort of protection is with you.

First Pinnacle 6: To begin, you will benefit from a child from a family context or tenderness, affection is usually present. . Very soon, you will have to take responsibility and get involved. You develop your creativity and sociability. You have a sensitivity to anything that relates to aesthetics.

Second or Third Pinnacle 6: You find harmonious achievement thanks to your ability to act responsibly. Investments are favored in particular regarding real estate. It's a good time to invest in partnerships, to express your ideas and values and to help others. An important life choice presents itself during this period and this requires your objectivity. Be careful though not to have a confused sense of service and servitude.

Fourth Pinnacle 6: Finally, it is a period marked by responsibility towards the family circle. Also socially, you agree to try to reconcile. Good advice, you mark spirits with your ability to properly assess situations. Benefitting from aid and support, you progress, while ensuring your back.

Sub-numbers of 6

15 (see also its meaning as a karmic debt): Reinforces excitement, accentuates the need to love. Forced to sort through responsibilities to be assumed. Makes you impatient. Gives a power of seduction. Demonstrates real generosity. Knows how to forgive. Prefers passion to reason. Emphasizes the need for movement, freedom. Made more tolerant. Develops the ability manage things for themselves. Anything related to adventure and travel is present. Gives the taste for experimentation. However, may profit from a tendency to listen to others for their own benefit.

24: Highlights a problem relating to a maternal link. Obliged to overcome a feeling of exclusion, an emotional lack, by asserting themselves and by taking their rightful place (see the chart parameters where this number is found). May benefit from female help and material resources.

33: Provides mental facilities that predispose the desire to study despite not always favorable conditions. Tendency to spread yourself too thin. Glorified and highlights a form of susceptibility. Develops an interest for the arts, humanities, medicine, the esoteric, information technology. Intensifies the need to be accepted.

42: Accentuates precariousness, brings about changing situations causing a difficult balance able to lead to forms of dependence where this number is found. Obliges them to assume their responsibilities.

51: Highlights certain obstacles that require a special effort needing an adaptation for a new departure. Despite a changing mood, confers enthusiasm, dynamism. Indicates divergent points of view, highlights contentious issues (litigation risks, in relation to the law). Emphasizes antagonisms leading to suspicions, cheap shots and determined enemies on their way.

60: Refers to the sense of responsibilities, affection, the need for protection, sensitivity, generosity and the imagination. Makes them whole but sometimes dependant on others. Loves the beautiful, the aesthetic. Concern. Favors material and social performance but can also mark the loss of these goods/and or their notoriety.

69: Indicates that associations are favorable. Commits them to a cause. Gives the sense of dedication, even sacrifice. Sometimes twisted. Spontaneous. Provides good abilities to convince and be heard.
Note: sub-number of 15 (6 + 9).

78: Boosts the ability to go through with their initiatives and to benefit from them. Predisposes to acquiring strong skills that will be proof of success and recognition. Duality between spiritual and material. Provides strength, ambition, sense of organization while showing compassion and warmth in human relationships. Sometimes completely focused on themselves, insensitive to others.
Note: sub-number of 15 (7 + 8).

87: Boosts the ability to go through with their initiatives and to benefit from them. Predisposes to acquiring strong skills that will be proof of success and recognition. Duality between spiritual and material. Provides strength, ambition, sense of organization while showing compassion and warmth in human relationships. Sometimes completely focused on themselves, insensitive to others.

Note: sub-number of 15 (8 + 7).

96: Oriented towards family, friends, loved ones etc Community spirit. Makes affectionate.
Note: sub-number of 15 (9 + 6).

When number 7 deepens...

Life Path 7: Everything will drive you to analyzing and researching. Destiny could give an original touch to your success. Your friendships will be very interesting.

In case of karma 7, you may have to live in a very independent way, which in fact does not suit you. Nevertheless, you will be asked to live your life from within. Your realizations will have to undergo some delays.

Tip: moderate by interpreting all the sub-numbers revealed by the 3 ways of calculating the life path (see Chapter V).

Expression 7: You are independent and you easily distance yourself by your ability to equate. You have a strong character. You are perceptive and know how to confuse those who lack loyalty. Deep in your analysis, criticism overlooks facts; you go beyond appearances and try to understand the reason for each situation. You find that each word has a meaning. Always on alert, you are sometimes sharp because of the exasperation aroused by others' behavior. Filled with doubt, you seek the certainties that allow you to move forward. Surely lucid and perfectionist, you do not leave anything to chance if possible. Sensitive and a diehard, you want to achieve your goals but you sometimes feel that fate is going after you.

Tip: see all sub-numbers behind this 7. Do not forget that Expression is also the reduced sum of the Aspiration and Potential numbers. This can reveal another sub-number. For example, Aspiration 3 + Potential 22 gives 25, sub-number of the Expression 7.

Aspiration 7: Your deep desire is to walk across the spectrum of intense emotions, joys and sorrows of the heart. You are a loyal friend, you do not like to gauge people and discover their true intentions. Giving emphasis to the friendship, you will have the opportunity to meet people who will energize you and give you beautiful insights or even a path leading to a deep spirituality. Independent by nature, you like to find your inner self. You enjoy and need physical activity. When you are moving into activities whose purpose is to improve the human condition, you can be sure to find support and protection in return.

Potential 7: You show restraint. You take time to assess a situation and judge according to your criteria on how to intervene if necessary. With an enormous capacity for work, even a workaholic if it serves your goals, you like to make your mark on the social area, often using an original approach. You aspire activities where you have levers. Behind a reserve, restraint is not to be confused with shyness, hiding emotionalism, and doubt assails you quickly when things do not turn out your way. Crafty, you can play on the heartstrings of the opponent. At ease with technology, advanced instrumentation, because you are sensitive to progress, you have to constantly keep learning, stay informed in your chosen fields. It is hard for you to rest on your laurels. As you never close the door to modernism, you are often one step ahead, and you know how to highlight your points of view.

First Name 7: You are somewhat concerned with daily tasks, particularly when you find them to be foreign to your field of investigation. Your insightful and inventive mind, puts you at ease in occupations requiring you to innovate, to seek, to develop, to find a solution. Colleagues are your friends. Your interest in social issues is evident.

1st Middle Name 7: Placid, contemplative, nature lover, sometimes pessimistic, you are also a reserved person. And this reserve can lead to excessive shyness in your associations. In fact, you are difficult to define, because you can give a false conciliatory appearance with your partners. Able to sacrifice yourself for good causes and for your loved one, you're a reliable person, able to cope with difficulties, contradictions, antagonisms. Despite everything, you tend to run away from your responsibilities which can lead you to seek a "monastic", peaceful, existence, free from constraints. You tend to meet mystics and/or people presenting non-standard life trajectories. Diplomatic, accommodating, sometimes fatalistic, you like to be supported by making your decisions depending on the circumstances of life. Blessed with strong empathy, however, you end up lacking consistency. You need to take your dreams and intuitions into account.

2nd Middle Name 7: Follower of a comfortable life, you like to enjoy life and surround yourself with luxury and beauty. A player, a little cunning, loves to feast, sometimes abusing the pleasures of the flesh, you like meeting with people of influence who you will enable you to ensure this lifestyle. Your conciliatory and flexible mind does not exclude a taste for excellence. A trustworthy person, kind, attractive, magnetic, creativity manifests itself in the search for beauty. Your inspiration is powerful, especially as you know how to harness your intuitions. The ordinary is not part of your daily life, you reject vulgarity. Be careful not to become a slave to your passions to the point of forgetting your loved ones. You also grant particular importance to your lineage, patronymic, to your offspring without showing a presence *vis à vis* your progeny, especially if it fails to satisfy your criteria.

Heredity 7: The family in which you grew up is serious, committed to its faith, not expressive and rather severe. It attaches great importance to the transmission of the name, sedimentation of knowledge passed from generation to generation. Anything related to learning of specific techniques is encouraged, the art field as well. You are always trying to make efforts to gain recognition from your peers, and especially not get away from the family pattern. That said, the respect of your family, even if unjust, is so strong that you try to avoid direct confrontation. Your mood is changing and this is caused by your environment (time and place) However, in time you detach yourself from the education you received and this opens a door to new ways and you finally find your own way. To do this, sudden upheavals uprooting may be needed so that you can develop. And then, your parents will participate in one way or another to the acquisition of your property.

Active 7: You need to act fairly and thoughtfully. It is through the action that you become aware.

For example, an Expression 7 is of course greatly amplified by this same Active number 7. In this case, the native's Expression will be more evident.

Maturity 7: Your social achievement and personal development will overcome research professions conform to your ideal and allow you to retain a certain freedom of action. There will be more emphasis on community service-oriented activities, technology, industries, research and more generally anything that requires a specialization. It will also be important to agree with what you do.

Intensity 7: You show an interest in advanced techniques, research and anything that uplifts the spirit. You are able to accurately analyze facts. Enthusiastic, you also know how to conceal your true nature and underlying intentions.

Karma 7 (no letter 7): With you, it 's either everything or nothing. You must admit your mind must be tamed. You look grumpy one minute and excessive the next. First, make peace with yourself. This is explained by a feeling of inferiority coming from your past lives. That your parents have encouraged you or not make no difference. You cultivate a sense of detail to do well, take each personal criticism as a personal attack, you think you suffer. To understand this, you need to look in the direction of your father, or of the person having held this role. Some are not known to cause difficulties. As a result, you are particularly responsive when you feel affected by integrity and moral values. However, not playing the victim at all costs. You have to find solutions. Your encounters with people who are often in more difficulty than you will allow you to put your situation into perspective.

1 letter worth 7: You are what is called an undaunted spirit, a rebel, especially when it comes to law, but of course, with the exception of your family. You are inhabited by the soul of a guru, a trade unionist, and the trips you plan, there must be, if possible, a goal, a mission to be accomplished. Eye-catching, sporty and curious about everything and anything, sometimes your ideas are a little too fixed. You have, undoubtedly, a great capacity to overcome many difficulties. Your empowered spirit of concentration, you can get started on many tasks that require deeper investigation. They must, above all, match your ideal, or you could become intoxicated without a port. Sometimes quarrelsome and vindictive, you enjoy sports and martial arts. You have a sharp eye that allows you to notice every detail. You can be obsessed with cleanliness and hygiene. Your preferred areas revolve around anything related to training and teaching. Ne careful not to be too idealistic, too attached to your quest for absolute faith. It is true that you like to believe you are the chosen one. Note that you are often the advocate of lost causes. Anything related to books is encouraged.

2 letters worth 7: You appreciate being surrounded by friends from different backgrounds, therefore often from cultures which are different from your own. Despite this desire to form all kinds of social circles, the fact remains that you stay very connected to your family. That which slows down your evolution, it is your heightened sensitivity, especially when it comes to bad emotional experiences that cause blockages. This may result from a mother who tended to want to make herself indispensable and/or demanded constant attention. A Noah of service, you have a propensity to create shelters for everyone, including animals. You're in love with the exotic and travel discoveries that allow you to free yourself from the weight of the family circle for a short time. A loving and professional association is possible with strangers. You are very attracted to sometimes esoteric groups. You attach great importance to sharing with people that have the same views and goals as you. Perhaps you might want to adopt a child. You need to collect and preserve all kinds of items (sometimes luxurious). You have an attraction for foreign languages and the facilities for learning them, even to the immersion in the countries concerned. The theatre is not for your displeasure, especially since you have a great memory. You tend to focus on the curriculum of your children, who may specialize in different fields and pursue studies which are sometimes very long. Possibility of secret children. You like to cultivate a taste for secrecy. You will certainly get a quiet life meeting your aspirations. Rely on your intuition and your dreams! And learn to control your emotions.

3 letters worth 7: Rebellious and refractory, you sometimes have real difficulty expressing your true inner nature. Fixed in your goals, you only look into your way. You may be the initiator of new projects, new laws, and even have an ability for writing. You are a lover of travel, exploration of all kinds and you love adventure. Accurate and efficient, undaunted, you do not let yourself be easily swayed. You look primarily for people who share the same views as you, and you readily associate with them. With a corporatist's, protestor's and union member's mind, you make a point of vigorously defending your ideas. You can sometimes be very litigious and become the advocate of lost causes. Everything you say should not be taken at face value because you have a theatrical mind. You have a great capacity for learning and can become a good trainer. Undoubtedly you are an idealist. You have a great sense of observation and a certain humor.

4 letters worth 7 *(uncommon)*: Attached to your professional success, you constantly pursue your goals with determination, even stubbornness. Uncommunicative, rather than explaining, you tend to highlight your work values. Obsessed with your performance (work well done) you are an artist/craftsman, designer, liking construction and interior design. You are a lover of nature, sometimes a little wild, or at least reserved or not very expressive. It is only when you really let go that you become very prolific and there is then no way to stop you talking. You must make the effort to overcome this "hard done by" nature that you show too often. You prefer long-term goals, refusing to display and explain your strategies until your goals are met. Anything related to technology is encouraged, you may even become a good teacher in this area. You have a capacity to pursue long studies, to redirect yourself in a particular area in order to specialize if your studies do not bring you what you desire. Everything related to the priesthood and/or monasteries may attract you, sometimes even inspire you to go on retreats. This does not prevent you from being very sensitive to the values of the family, even of the country. Companion of duty or freemason.

5 letters worth 7 *(uncommon)*: You are the archetype of the idealist, vibrating as the most exalted of wild horses. Driven by groundbreaking ideas, you are a missionary who never stops trying to impose a new society and new structures in your chosen fields. Intelligent, able to learn a lot about anything and everything, you're without barriers, despite a sometimes conventional appearance. A mythomaniac in some ways, you put your faith in what you judge to be fair. You feel a great attraction for long journeys and discoveries. Despite a discrete, even secretive nature that allows you to conceal what you are looking for from prying eyes, you like to showcase yourself and sometimes take unnecessary risks. Above all, you like doing what you like. You will need to beware of suspicious groups (sects, etc.) because you always want to find people who share your viewpoints to create closed clubs. You swing between extrovert and introvert. You often study new forms of action by leaving nothing to chance. An inquisitive mind, your original side sometimes makes you strange and elusive. There is a guru in you.

6 letters worth 7 *(rare)*: An aesthetic, you have a taste for everything related to luxury and the arts (theatre in particular). You can become a true perfectionist sometimes too obsessed with the pursuit of your goals. You like to invent methods, organize and plan. Your rhetoric may lead you to become too critical. Attracted by discussion groups, you like debating. You can prove to be a good adviser, effectively the right hand of the person who puts their trust in you, an outstanding leader. You prefer married life and community life with people who complement your life goals. You find it particularly easy to meet influential people who can bring you a lot. You are what is known as a pragmatic idealist, led by a lively curiosity, able to see details that others can't, be careful not to get too focused on specific issues that bother you.

7 letters worth 7 *(rare)*: The ultimate eminence grise, trainer, guru, looking to be part of an elite, and especially to surround yourself with people who share the same opinions as you. You are a follower of travel, expeditions and you may experience sudden changes of direction in your life. You have a certain love for beautiful books, either written in your native language or not. You can be very secretive and reserved because you often feel misunderstood when you express yourself with this feeling that others do not understand your depth. You enjoy tranquility and peace, but despite everything, you're still a quarrelsome person. You must try not to be too dramatic, and especially be careful not to fall into mythomania. You're able to invent worlds of your own. You are blessed with great curiosity, especially for history. You are a polarized being who sometimes too often has fixed ideas. You must be careful not to fall into primary idolatry and even less into some fanaticism. You can often/sometimes be little too wild and/or too distanced from your family's concerns. You can be a great adviser.

8 letters worth 7 *(rare):* You find it very easy to maintain special relationships with groups that tend to conceal their true identity, you like to spend time with people who are outside the norm, sometimes living on the margins of society. You look mainly for work in line with your mysterious nature and your taste for secrecy. You find it difficult to engage. You are inclined to experience sudden changes in your social and professional life. Your unusual, sometimes deviant and fetishist sexuality may lead to you living a disjointed romantic life, especially if you cannot find the right partner. You like to transform your environment while leaving others to apply your teachings, your visions and your views. Your search for a certain spirituality focuses more on psychic powers and finding people with these powers. Sudden changes in life can lead you to live in a monastery, an ashram or a place which is a little too isolated, for a long time. You have a alchemist and researcher's soul. All ways are good to get what you want.

9 letters worth 7 *(rare):* A diplomat, mystic and visionary with great sensitivity, you are at odds with society and the reality of our world. You are able to face violent opposition to contrary winds, by keeping a low profile. You have an intuitive nature, you often let yourself go with the flow of life, which tends to make you appear lymphatic and unable to make the right decisions. In search of paradise, you must beware of artificial paradises. You tend to be overconfident when it comes to solving your problems. The pursuit of your goals may seem impalpable by those around you. You can give others a fresh perception of life. It may be that you are disabled by chronic illness that requires you to toughen up a bit, allowing you to cope with adversity more easily.

More than 9 letters worth 7 *(rare)*: See above for the interpretation of the reduction of this number.

Example: If you have 13 letters at a value of 7, you get a 4 by adding 1 + 3. Refer to this value, that is to say 4 letters at a value of 7. Remember to also take into account the 1 and 3 which makes up your 13 because they also refer to sub numbers. You must, therefore, interpret them by taking into account the definition of these two figures from the definition of the sub numbers given below. Remember, this concerns mainly that which relates to faith, certainty, doubt, intellectual abilities and knowledge etc.

7 Mental letters: You have mental skills which are ideal for research and areas of experimentation because you are able to think outside the box to address a problem. For you, all knowledge is based on the individual's experience. You analyze the phenomena; deduce the consequences meticulously and originally. Abstraction does not put you off when it comes to furthering your knowledge. There is far less to satisfy you when you need to find an answer. You're not very inclined to pass on your knowledge. With each one, you find a personal method for discovering what you think. This refers to information technology, health and/or psychology which will one day or another come into the scope of your research.

7 Emotional letters: It is difficult for you to fathom matters of the heart. You keep your emotions inside and only betray, most of the time, a small amount of information to your loved ones. However, you are very sensitive; your sensations are intense even if more often than not it is spirit that you provide.

7 Intuitive letters: Were you told one day that you are good when it comes to establishing a diagnosis or seeking a solution? But maybe you already feel your tremendous potential for feeling, perceiving and imagining? These abilities help you to be innovative and effective in your creations. You also grant importance to your dreams. Learn how to interpret them.

7 Physical letters: Sensitive to people in need, you love to give your support to those in difficulty. Loneliness, a sometimes depressive condition can be a prerequisite to awareness. Rivalries, jealousies, particularly within the family but also among friends, can occur. Your magnetism is powerful. If not daily, you like more physical activity that brings you back to yourself, pushing you to analyze and to look deeper. The body must be able to allow the mind to be clear, lucid. Some individual Asian disciplines may suit you.

7 Creative letters: Your creativity is expressed in cutting-edge and innovative areas. Your creations can experience one type of audience.

7 Balanced letters: You are fond of giving yourself moments of relaxation, meditation, because it is in the withdrawal into yourself, even the power of prayer, that you find your balance and ways to find greater stability.

7 Dual letters: Your ability to detach yourself, to take a step back will be proportional to your ability to open yourself up to new ways of thinking and understanding reality. Tests can serve as a springboard for this transformation.

Challenge 7: You should avoid spreading yourself too thinly by pursuing too many objectives at once. You often give the impression that you feel above the fray. It will be overcoming a form of bad faith and a tendency not to be the opportunist of service through your ability to use yourself for the ease of relatives in public, to get what you want through them. In fact this challenge should teach you how to focus, to set yourself up to complete what you plan but without isolating yourself from the world. The rationale for some events is to train yourself or retrain yourself for it. Furthermore, you shall fear neither introspection nor self-criticism. You humbly open up to others as to the forces of the Spirit, expressing your faith more deeply in what you do and in life.

First Cycle 7: Childhood is sometimes lived in secret. You live in the dreams of your inner world. You do not easily go to others, especially when you are emotional and manage conflicts and criticism aimed at you badly. Your originality is marked and for you to develop, you need to feel a safe family and educational atmosphere. Even bigger, you mark your difference fairly quickly and are looking to achieve quickly. Your maturity is premature.

Second Cycle 7: The environment should lead you to implement your desire to assert yourself in an original way. You need to mark your values with an activity. Vibration promotes research, discovery, and initiation. If you are married, this return to yourself is sometimes synonymous with the spiritual quest, which should not hamper your married life. That said, it's a great period for the development of the inner being. Writing is particularly favored as is the mastery of techniques and esoteric knowledge.

Third Cycle 7: The context allows the development of your inner self, sometimes resonating with deep faith. You are passionate, focused on your interests. The search for knowledge continues to be your goal. This refers to creation, publishing, education, psychology, spirituality which may affect you.

First Pinnacle 7: You will often withdraw into your inner world. You're looking for a refuge. Your originality can take you to the edge. You suffer from a lack of understanding from some of your loved ones. You are not short of intellectual abilities but the educational context does not seem appropriate. So you can surround yourself with people very different from the norm, to oppose yourself, to run away. Early marriages and associations are not recommended during this period.

Second or Third Pinnacle 7: You act for a new life design. You study and socialize with surprising and rewarding people. Writing, humanities, IT, education, and/or research are areas in tune with your needs. Sometimes it is a sign of deep faith, a new commitment for a collective cause. In all cases, no need to force the hand of fate. Opportunities will arise which could lead you to profoundly transform your life. It is necessary to properly manage the financial and material life which can sometimes be complicated.

Fourth Pinnacle 7: Finally, you feel the need to retranscribe or to transmit the reflection inspired by your experiences. You devote time to reading, watching television, gaming and/or any activity that promotes a return to self reflection, analysis. It is therefore best not to shut out the world. You need to passionately enjoy your main interests. Be careful not to be too offensive to some people.

Sub-numbers of 7

16 (see also its meaning as a karmic debt): Predisposes to a life of secrets. Can lead to withdrawal, to favoring retirement. Sometimes living next to others rather than with others. Makes inner life intense. Gets to the bottom of things. Difference that gives the feeling of being misunderstood. Duality between high self-esteem and an obvious lack of confidence. Frustrations. Stubbornness Self-esteem. Rebirth.

25: Predisposes to living in a dream world rather than in reality. Taste for leisure, pleasure. Strategies for shunning conflict, adversity, responsibilities, effort, unless the effort is worth it. Works with envy, motivation. Become aware of the consequences of their choices over time.

34: Predisposes to living in a dream world rather than in reality. Taste for leisure, pleasure. Strategies for shunning conflict, adversity, responsibilities, effort, unless the effort is worth it. Works with envy, motivation. Become aware of the consequences of their choices over time.

43: Have a good overview to direct their life. Promotes concentration, stability, the analytical mind, a sense of detail, the practical and productive initiatives. Adjustments necessary to address some aspects of life. Particularly predisposes to whims, mood swings, depressive states, feelings of inferiority. Issues often favorable.

52: Importance of a woman in development. Rivalry, jealousy contexts which might hinder the freedom of action. Renunciation.

61: Highlights a problem linked to the established relationship with hierarchy. Direction particularly dependent on studies. Perseverance is rewarded. Harmonious with respect to the fields of law and research. Need for family, friendship. Problematic romantic relationships. Sometimes looking for a higher partner in spiritual terms.

70: Refers to a form of solitude and a quest for the truth to the point of losing contact with the material aspect of life. Loves living eccentricity and instinctively; sensuality; sensitivity; spontaneity but also the ability to persuade. May want to help others even if they have to resist. Confers real abilities for innovation. Highlights everything affecting the native's inventiveness.

79: Indicates a native seeking power (social, political, spiritual) but without forgetting their humanistic motivations, which sometimes don't prevent them from being ruthless. Productive, whole but taking criticism badly. Looks for truth. Taste for culture.
Note: sub-number of 16 (7 + 9).

88: Accentuates the spirit of contradictions. Tends to favor business over emotional relationships. Insensitive. With time ends up finding more advantages in spiritual steps than in the accumulation of material goods.
Note: sub-number of 16 (8 + 8).

97: Provides great sensitivity. Often highlights a humanistic side in all reflections, which leads the native frequently turn to others.
Note: sub-number of 16 (9 + 7).

When number 8 comes up...

Life Path 8: Your projects will be fueled and supported. You will meet your material goals. Your relationship to money is fair enough. Although you will encounter some tests, it is the prize to pay for success and it is worth it.

In case of karma 8, your material way of life might lead you into delusion. Turn your ambition down a step, or you might have to live through tough tests. I say this for your own good.

Tip: moderate by interpreting all the sub numbers revealed by the 3 ways of calculating the life path (see Chapter V).

Expression 8: You have desire and energy! Courage, vitality and perseverance do not make you default when it comes to succeed socially. You need everything to run smoothly, you do not let details escape. On the one side, you still have some inner turmoil. With a deep, lucid, curious, intuitive and stubborn personality, you know how to fight for your point of view, and your words can become a weapon. You are not indifferent. You know how to lead, organize and synthesize what is best. You decide ... and others must follow. Finally, you play your game well in tense situations. Making others give up is an art. You like provocation and let no one tell you what you need to do if it does not match your point of view. But you are also able to mellow if the situation requires. In fact, you are a passionate, capable of large expenditures of energy to achieve your goals, which sometimes make you feel down.

Tip: see all sub-numbers behind this 8. Do not forget that Expression is also the reduced sum of the Aspiration and Potential numbers. This can reveal another sub-number. For example, Aspiration 11 + Potential 6 gives 17, sub-number of the Expression 8.

Aspiration 8: Your deep desire is to find a bridge between the spiritual and material, to achieve your existence on these two planes, to show that one does not exclude the other. Suddenly, you appear double to those who know you well. Alternately, you are capable of empathy and sensitivity more than hardness and intransigence. You are comprehensive one day and a manipulator the next. You are open towards others and then you are closed, alone. The fact remains that your loyalty is unwavering among beings who find favor in your eyes. Genuine cooperation can even move with them. A partner of the opposite sex will play an important role to make you aware of your influence on others duality, but also your magnetism. In fact, your soul longs to transcend on a selfish use of power. Over time, you will want your success and also want to have positive also have positive consequences. Enter sum of the right to abundance. This development will inevitably take some time but it is likely to occur.

Potential 8: You flaunt your ambition, your desire to succeed, your tenacity to defend your ideas and projects. You are never at loss for an answer and you are efficient to the point that you run out opponents. Stubbornness is not the least of your flaws when it comes to a project. Curiously your independence does not accommodate your need for confrontation. You want the other to react to your comments. You can not stand anyone interfering in your affairs. Despite a real emotion, you show a hardness that forces to tilt or conversely may lead to serious confrontations. Fortunately, you also have the ability to analyze yourself, and if you detect something in your personality that is not suitable, you can fix it. Finally, transforming yourself is not insurmountable, as you see it as a way to be even more effective. You perceive depth through touch. The presence of minerals strengthens you. This feeling is coupled with an ability to discover the hidden meaning of things; the esotericism appeals to you. You will have the opportunity to approach these mysteries thanks to relatives. Your potential allows you to build your wealth.

First Name 8: Sensitive and reactive to anything said about you, you hate that it imposes what you should do on you because you need to be able to decide when and how to act on a daily basis. To achieve your goals, you are able to work in a group, to call on your legendary endurance and to use your creativity. While keeping your life space of course.

1ˢᵗ Middle Name 8: Your romantic relationships are curious within your couple, often finding yourself off the beaten track... You are attracted to strange, unusual partners. Your associations are realized within the context of singular (even mysterious) projects, all of which can lead to taking apart, even destruction. This is in part due to a seduction/attraction/repulsion issue. A form of naivety can lead you to lack judgment towards your partners. You like to play up to your magnetic and enigmatic side to capture another. You like a sort of fascination re-fashion the physical disgraces or to remodel the other person's character.

2ⁿᵈ Middle Name 8: You like to defy prohibitions, experience impossible lives. A very strong sexuality motivates you. There may be a big age difference with some partners. Being unfaithful does not make you uncomfortable. A force of nature, you are a charismatic person, magnetic, enigmatic, attractive and annoying at times. You have this ability to find everything you need to satisfy your needs. You are a big-spender and have a desire for recognition affected by the taste for the secret in the sense that you love to be recognized without being revealed. Ironic surely? In fact, you like to keep all or part of yourself hidden as much as your strategies. Adapt to transcendence, you surround yourself with influential people who promote your progress. Like a Godfather, like you pull the strings, by subtly playing to your influences. You might have illegitimate children just like you may adopt. You also have a pronounced taste for good food, and an aptitude for music.

Heredity 8: Your family (parental home) is associated with forms of power (social, financial domination in a field ...) Issues derived from and directly affect individual members A wife, mother often represented the authority in your early youth and has deeply influenced your personality, including giving you the ability to cope, bounce back, to be reborn if events require. This family history sounds plays an important part in your development and your willingness to assert yourself socially You can be both passionate and detached depending on the things that interest you and the people who are around you. In fact, you do not let your opponents have control. Your magnetism is powerful. Your life will be marked by legacies that will count towards your successive orientations. Your place of residence must be a nest where you can relax.

Active 8: You act by being able to make use of a lot of energy to achieve your goals.

For example, a 9 Expression colored by an Active number 8 amplifies tension and nervousness but makes the character more able to assess a situation and adapt to it.

Maturity 8: Very willful, stubborn and combative faced with challenges and adversity, you will continually increase your knowledge of the environment in which you thrive. You like to have enough money to feel secure. You fight any feelings of lacking or frustration experienced when you were younger ensuring material tranquility. So you commit yourself to work to make up this heritage. Even if, along the way, you have to guide your career differently due to your interests or a sudden calling. Meanwhile, you will be wiser with time, mostly thanks to the influence of a partner.

Intensity 8: You are concerned by anything that affects their success. Ambitious, persuasive, you have a real ability to mobilize energies and to succeed in your endeavors.

Karma 8 (no letter 8): Your relationship with money and power is very different from the norm. This is why you might live situations in which your way of considering things will not be understood. Be careful! In fact, there is need to overcome a tendency to not dare to confirm your ambition, to think that this is impossible. This doubt, this hindrance comes from the influence of bad-intentioned people, often from childhood. A form of sadism, of destructive behavior (pressure, blackmail, guilt etc) left and perhaps left their mark on you. These pressures can also be exercised by any established authority (police, justice etc). It is recommended that you identify these people and machines that exercise them, understand why adults are always there and step back and take the necessary steps to avoid these situations. From now on, achievement and success become possible, if you show yourself to be determined, courageous and persistent, and avoid the reproduction of these rather destructive patterns. Surgery and/or risk of falls, accidents are likely to punctuate your existence especially during cycles and achievements 8. Therefore caution is called for. During these periods, your financial stability is marked by ups and downs (money coming in, big spending, difficulty in distributing money, inheritance too). Be careful to exercise caution without becoming paranoid.

1 letter worth 8: The strength and anger arising from the depths of your being, like a volcano eruption starts in particular situations. Despite your naive mind, you have an unusual strength to overcome difficult situations and conflicts. A volunteer fire-fighter, loving risk and the foreign, you love to measure yourself against the forces of nature. An instinctive medium, people shouldn't ask you the how and why of your actions, you would be unable to answer. Frank, direct and straightforward, you need an intense, sometimes uncontrolled sexual life. You have a dense inner life, which is difficult to perceive by those around you, often forcing you to believe that it is necessary to fight and that it is necessary to get rid of all impossible situations. There is no need to always face difficulties head on and it is not necessary to prove suffering is necessary, other paths can be considered. You have a masochistic side to you. You are a person who can be counted on. Learn to moderate your expectations, you're not going to conquer the whole world. Few things frighten you. However, you must learn to measure your words, which sometimes border on vulgarity. All sorts of accidents may occur in your life but you have an unusual power to regenerate, which can get you out of extreme situations, sometimes to the point of being an enigma to medicine.

2 letters worth 8: You have a rather feminine sensibility. Your search for your sacrosanct family life may have been disturbed from birth through difficult circumstances. The presence of the mother, or lack thereof, may have left you with a very strong intimate impression. You can be very attached to money, deploying a certain courage to face all kinds of situations when it comes to materially guaranteeing the safety of your own family. You may invest in various activities provided they are lucrative. There is a dichotomy between the trust that you view and the doubt that you feel in your everyday life. You do not hesitate to give yourself completely in love for a second. You are attracted to all kinds of sexual experiences despite a certain modesty that you can easily overcome with intimacy, if you're confident. You have a tendency to hide your emotions, to not let them show because you know you're very excited, and it is your insight that drives you to hide everything. This often causes great anxiety because you are upset by this dichotomy. You are the sum of intuition and rationality. Your love life may be marked by deaths, separations and by profound transformations in your life, sudden changes of home, loss of property and uprooting. Be wary of activities related to water. With time and experience, you will, gain a certain interest in the afterlife and all that relates to death. You are subject to material and spiritual heritage. You have real magnetic and/or psychic talents.

3 letters worth 8: Blessed with a secretive, cold and impermeable mind, you are attracted by that which is mysterious and hidden. Anything that relates to psychiatry, death and the afterlife interests you. An instinctive medium, you can sometimes be a little too direct without embarrassment, you're not very smiley by nature, leaving the people around you feeling that you are always putting distance between you and them. Strong magnetism emanates from you and you have a deadpan, sometimes cynical and violent sense of humor. You have an extraordinary ability to quickly learn the lessons of life. You can be a fantastic character, not always easy to identify, but the fact remains that you love to prove your skills and prove that you can be firm and stubborn, once decided. You have a very great power of concentration. Anything that relates the field of cinema, espionage and writing attracts you. You are often the ideal person to solve difficult situations, even outside the norm, it is important to recognize that you are unimpressed by difficulty. Your interest is great for everything that relates to sex and money. You have many strings to your bow: for example, everything related to cooking and research, sometimes with a great capacity to invent. Difficulties with your brothers and sisters can affect the family environment, even disrupt it significantly. You like the dark and the night and you love to take the indefinable aura of the uprooted and the elusive. Somewhere in you is the ideal "channel".

4 letters worth 8 *(uncommon):* Sensual and greedy, you like the pleasures of life. You do not necessarily share your long term goals with others. You are blessed with a certain strength and you are able to develop practical skills that lead you to be very skilled in your chosen fields. You are able to create from scratch. Behind your unsmiling, even distant appearance, you need to live intensely. It is not easy to locate you, because beyond your apparent fixity, you experience changing life contexts which often tend to disrupt your routine. Frequent U-turns should be expected, you are often the instigator without even realizing it. You have an elusive character. A hard worker, you want to change but above all, you do not want to lose your assets, and you prefer to subscribe to a certain continuity. You are able to continue the activities of your peers and/or your parents, but this does not prevent you from being attracted to people who are younger than yourself.

Note: It is rare to find more than 4 letters in 8 in French nationals or French-speakers. H, Q and Z are more frequently found in Anglo-Saxons.

5 letters worth 8 *(rare):* You have a taste for everything related to mystery and magical worlds. A born medium, you love everything that is strange and extraordinary. You tend to use your free, direct and conformist mind as if you were alone in the world. You like to experience all kinds of relationships, no matter where they come from. You will need to be particularly vigilant, you will need to be careful not to end up with the wolf in the woods. You are attracted by secret and nightlife that you like to share with your friends. Death can exert a certain fascination in you, leading you straight to explore faraway worlds, this is your second nature. In your areas of choice, you have the ability to highlight your ingenuity. More instinctive than reflective, the experiences you like which lead to all sorts of areas can naturally lead to experience a sometimes unbridled sex life. Your excessive side makes you reckless, you should be extra vigilant with regard to anything related to cars because you can be a daredevil. You have an unsmiling nature, but paradoxically, in certain situations, your voluble side makes you show a smile that can be disarming, even enigmatic. In any case, you are very magnetic and sometimes a little careless.

6 letters worth 8 *(rare):* You are blessed with a real ability to care for others, everything related to medicine and psychiatry is favored. You have difficulty getting things in perspective between the rational and the hidden meaning of life, between what is definable and what is not. Profound insights will be derived from anything that is connected to the physical and aesthetic. You're more comfortable in difficult situations than in small everyday hassles, where you tend to get overwhelmed - you often see them as worthless. You like getting started on a task and completing it methodically and efficiently regardless of the adversity encountered. Loss or separation from a brother, sister or child may affect you. You feel an interest in matters relating to food. The completeness of your sexuality must pass through the head. Beyond your moralizing side, you are able to meet and accept people opposed to how you operate.

7 letters worth 8 *(rare):* Very ambitious to say the least, you're capable of anything, to get what you want. You are able to find people and resources needed to achieve your goals, even if you side with the devil. You are a clairvoyant and a visionary and you have a great attraction to everything related to mystery, the unfathomable and the strange. You like to invest and explore in search of hidden treasures. You are the perfect adventurer who can live their life from the other side of the world to share it with ethnic groups and people who are radically different. You will probably experience sudden events which will undeniably cause drastic changes in your outlook on life. No doubt this will cause a particular interest in the mysteries of existence, and consequently, will lead you to take an interest in these areas. You have an unbridled sexuality which is sometimes tinged with a sporty aura because you are looking primarily to satisfy your impulses and to confront your stamina.

8 letters worth 8 *(rare):* You are a determined character, adaptable to all sorts of situations, but you have a tendency to be naive, even innocent. You are a naturally spontaneous, sometimes straightforward person, you often disconcert your friends with your words and your way of being and doing. You can sometimes be locked in your silence. Your life may be strewn with many pitfalls, mishaps, meetings and bizarre situations. You cultivate a particular taste for everything that is secret which may lead you to live away from the eyes of ordinary people (in appearance only). You have a taste for the night. Your strong and free sexuality, may surprise or even upset your partners. You are prone to unexpected windfalls. Above all, you have to overcome your legendary temper and not always give in to the desire to destroy everything that you've started to build.

9 letters worth 8 *(rare):* You are an inspired medium in the purist form, who is able to hear celestial music, channeling higher spirits. You have an excessive taste for fairy tales, for the unreal and for parallel worlds. Your fine ability to perceive the world around you makes you very sensitive to perfumes, odors and the vibrations of places whether they be beneficial or not. Romantic and sentimental, your strong sexuality requires a delicate approach (atmosphere, perfumes and fairy tales etc), without, of course, forgetting extreme sensations. You have a particular ambition, being much more interested in immediate well-being. You are very sensitive to the world of the Elves and to the forces of nature which makes you naturally very respectful of the environment in which you live. You like to devote yourself to a good cause. You may live in a bizarre world or mix with strange people.

More than 9 letters worth 8 *(rare):* See above for the interpretation of the reduction of this number.
Example: If you have 12 letters at a value of 8, you get a 3 by adding 1 + 2. Refer to this value, that is to say 3 letters at a value of 8. Remember to also take into account the 1 and 2 which makes up your 12 because they also refer to sub numbers. You must, therefore, interpret them by taking into account the definition of these two figures from the definition of the sub numbers given below. Remember, this mainly concerns personal development, knowledge, transformations, sexuality, ambition, power and death etc.

8 Mental letters: Your reasoning emphasizes pragmatism. Any action must be served by logic, reasoning and flawless reasoning. You know how to deepen your knowledge. You can sometimes appear uncompromising in your demonstrations, even if you are skilled and efficient when it comes to passing on knowledge. Intellect should serve your purposes. Your attraction to mysteries and the unknown is strong. You explore and analyze the essential, often using esoteric methods. Your inner life is very rich, marked by an interest, even a passion for the afterlife. Capable of introspection, psychotherapy and all kinds of research in the field of psychology and/or the paranormal will lead you to evolve favorably.

8 Emotional letters: You have a strong magnetism around you. You live in a way as intense as your emotions; you do not hide them and even learn to use them in your relationships. In fact, it is your emotions that guide you, influence you, you move from a state of euphoria to a feeling of helplessness.

8 Intuitive letters: You are so intuitive that you're using it to carry you physically. Your hunches are terribly accurate. They know how to guide you. You take advantage of them without the expense of others and respecting the truth of each. This predisposition can also feel everything related to death (perception of missing beings etc).

8 Physical letters: Your life will be marked by a profound transformation following a death or renunciation. You have a sense of sacrifice. You encounter adversity in relation to your views on sexuality, finances and authority. The partner will have difficulties in relation to their sexuality. Your passions are characterized by a kind of secrecy. Tests encountered have the effect of lifting you to a more detailed understanding of the world. Your magnetism and your psychic talents will grow over time. Day by day, you like to impose yourself physically. You have a lot of energy to burn. You must fight and win. You enjoy a challenge, the challenge to come. All your efforts are working towards a greater affirmation of your physical qualities.

8 Creative letters: Your creativity is expressed from the moment that you are researching. So you are inventive, sometimes turned towards the occult, insightful.

8 Balanced letters: You are fond of conquering new horizons. It is within your power relations that often, you find the balance that you need. For you, stability is gained in the field; it does not come about by chance.

8 Dual letters: You'll stand back and direct your life differently after you become aware that you are not being judged at your true value. You may also be a victim of theft.

Challenge 8: You must learn to channel your strength and your willingness in such a way as to avoid the excesses of accumulating, possessing, and manipulating. In short, it is about becoming aware of your power and your ability to overcome difficult situations. You must find the strength to accept the great opportunities that life presents to you, especially if they fall outside of the scope of your habits, your expectations and your familiar surroundings. In other words: overcome fear of the unknown. As a child, you tended to want to accumulate, possess, be the leader of the group. Some friends may have found you pretentious.

First Cycle 8: The context promotes advanced education that leads you to premature social success in spite of any material difficulty. You affirm your identity very early. As a child, everything that helped you to understand how to manage pocket money and power for example (being a class representative, a team captain etc) is a real asset for your future success. You model yourself on people who have a positive influence on you. Therefore, quickly, opportunities for social upward mobility present themselves, made possible by the affirmed expression of your potential.

Second Cycle 8: The context is perfect for socioprofessional accomplishment even if it requires a lot of willpower, fighting spirit and courage. The vagaries of life have implications on the internal balance. Acquisitions, property, personal and social affairs take an important place.

Third Cycle 8: The context favors the maintenance of an activity. Your energy drives you to undertake further investments, to plan for the medium, even long term. It is possible to successfully complete social achievements.

First Pinnacle 8: To begin, you are able to quickly develop socially. You're nervous and impulsive when it comes to satisfying your desires. You want to reach your objectives. Long studies are encouraged if that is your choice. In all ways, some social success is likely to occur quickly.

Second or Third Pinnacle 8: Time has come to improve your physical condition. You also know yourself better. A welcome development on the financial, social and professional fronts is achieved if you want it and you give yourself the means.

Fourth Pinnacle 8: Finally, you do not really want to or cannot withdraw from any activity. This period is characterized by a lack of commitment in the field of business and everything related directly or indirectly to a power. The energy, combativeness are often at the meeting. Away from you, the idea of experiencing a very quiet retirement. Instead, you can invest and in return even receive a social status, sometimes even a certain notoriety.

Sub-numbers of 8

17 (see also its meaning as a karmic debt): Have a material increase in proportion to their faith, the respect of their values. Allows for discovery that the manifestation of their spirituality is not antagonistic to their material achievement. Willingness, firmness and ability to master their life. Sense of reality. Creativity. Promotion. Protection. Providence. Make sure they are surrounded by stable friends, influential relationships, on which they can count. Sometimes impatient.

26: Elation. Impulsivity. Search for new situations. Enthusiasm sometimes leading to finding a new approach. Need to better manage certain aspects of life. Tendency to inertia when the passion is missing. Interest in everything with a social character. Allows them to be appreciated by their loved ones for their actions and attentions. Sensitivity which predisposes them to seek others, to be useful, to appreciate comfort. Emotional dependency in the area concerned.

35: Need to overcome a restrictive context (often on the financial or emotional front) in order to gain in maturity and to broaden an overly set vision on things. Good intellectual dispositions and/or abilities to cope with their commitments facilitating an ascent. High expectations.

44: Confers ambition and fixity in the goals to be reached. Has a business sense, the potential necessary to undertake a military career and a visionary side. Refers to charm, power, power that is acquired step by step. Confers the sense of responsibility and the need to pass it on. Survival instinct, sometimes overloaded, overwhelmed, fleeing the overflow. The need to feel safe. Increased skills and knowledge. Action based on guiding principles. Sometimes intolerant to those who display a lifestyle opposed to theirs. More attached to basic realities than to philosophical discourse. Lack of imagination. Need to be flexible. Delays. Refers to feelings of culpability (poorly managed passions).

53: Turned towards creativity, words, business but also games, distractions. Predisposes to act hastily (even ill-considered). However, able to go ahead and succeed when impulsivity and scattering is controlled. Confers energy, inspiration.

62: Turned towards creativity, words, business but also games, distractions. Predisposes to act hastily (even ill-considered). However, able to go ahead and succeed when impulsivity and scattering is controlled. Confers energy, inspiration.

71: Has determination and enthusiasm but also an intransigent, even harsh side. Looks for ideas but also their concretization.   Is not insensitive to success. Ability to make decisions, to guide reflection, to assume the role of a leader. Material aspects of life are also important. Favorable development. Growth. Success.

80: Has determination and enthusiasm but also an intransigent, even harsh side. Looks for ideas but also their concretization.   Is not insensitive to success. Ability to make decisions, to guide reflection, to assume the role of a leader. Material aspects of life are also important. Favorable development. Growth. Success.

89: Confers noble sentiments in the service of all that is undertaken. Makes loneliness telling. Highlights the need to belong to groups and/or communities. Predisposes to travels.
Note: See also 17, which is a sub number of 17 (9 + 8).

98: Characterizes difficulties in expressing themselves, being understood or showing their emotions which confer an apparent indifference. Idealist.
Note: see also 17, which is a sub number of 17 (9 + 8).

When Number 9 humanizes ...

Life Path 9: Your destiny is that of a traveler's. You belong to those who explore and seek for an ideal, be it on earth or in the mind, it doesn't matter. It is also the promise of varied encounters and experiences.

In case of karma 9, your destiny looks like running after a dream, an ideal or an urge to escape. Nevertheless, beware of traps of reality which will implement devotion, courage and an open mind.

Tip: moderate by interpreting all the sub numbers revealed by the 3 ways of calculating the life path (see Chapter V).

Expression 9: You would give the shirt off of your back for a good cause. You are sensitive, humanistic. Injustice offends you. You are looking for balance but flee from everything that does not elevate the spirit. On the heart, animated by noble sentiments, you easily project in an idyllic vision of your relationship when the reality is more complex. So, the communication does not go, as you'd like. In this field, you will have to clarify the situation; otherwise you and your partner will have misunderstandings. Be careful also not to sound too demanding or temperamental at times. It is true that expressing your deepest feelings is far from obvious to you. You prefer to protect your privacy when your relationship becomes too intrusive or confrontational. With time you become more suspicious. Dedicated by nature, your stamina will push you to act to serve, to add value to your neighbor. You also have the ability to see and understand what others do not perceive or let escape. You need external circumstances to prompt you to undertake. You need a very special atmosphere, leaving you with beautiful leeway. Your actions are almost always thoughtful. An innovator at heart, you can put a lot of strength and energy in the realization of a project if it suits your ideals.

Tip: see all sub-numbers behind this 9. Do not forget that Expression is also the reduced sum of the Aspiration and Potential numbers. This can reveal another sub-number. For example, Aspiration 9 + Potential 9 gives 18, sub-number of the Expression 9.

Aspiration 9: Your deep desire is to live your experiences unhindered. Generous, you have a very open conception of life. You like the challenge that allows you to claim your freedom and you encourage people to do the same. Early on, you let yourself be carried away by your dreams, agreeing to probably explore young sensuality. Basically, romantic at heart, you search for your great passion is so passionate that it sometimes harshly bumps into reality. Often impervious to advice, you are nonetheless a devoted friend. Friendship is essential to your balance. The foreign, travel, people of different backgrounds have opportunities to rekindle your flame.

Potential 9: You have a natural tact in your everyday relationships and know how to maintain these relations. Listening, you inspire confidence. You make the choice to carry through what motivates you, even if this should occur later in your life. Your humanism does not prevent you from having a sense of business and commerce. Once decided, you act with courage and boldness. To do this, you need broad perspectives and sufficient remedies. You do not like framed situations. You rely on your knowledge. You love to learn, expand your knowledge. Modernism does not scare you when it is useful. Breaking habits and providing solutions allows for social progress that gives you reason to act and to easily be involved. The problem here is for you not to impose your vision. When you are confronted with situations of injustice, you are lead to violently express your emotions.

First Name 9: You devote a lot of attention to others. You like to help in your work. You are able to give until exhaustion when a cause or a project fascinates you, with a need to be impressed to commit. For you, your profession must correspond to your desires. Music, reading and writing, travel, the sea is essential for your emotional balance.

1st Middle Name 9: You idealize your partner by looking for a beautiful person who is not indifferent. You want to live your relationships in connection with your privacy and your feelings. You show kindness. Liking to put yourself out for common success, you are totally committed to your partner, while excluding the idea of this solitude what you don't really like. Be careful not to become a slave to your spouse's obligations. Aesthetic, you are sensitive to perfumes, atmospheres, your environment and the comfort of your associates/spouse. That said you don't like it when others disturb your tranquility. You do all you can to live in a harmonious environment by developing a particular sensitivity to music. You have a great capacity for discerning that which is amiss in your associative relationships. However, you need to listen more to what your associates/spouse say, even if it is hampers your options and/or disturbs your beauty sleep.

2nd **Middle Name 9**: Trainer, protector, idealist to the extreme, you tirelessly pursue your goals. Bemused by success whilst knowing how to preserve a certain harmony, this does not prevent you from being intransigent towards your loved ones (progeny included). You also have a guru side having a tendency to dictate laws that you do not follow yourself. Defender of the merits of your objectives and those for which you work, you are a lawyer at heart. You idealize your loves to the point that you commit body and soul. Creative, inspired, original, you push the taste of aesthetics away. You have the spirit of consensus while you keep the leadership. You like continuing or resuming studies. You have talents for teaching, writing. You encourage your progeny to undertake long studies. Your dissatisfaction is significant when you cannot find the object of your desires and your aspirations. You look for the presence of water through nautical activities. You know tame animals.

Heredity 9: The parental home is marked by the influence of a man (the father) and grandparents. You idealize the members of your family and this sometimes disappoints you if they do not turn out to be at the height of your expectations. Family issues revolve around patrimony, sometimes creating sacrifices, difficulties in relation to money. This family background leads you to like traveling and activities that let you get away. Attracted to places near water (sea, lake, river ...) and the great outdoors, you gradually move farther in your life without neglecting the importance of your roots. In doing so, it is necessary to find a balance between a good

240

adaptation to material vicissitudes and your desire to get away from this world (travel, games ...).

Active 9: You act by trying to give yourself your ideals. Your actions are influenced by your (hyper) sensitivity to others and the environment, so you still like to keep some kind of distance in the action to protect yourself.

For example, an Expression 8 tainted by this Active number leads the native to a need to succeed exclusively in a field close to their heart that they idealize.

Maturity 9: You like to use your perceptive mind, enrich your knowledge and give free rein to your imagination. On the other hand, you have trouble when the context seems fixed or when you work in a way that is too centered on yourself. Your mother has played a significant role in your direction. Eventually you will realize that it is by giving to others, by serving a just cause, that you get the greatest satisfaction.

Intensity 9: You appear concerned by the lives of others. Idealistic, generous, a good speaker, a teacher at heart, good at art, you are nonetheless impressionable and take your strong emotions into account, you have the art of disguise.

Karma 9 (no letter 9): You are often selfish. Learn how to care more for people around you, in the first place, and then for the world. It's not such a big deal, after all. Your high emotionalism leads you to appear possessive and jealous among your loved ones. Let others breath, accept their differences and preserve their space. Your journey will be characterized by a loss of identity, benchmarks, motivations which are probably a result of an event affecting your beliefs, your faith. Hence the disinterest of others and society. However, this can lead to significant spiritual awareness. By keeping your distance, it can be high and then you embrace a broader vision of the world.

1 letter worth 9: Able to accept adversity, you have a great ability to take all kinds of knocks. Often involved with the issues of your loved ones, you often experience hopeless situations, which

241

require you to flee, to keep a low profile, not to take the bull by the horns and therefore you let the situation fester. You must be careful not to wait until the very limit before you decide and act accordingly. Yet you're made of the right stuff because it is in the most desperate of situations that you reveal your amazing ability to solve conflicts. You are blessed with a great imagination and your spontaneous inspirations can help solve many problems which are sometimes inextricable. You must be careful not to consider yourself to be a victim of the vicissitudes of life. Sure of your mystical or religious beliefs, or in any case giving yourself over to the will of fate, it seems to you that life decides for you. You have a great ability to reconcile contradictions, and even to not let yourself eat with your legendary generosity. You may be prone to chronic diseases, which require you to take care of your health by adopting a healthy life, otherwise you risk loss of energy. Learn to relax. Anything that relates to psychology may interest you.

2 letters worth 9: You are a person who is particularly shy, sensitive and emotional, with a slightly childlike side. You can be very committed vis-à-vis your family. In extreme cases, you tend to take refuge in your dreams and the imaginary worlds that you invent, it may be that you put yourself in adventures by proxy to escape a fact of everyday life, you sometimes think too much. You're not particularly committed to your success because you are not fundamentally careerist, which, of course, does not favor studies. This can lead to your becoming too interested in the success of your loved ones, especially that of your children. Everything related to the arts is especially favored. You are a magnetic, intuitive, quite attractive person with a certain "je ne sais quoi" which makes you want to protect yourself. The fact remains that you pursue your own goals, even your ideals of peace, and your charitable or other commitments. You like to study at your own pace. Anything related to books, certain collections, fashion shows, fashion can be part of your interests. You will learn to express your feelings, your emotions and to finally say who you are. You will enjoy some popularity, but you must be careful not to yield to a form of selfishness, a form of disinterest vis-à-vis that which bothers you, this is often dictated by your restricted life. You need to feel loved. Blessed with a powerful mind, you feel particularly at ease in your environment, if the vibrations, odors and climates generated are harmonious. It is likely that some members of your family, like an uncle or an aunt played a big role in your childhood. Mysticism and religion are not foreign to your upbringing or your environment. You may experience difficulties of choice in many areas, including love. You are a poet at heart.

3 letters worth 9: There is a very strong opposition in you between your religious and mystical mind and your analytical side. You are particularly attracted by psychoanalysis, the cognitive and understanding of the subtle mechanisms that drive humans. You are a dreamer and a Cartesian who wants to explain everything. Your subtle language can make you a great diplomat, someone very dedicated who is not afraid by adversity. What distinguishes you as is your split personality with which you play depending on the circumstances, giving you a seemingly conciliatory appearance. You look for harmony and beauty and you have an ability to channel information from higher spheres and to express them without being sure of their provenance. Your personality is hard to define and has multiple facets because it is often modeled on how you think of your friends. You are a young dreamer idealizing a perfect and non-violent world which may lead you to escape reality and/or experience periods of loneliness, seclusion and withdrawal. The quest for paradise is strong, even if it's an artificial paradise. You are a romantic and sentimental lover. You sometimes lack commitment, difficulty in choosing what you really want in your life, which may have led to a difficult schooling. You're a musician, able to hear heavenly music. You are very intuitive, with a great ability to concretize what you feel.

4 letters worth 9: You're torn between your penchant for a stable life and the proven attraction vis-à-vis what you think is new, which can push the boundaries of your usual environment. You still get to marry these two aspects by investing in education and learning that whilst allows you to benefit from new horizons, means you don't lose what you've patiently acquired or constructed over time. You constantly look for what can bring you a more comfortable life, emphasizing your independence in what you intend to undertake. You need to understand the ins and outs of what is presented to you before you commit. Crafts and antiques prompt you to find people with whom you can share your perfectionist, even elitist views. It is very difficult to know which purpose you pursue and what you're undertaking as you give little away. Deep contacts will often be made with people with whom you can share everything that relates to the mastery of creation. You like to find lucrative, producing and efficient occupations. Real estate, construction and restoration is particularly encouraged. Trips can be taken if you find your routines. It is an essential condition, because otherwise, you get bored very quickly, resulting in a hasty return. You have a collector's soul and you're attracted to nature and animals. You will seek to protect your life by all sorts of means (insurance and securities etc). Politics may also interest you, if it is lucrative. You must not give in to resentment or brood on hard feelings.

5 letters worth 9: You appear to be shared between an unconventional and monastic life. You are a dreamer, blessed with a very friendly nature, but you assert your true personality. You are attracted to everything related to the mystical, the foreign and unconventional, and you're often driven by sometimes utopian ideals. You have a great fondness for travel, exploration and discovery of new horizons and cultures. You may express a strong debilitating shyness as well as a strong extroversion. You dislike conflict, you prefer to use diplomatic channels, but often, whether you like it or not, you are unwittingly the cause of many headaches. You have a tendency to escape certain responsibilities, because deep within yourself, you feel that you are not concerned, that it does not belong to you Your nervous system is fragile and you need rest and tranquility. Surround yourself with calm friends, support a Zen attitude. You will experience difficulties in expressing what you really live for because you are blessed with transcendental intuitions that your loved ones find hard to determine, you will learn to trust them. You are unpredictable which often occurs where you least expect it. You have a great ability to bounce back when you are hurt by life. Beneath a sometimes placid expression, you have a strength that allows you to roll with the punches and get out of really difficult situations. You are very attracted to the esoteric, so beware of pseudo-mystical groups. You need the presence of water but you also need to anchor yourself, to root yourself in our good old earth.

6 letters worth 9: You like to dissect everything, you invest in areas that affect the brain. A psychoanalyst, you must learn not to over strain your intellect through constant questioning. You often tire yourself out in your philosophies of life, in your remarks about everything and anything. You're just as non-religious as you are religious. You enjoy organizing and structuring your life and that of those around you in your own way. You will learn to respect the quiet lives of others. You feel the need to be reassured about the love people have for you, while displaying a kind of independence of action and thought. You impose an order that you do not always respect yourself, or else in your own way. You will need to exceed a certain phobia you may have vis-à-vis all that is dirty and vulgar. You commit more easily to your loved ones when you feel useful or when you're responding to an urgent desire of your intellect. All this lacks a bit of spontaneity. You love talking and/or singing. The academic achievement of children can be a big concern. Medical careers may suit you as well as everything related to paperwork. Marriage can be done with a stranger. You are a person with high morals.

7 letters worth 9: You prefer anything that can bring protection to your loved ones and yourself. Part of you still lives in areas that are not easily discernible by most of your contemporaries. You are a spiritual light listening to heavenly music. A misunderstanding of the system in which you work (company, family) sometimes leads you to a form of autism, a refusal to leave your inner world. You are an idealist, you need to meet people who share the same experiences as you, and you're even a humanist who needs to feel useful with regard to difficulties encountered by the world in general and your loved ones in particular. Your taste for the extraordinary and the mystical can sometimes lead you to mix with sects which are not always recommended. Beware of delusions that can result from commitments which are overly idealized. You are a real or virtual traveler and a dreamer. Numerous solutions can be found while you sleep. You will learn to be wary of your particularly fertile imagination, not to think the moon is made of green cheese and to control your excess emotions that fuel you. Looking for approval and a spiritual bond for what you do. Volunteering and charity is advised. You're looking for icons and figures through whom you can easily identify yourself. You need to have a retreat, a peaceful place where you can relax. Anything related to literature and to novels is particularly present. Your nature is sweet, you're a conciliator and an excellent diplomat. Musician, very artistic.

8 letters worth 9: Especially enamored by all that is obscure and not easily discernible, you easily present your environment and people around you but you do not always take them into account. Despite your sharp eye on your fellows, you can show disconcerting naiveté. You are the innocent who loves to fight for lost causes or at least appears as such. You have unusual resources to cope with adversity and people can trust you to solve all sorts of problems. Driven by instinct, you're not very consistent in your work, you tend to act one step at a time. You still have a great ability to get involved and you are blessed with a very high resistance to pain. You tend to focus on the ephemeral, frequently changing activities with regard to seasonal work or tasks. All kinds of businesses are favorable to you, including foreign connections. You like to go where you feel good where you are needed. You are a medium, everything that relates to the afterlife and death concerns you - no doubt this will all become one of your primary occupations. Your proximity of water is particularly recommended and you may enjoy scuba diving. You do not hesitate to challenge yourself, to meet strangers, including in love. You can easily build a network of relationships and friendships from very different backgrounds. Be vigilant vis-à-vis all kinds of drugs, even medication. Be more organized! The father figure plays a role in your identity. Everything related to the relaxation therapy and the paramedical.

9 letters worth 9: You're too idealistic and sometimes outside of a certain reality, to share a satisfactory life as it is usually understood. You are animated by a great desire to reach an ideal, a goal, a reason for being. Your soul is that of a traveler, a priest, a guru who tries to defend their ideas and who likes to live without limits and without attachments. You must learn to listen carefully to others to hear what they're really saying, not what you think they're saying. Driven by your ideal, you sometimes tend to believe you are alone in the world, wanting to do exactly as your head sees it, not listening to any advice. However, you are able to impose laws on yourself, to give yourself directions and to organize your life as that of others and to define what it is best to do. All this is not always practical, you will undertake work to streamline your ideas and to put some order in what you intend to do or are undertaking. You have a strong tendency to live beyond time and space, especially when nothing works the way you want it to. Need to return to reality. Still, you can be a good diplomat, able to deftly resolve conflicts or to anticipate and avoid them. You can be courteous, helpful and dedicated especially if you can get something out of it. You are charming, theatrical and sensitive and you may even not want to leave fingerprints on your way. Are you really meant to live on earth? You need to live near water. Lovesick. Studies and the pursuit of knowledge are encouraged.

More than 9 letters worth 9: See above for the interpretation of the reduction of this number.

Example: If you have 15 letters at a value of 9, you get a 6 by adding 1 + 5. Refer to this value, that is to say 6 letters at a value of 9. Remember to also take into account the 1 and 5 which makes up your 15 because they also refer to sub numbers. You must, therefore, interpret them by taking into account the definition of these two figures from the definition of the sub numbers given below. Remember, this mainly concerns everything related to ideals, knowledge in the broadest sense of the term, travel, dreams, charity, activism, sacrifice, grandparents, brothers, step-sisters, uncles and aunts.

9 Mental letters: Your knowledge is part of a holistic type of thinking. You include the world in its entirety. It should not be split into many separate domains. Everything converges from your particular mode of reasoning which is not always logical but rather intuitive. However, this representation of things can move away from material reality and its contingencies. Your powerful imagination and the pleasure you take in letting it guide you can blur your message and make your goals in life less accessible. You have a good memory and are able to concentrate.

9 Emotional letters: You are very sensitive to the feelings that others have towards you, to love itself, in the universal sense of the term, because your world is made of subtle perceptions easily discernible by those around you. Your inner world is enamored from humanism. Your empathy makes you perceive emotional fields, underlying motivations and even others' inner disturbances, as you learn to protect yourself from outside influences that may disrupt and profoundly change your basic nature. That is why sometimes you appear diminished, absent, or radiant. Doubt easily creeps in if this work has not been done, and this causes you to flee, which some people will criticize you for.

9 Intuitive letters: You have great, if not exceptional, talent for mediumship. In many ways, you are visionary. Serving others, this potential may be expressed at the highest level.

9 Physical letters: You are characterized by a heightened and mystical temperament. You need to establish yourself within a group by expressing great ideas. A particular interest in the esoteric will show itself sooner or later likely to support your ability to feel and guess. Some of your dreams seem unattainable to you. Relatives and/or you yourself are intimately concerned with separations, break-ups (relative to the law) leading to periods of withdrawal into yourself or even abandonment to superficial paradises. Otherwise, you like to be physically accomplished therefore you feel recognition and sympathy from others for your efforts. You need to be encouraged. Although often sport appears to be the way for you to overcome conflicts to reach a broader ideal.

9 Creative letters: Your creativity is expressed through a powerful ideal. The others are your engine. You enjoy sports precision and skill as much as you do teaching and writing.

9 Balanced letters: You are committed to providing support, aid around you. Finally, your balance is proportional to that of the people you help. Moreover, it seems to you that teaching and knowledge can bring you a form of security.

9 Dual letters: You gain height after having made a sacrifice, loneliness. States of anxiety, or gloom may generate a subsequent spiritual elevation.

Challenge 9: You must overcome a tendency to believe out of this world, to exonerate yourself from stress and contingencies that do not implement your ideals. You will learn how to land, to remove yourself from your utopias. If is also necessary that you do not always highlight your sacrosanct humanity, or any other spurious reasons, to excuse your inaction in areas which do not concern you. Eventually discover that you are not alone in holding down a job or that only your mission is commendable. By learning to overcome your fears, you will no longer systematically blame your failures on others. You will discover how to better communicate and express what you really think.

First Cycle 9: The environment brings out the sensitive child in you, empathetic, but also secret. Very soon you're thirsty to learn, to open up to the world, to discover. Your parents must not stifle this need which is a source of success. Their attitude will be key in giving you that required confidence when you rightly stay reserved in case of external tension.

Second Cycle 9: The context predisposes you to advancing in your projects but you sometimes feel you don't receive as much as you give. Any association (marriage, partnership etc) should be carefully considered before you commit. Moreover, the family circle can sometimes suffer because of your lack of your commitments. It is easier to get involved with others than to provide for your own needs. Opportunities relating to the foreign, travel, humanitarian careers, social, political and/or education arise. If you write, your writings receive a favorable reception. To summarize, the more disinterested your action is, the more benefits are certain in return.

Third Cycle 9: Now is the time for a constructive retreat, rewarding when you develop listening skills, humanism towards your neighbor. A commitment to a cause is likely. You do not have to fear insoluble worries while you continue to awaken yourself to the mysteries of this world, by traveling for example.

First Pinnacle 9: To begin, you open up to the world around you very early. However you should be able to deal with your emotional nature. Travel and moves leave their mark. You want to discover and live intensely, feeling strong emotions, even if it means experiencing a few tensions. You develop your artistic and intellectual abilities.

Second or Third Pinnacle 9: It is time for a dedication to a task, sometimes a humanitarian or social mission or even an activity related to education, humanities, writing and/or business. In all cases, you show interest in others. You open up and develop cutting-edge capabilities. Evolution is high on the artistic and/or spiritual plan. There may also be contacts with the foreign (meeting people and/or moves). The vibration predisposes you to perceiving others' moods and emotional imbalances to the point of taking them upon yourself. Your sensitivity can become hypersensitivity. Your feelings are strong. It is necessary to find ways to keep a balance in these areas.

Fourth Pinnacle 9: Finally, you realize with others, focusing on group activities, spiritual opening, sometimes writing. You make new friends. The appeal is also the love of travel and a strong interest in spirituality.

Sub-numbers of 9

18 (see also its meaning as a karmic debt): Allows you to get involved in large enterprises with perseverance. Difficult to find a balance between appetites and selfish desires and higher ideals. Indicates contexts conducive to treachery. Precarious emotional balance partly due to hypersensitivity. Makes you nostalgic. Meet psychologically fragile people in the sectors concerned. Tendency to judge, to engage in struggles for influence, to seek power in the relevant field. The distinction, even the reappointed are researched.

27: Characterizes the simplicity, honesty, the sense of commitment but also a fragility and a vulnerability in emotional terms. Gives real possibilities for developing projects. Gives an independent character, a thought that wants to be free, a rigid side too. Searches for others. Likes to be included whilst having the necessary room for maneuver. Developed artistic sense.

36: Makes it necessary for them to adapt to their changing environment whilst allowing success. Recognition. Has some comfort in their relationships.

45: Highlights jealousy, mistrust, ingratitude and signals handling issues. Wary of the betrayal of someone close. Attracts people in difficulty. Works to focus on comfort first of all. A spirit well anchored in their convictions, able to teach, orientated towards knowledge, sometimes cynical and discriminating. In connection with money, finance, management, the international.

54: Makes controversial situations possible, made of intrigue, indiscretions. Refers to the sense of organization, to discipline but also to ideals, creativity. In connection with knowledge, wisdom, disinterest.

63: Be careful not to mess anything up. Make sure you move forward on your tiptoes, remain resolute faced with obstacles, so as not to compromise the success of their projects. A sometimes scattered mind.

72: Leads to a form of laziness not very conducive to the implementation of their projects. Needs to form a willingness, to take initiatives, to put themselves out. Confers the taste for conversation and reading, assets to please others. Sensitive, intuitive, honest, frank, not short of humor. Signals a form of wisdom but also the refusal to listen.

81: Gives a taste for money. Confers a certain aggressiveness, the need to manage, to change, to open up new directions. Be careful not to discriminate against anything, remain conciliatory. Developed imagination and sense of humor. Authority, manipulations.

90: Amplifies the fervor for the spiritual world, accentuates the sense of sacrifice, of selflessness. Commands the respect of others through a sincere disinterest, which sometimes leads to distance.

99: Confers artistic talents. Emphasizes contexts of jealousy, possessiveness. Relationships often complicated due to malicious gossip.

Note: sub-number of 18 (9 + 9).

When Master Number 11 transcends...

Life Path 11: You will accomplish beautiful things in this existence for you have the potential to do so. You will be inspired, and your own magnetism will help along.

Tip: moderate by interpreting all the sub-numbers revealed by the 3 ways of calculating the life path (see Chapter V). Note that if there is a 20 in the sub-numbers, Life Path is 11/2, otherwise, it is 11.

Expression 11: You show your willingness to help your neighbor, to support and act in this direction. Your strength, your determination is great and always driven by the need to move toward something higher, according to your thirst for ethics and fairness. Independent, you know what you do and do not like that others tell you what to do. You need to hold the steering wheel, able to take off in an instant, but as you are unpredictable, it is sometimes hard to follow. Your vitality is proportional to your interest for an activity. Committed, determined, opinionated, you can show to be reserved while you are bubbling inside. Although more emotional and nervous as it sounds, you can have tantrums but you quickly return to your ideal of generosity and kindness. You know your past you has influenced you and you are trying to be more authentic. You are always dissatisfied because you are always putting the bar very high. Life would be easier if you were less demanding.

Tip: see all sub-numbers behind this 11. Do not forget that Expression is also the reduced sum of the Aspiration and Potential numbers. This can reveal another sub-number. For example, Aspiration 7 + Potential 22 gives 29, sub-number of the Expression 11.

Aspiration 11: Your deep desire is to go where your inspiration takes you. You know how to see the positive in every situation. Everything is based on your evolution. Friends and family can count on you because you are sincere and faithful. For this reason, you attract interesting and spiritually advanced people who often share common values. Some of them will play a beneficial role in your career. The ego is developed at home but over time, you'll find a balance and you enroll in a class action. An emotional deprivation has been experienced during childhood, thus you are both independent, very committed to your freedom, but also eager to find love, tenderness, warmth and comfort.

Potential 11: You display a real ambition to match the esteem you have of your abilities. Powered by a model to follow your principle, you naturally flow from what you feel is your duty. You are also able to not express everything that you feel, as if you have a superior reason to accept in silence. Generous, you are not less selective in your activities, leaving aside anything that you feel insignificant and mediocre. Attention to progress, you constantly improve your projects to the point of no longer having the energy to manage your emotional life, which can often be tense.

First Name 11: You blossom most in occupations with a social and humanitarian character, anywhere you feel useful. However, you must learn not to lock yourself away exclusively in your projects, and learn to take a necessary step back to broaden your scope. If you focus on your goals too much, if not to say fights, you end up forgetting the world that surrounds you. You need to move. It is difficult for you to stay in the same place for too long.

1ˢᵗ Middle Name 11: You have a tendency to want to impose your view of the world on your associates/partner. You look to go beyond the limits imposed by a society that you judge to be too restrictive. A real driving force leading your family in your new ventures (sometimes unrealistic), you reluctantly agree to question your knowledge or to revise your goals. You like to surround yourself with diverse relationships, coming from very different backgrounds by looking to maintain leadership. You refuse any form of emotional dependence. For you, there is a quest for absolute love (physic, brain, heart) which must combine with this ambivalence between your spirit of independence and your commitment to each other. You look to communicate your taste for the esoteric, new technologies and/or travel. You attach specific importance to the fruit of your experiences that you share with your partners. You like to go beyond your limits. Independent, free, proud, you do not look for anything less from the other person.

2nd Middle Name 11: An artist at heart, you have a pronounced taste for music. A player, you are always ready to discover new experiences as long as the notion of achievement is present. You go where your heart and your passions take you, with this perpetual need to live intensely. Good organizer of meetings in varied areas (sport, arts, etc), "Egocentric" at will, you like to be recognized for what you do and create. In the quest for intense romantic relationships, exclusive, this does not always lead you to exemplary fidelity. Sudden uncontrolled changes have a tendency to cause you profound dissatisfaction. You are better as a boyfriend/girlfriend than a father or mother, able to accept the progeny of others. You have a taste for leisure travel and love for a certain freedom of life, without specific material attachment, which doesn't however, prevent you from appreciating beautiful things. Reactive, touchy, you like to be worshipped by your family, while giving a preference to people with a certain aura. You still need to be aware of flatterers.

Heredity 11: As a child, you have evolved into a family different from the norm, whose history is marked by changing events, alterations, relocations, and/or a desire to infuse it original way of seeing things. Moreover, it is possible to find a close interest in the esoteric field or avant-garde in your family circle. You then seek to get away from family boundaries, surpassing anything that could restrict your freedom during your youth and affirm your differences. This family home has made you easily influenced, uncompromising, so conflicts could occur with parental authority. In response, you easily mistreated any member of the family who you think is narrow of mind. You have a strong will to increase your wealth, acquiring property through a will that rarely fails. You do not live a cramped lifestyle. Looking for novelty, a change of place. Your home reflects your taste for all that is modern. Over time, your living will change radically.

Active 11: Your behavior will lead you to put yourself at the forefront like a conductor so that you feel free and recognized. The way you act is original. It can also sometimes cause surprise. Your inspiration guides your actions. Firstly, you act according to your plans and desires. On the other hand, it is more difficult for you to act on demand.

For example, a Realization 1 modulated by a 11 on this parameter multiplies the native's desire to live their life as they see fit, not without a certain originality in their non-conformism.

Maturity 11: Incidentally, why not direct yourself towards these cutting-edge disciplines that appeal to you? With this feeling of being on a mission, you will blossom wherever you feel useful, to be able to come to the aid of your neighbor. You then rely on your intelligence, your individuality and your vision for success. Knowing that you like to have the ascendance in your areas of choice, be sure not to impose your views on others. Life might lead you to experience sudden changes in your emotional and/or social state so you get an awareness of the consequences of the interaction between the material and the spiritual. One does not go without the other.

11 Mental letters: Your intellect is sharp, driven by an ideal, capable of surprising and innovative ideas. Your mental skills bring you to galvanize others to push them to explore new possibilities for themselves. Forward-thinking, always on the lookout for new knowledge, you often enthuse others when you do not confuse them. You also know how to make the most of your intellectual abilities, be careful not to use this to get a grip on others. Some events may upset your studies.

11 Emotional letters: Free character, only listening to your willingness and motivation, enduring evil that imposes what you should do on you, you search for entire characters with high spiritual values. Your sexuality is strong. The management of your emotions is not always simple. Your impatience is often the main cause of your anger.

11 Intuitive letters: In a certain way, you have the option of connecting to the Mind. Suddenly, your insights are most often founded. This also gives you a great ability to lead your projects thanks to this ability to sense and develop.

11 Physical letters: You will have the opportunity to sensitively invest in many areas. Your ability to reap the benefits of work already undertaken in other existences will meet with hostility, jealousy and the treachery of false friends. Your nervousness is related to the changing environment causing you to revolt, to overcome a situation even if it means taking a new direction. You must accept and cope with adversity by using your spiritual gifts wisely.

11 Creative letters: Your creativity is often expressed through challenges. Human adventures inspire you as well as speed and everything that requires innovation and originality.

11 Balanced letters: You are inclined to find situations where your intelligence is fully expressed. It is through this and your discoveries that you find your strength and security.

11 Dual letters: You have to detach yourself from the influence of your mother. Also watch your tendency to impose your way of seeing and thinking and trust in your talent for mediumship.

Challenge 11: You will learn to combine your initiatives taken with the constraints inherent to your associations and collaborations, while not erasing one for the benefit of another, by somehow managing to cope without sacrificing your individuality. You need to avoid burdening others with the way you operate, while knowing to respect those people in your family who may be diametrically opposed to yours. Learn to delegate by trusting. You demonstrate the ability to upset the established order when you feel the need, and finally you adapt to any unexpected disruptions and that will inevitably arise in your life.

First Cycle 11: You are very sensitive to your environment which can make you nervous and anxious. You need emotional presence otherwise frustration may lead you to rebel. It is necessary that boundaries are imposed on you but without aggressiveness. In fact you want to attract attention and show that you are able. This strength will assist you with your entry into working life.

Second Cycle 11: The context is favorable for creating new ideas and feeding projects through your inspiration. On the other hand, do not expect to receive too much in terms of everything related to business, to purely speculative transactions. If a form of success characterizes your action, significant fluctuations at the level of emotional balance need to be controlled. This cycle may be marked by a period of isolation and/or significant transformation in your life. Events highlight your uniqueness but also your instincts.

Third Cycle 11: It is a time offering many opportunities to help, guide and advise others in friendship. You feel inspired with the desire to get away from material constraints. A creative breath can lead you towards creative writing and/or engage you in an action having an impact to bring collective progress. However, this cycle is also a factor in nervousness because of community life, married life is not always smooth sailing.

First Pinnacle 11: To begin, you like to move, experiment. Anything that relates to movement, speed, technology fascinates you. You are often on your toes, alert to that which is innovative, a little touch of everything, daredevil. A form of nervousness characterizes you. Slightly larger issues of a philosophical, humanistic, spiritual nature outweigh the material aspect of things.

Second or Third Pinnacle 11: You show your willingness to assert your individuality. You feel inspired to the point of expecting significant success given that greed is not an end in itself. The action is part of a collective framework while emphasizing your uniqueness and your ability to innovate. Your lifestyle may change.

Fourth Pinnacle 11: You now look to develop yourself personally. Responsive to your needs, you could take a new direction in your life. You let yourself be inspired and widen your circle of relationships. You invest in original actions seeking to avoid conflicts if possible.

Sub-numbers of 11

29: Limited in their actions and ideas. A form of rebellion which may lead to personal consequences. Shows boldness. Enables success thanks to courage and tenacity. Charm, Magnetism. Endeared to their family, their home must be a haven of peace. Facilitates the emergence of new abilities. Emotional instability. Risk of separation. Fear of tomorrow. In connection with inspiration, intuition, knowledge and a need to be fair.

38: Alternating successes and failures. A need to fight at social level. However, confers a strong capacity to find fulfillment. Security of a harmonious and blossoming emotional life.

47: Promotes success. Guarantee of material success. Completion of projects. Allows for friendly support. Brings out the best in them. Confers tenderness and availability.

56: Leads to discussions, even complications. Leads to divergent views and interests. A need to adapt, cut corners, otherwise the action is fraught with resistance. Indicates a certain duality between sensitivity, sense of family responsibilities and desire for freedom.

65: Refers to the need to balance their quest for freedom and their obligations (family in particular). Defines contexts involving the law. Confers inspiration, magnetism, charm. Devoted, diplomatic. Emotions are difficult to manage. Has a slightly explosive side that can be turned against itself.

74: Leads to financial difficulties and the taste for risky business. Shilly-shallying. Possibility however, of unexpected earnings. Increases premonitions and intense dreams. Emotional disorder. Searches for a form of recognition sometimes through artistic mastery (music, painting). Sometimes highlights a vague sense of insecurity which may harm motivation.

83: Favors exchanges. Makes good business sense. Creates character. Gives a sense of invulnerability but also a form of insensitivity.

92: Confers a humanistic breath. Inspires. Sometimes leads to emotional dependence.

When Master Number 22 builds...

Life Path 22: You belong to those who have the necessary potential to accomplish a great task, a noble goal, aiming at others. Grasp your chance when it shows up.

Tip: moderate by interpreting all the sub numbers revealed by the 3 ways of calculating the life path (see Chapter V) for it is rare to get only 22. There is often sub-numbers of 4 (13, 31, 40...). In this case, you got a Life Path 22/4.

Expression 22: Aware of your strength and your potential, you need to prove your achievements in what you can do. You love performance; your pride is your engine. Rarely satisfied, your projects are carried out with consistency, thoroughness, depth and determination. You act as if you have faith in what you do. Even in cases of force majeure, you do not act against the crosscurrent of your beliefs. In fact, you are one of those who are incarnated to build on the basis of their own ideas and sometimes visionaries. Beyond the calm and cautious character that distinguishes you at first you are much more nervous. Your magnetism and your aura are great and will rarely make you indifferent. Your positions are frank and clear, and can sometimes arise reprobation so your opinions are sometimes unqualified. Sure of your acts, you know how to use psychological pressure to achieve your goals but you hate those who use blackmail against you. It is certain that you will take action in this life; you will leave a mark and become a model or a precursor of your time.

Tip: moderate by interpreting all the sub-numbers for it is rare to get only 22. There are often sub-numbers of 4 (13, 31, 40...). In this case, you got an Expression 22/4.

Aspiration 22: The impulses of your heart give you the ambition, perseverance and courage to carry you socially, using your models as example. You need the presence of friends who often have a radical vision. You may feel the need to live a strong and passionate sexuality. This decided spirit can lead you to deafening anger that then turns you into a hard-liner person. You also like to take under your wing by blowing your righteousness and this results in a tendency towards paternalism.

Potential 22: You basically know how to act with determination and seriousness. You have a real ability to galvanize others into action. With a great skill you that know to put forward, you are able to solve problems in dealing lucidly organized and difficult situations. You know, archive, manage, measure You know to be responsible in your actions. Your concern is to do well with your feet on the ground. You carefully apply an ethic to define your values and principles that you have established. Very resilient in the face of adversity, sensitive to the material aspects of existence, you can sometimes be tactless, be under stress, and be extremely austere and/or demanding. You have the creativity to spare. You have important plans and you are able to achieve them.

First Name 22: You show an interest in anything related to beginnings (history, archeology, genealogy etc). Pugnacious and determined in your activities, you can exhibit enthusiasm for political action and concrete commitments in the service of moral values that you defend. All this subtends an inner fight between the exemplarity that you display and your secret desires, which sometimes leads you carry around a form of culpability.

1st Middle Name 22: You prefer strong and lasting commitments with your associates as well as your spouse. Often emotionally dependant on others, you combine family and professional lives. According to other aspects of the chart, you may well have experienced major difficulties in your life. You are a serious person, lacking enthusiasm, however, you find very often find yourself in connection with persons displaying an identical or completely opposite character to yours. You hide your sensitivity with a form of reservedness, even coldness. As a child, you were too serious, what led you to have inhibitions very early. Easily won over by pessimism when your expectations are not met, you then exercise authoritarianism through emotional blackmail.

2nd Middle Name 22: You are an undisputed leader with an unusual strength of character. You have a very special, even intimidating area. In fact you are probably an old soul blessed with great knowledge, often interested in genealogy and research into past lives. You love to impose your abilities, your visions, your way of managing your projects. Able to throw yourself into long term projects, you will pursue them relentlessly. A sympathetic, trustworthy character, friendly when your environment meets your expectations, you can nevertheless sometimes appear unpleasant, even cynical, *vis à vis* people who don't meet your standards. An attraction to political (Mayor, Councilor etc) and/or military life may be felt. You like concrete action on the ground. You display great sensitivity for the aesthetic and the plastic in your romantic relationships. You know how to take care of the comfort of your family while taking care not to invest too much emotionally. Very attached to the success of your progeny, you nevertheless do it sometimes too rigidly, which then causes a reaction diametrically opposed to the research effect.

Heredity 22: Your family gives prominence to the surname and the facts of its history. Memory tests crossings, deaths and everything that relates to his heritage is essential. You keep a deep imprint of the past. There is the strong influence of the father or grandfather, who mostly lived a restrictive childhood (boarding, etc ...). The educational principles focus on honesty, exemplary, work. Education requires a strong authority that can exercise pressure, you sometimes feel guilty. In fact either you accept or you reject them without reservation this family model. Still, you take everything you do seriously. You also have inherited a greater sensitivity to the places visited. You often search your roots beyond the known family (genealogy, past lives ...). This childhood stays with you, you are sometimes very serious, pessimistic and you are prone to bitterness.

Active 22: You act by using your skills. Your actions are often motivated by a need to think big. Once you have decided something, you are very determined to reach your goal.

For example, Aspiration 3 with this active number reveals a nature that means the native expresses what they desire to express and achieve as far as possible. Friends of the native will be needed to foster this desire.

Maturity 22: You will need to make sense of things by asking yourself whether the influence of received educational modes and the family in general, doesn't distract you from your true motivations. Once this certainty is acquired, you'll invest in yourself thoroughly, demonstrating mastery and determination. You will weigh every decision up whilst not taking unnecessary risks by having a clear vision of the ins and outs of every situation. You can then commit properly, driven by your values and your pride, recognizing the importance of your actions, able to withstand heavy workloads.

22 Creative letters *(rare)*: Your creativity is expressed in a very earthly manner through concrete achievements. Your inspiration should be able to find a purpose. Ecology can please you or else everything related to wealth management, real estate.

Challenge 22: You will learn to go beyond this vague feeling that the world conspires against you to prevent you from achieving and establishing your ambition. You'll need to put your coldness and your pride aside in order to share your life force with the most humble, and avoid getting caught up in pessimism. You can then build and promote your worldview with the greatest possible humanity. Your childhood will not be a stranger to your destiny.

There is no 22 in the first cycle.

Second Cycle 22: The context offers you the opportunity to invest in projects where your abilities to complete and to finish are required. Your involvement requires deep convictions and appeals to your tenacity. Your quality of life changes during this cycle and certain times lead you have to deal with some nervousness.

Third Cycle 22: During the latter, you will develop great sensitivity. Very responsive to your surroundings, you need to act accordingly. You seek security. As experiences dictate, you learn to better control, to channel your nervousness in order to find the necessary balance for your achievement.

First Pinnacle 22: To begin, you will develop great sensitivity. Very responsive to your surroundings, you need to act accordingly. You seek security. As experiences dictate, you learn to better control, to channel your nervousness in order to find the necessary balance for your achievement.

Second or Third Pinnacle 22: Good chances to improve your lifestyle (home, occupation etc) by using your talents. Thanks to your perseverance (it is the condition), you succeed in your endeavors. It is also a time when you display profound convictions. This commitment may occur within tailored structures to highlight and allow you to exercise your abilities.

Fourth Pinnacle 22: Finally, during this period you will access significant responsibilities and you will remain still very invested in activities (this may be your family, improving your quality of life or projects with a political significance). Your universal vision is in terms of teaching, a project enabling an elevation of beings. It is necessary to stay focused to avoid spreading yourself too thinly faced with many demands. Your offspring demand all your attention.

Aspects between the numbers

Aspects which are deemed harmonious or discordant are to be treated with precaution. It all depends on their intensity and strength. Aspects which are too harmonious can lead to a sort of immobility and unquestioning comfort while so-called discordant aspects tend to stimulate exchanges, even if they are conflictual, by creating awareness. Excess in either direction is never a good thing.

These aspects can be more or less favorable depending on the life choices of the affected parties (sport, outings, family, professional choices and travel, etc.).

The essential point, and the one that is often forgotten, is that love and the heart have the advantage over all antagonisms, which come from the expression of the ego.

1 vs. 1: All or nothing. Common understanding for common objectives or rivalry of authority, personality. The main quality of this association is based on intelligence.

1 vs. 2 (1 + 2 = 3): Strength and softness. Connects the dominant to the dominated. Many antagonisms may be sublimated through dialogue, communication. If everyone plays their role by accepting one another, perfect couple. 2 looks for the strength of 1's character. And 1 enjoys listening to 2.

1 vs. 3 (1 + 3 = 4): The king and the jester. In the long term: dialogue of the deaf, difficult relationships. The susceptibility and the brilliance of 1 doesn't go well with the critical logical mind of 3, their incessant questioning. 3's need to communicate, to analyze makes it difficult to agree with the authoritarianism and impulsivity of 1.

1 vs. 4 (1 + 4 = 5): Fire and ice. Apparent conflict of authority. They don't have the same way of operating at all when it comes to leading their lives. 1 is lively and impulsive and 4 is pragmatic and stubborn. They need to agree on common and strong goals by distributing the tasks perfectly in order to achieve them. Need to know oneself properly and to accept the very vast difference in design of life. Surprising, unconventional and unpredictable association in these outcomes.

1 vs. 5 (1 + 5 = 6): Entente cordiale. Personality and ego conflicts are not absent but a mutual admiration links them as well as a mutual understanding. Many common objectives. However, 1 is disconcerted by 5 and 5 may more or less gently mock the pride of 1. Humor, curiosity and the game may be central to their exchanges.

1 vs. 6 (1 + 6 = 7): The master and the servant. If 1 works for the aspirations of 6 all goes well, otherwise, relationships are impossible, 1 doesn't meet 6's expectations (love, respect, life principles, protection). Similarly, if 6 does not give 1 recognition for their action, the harmony becomes difficult. Finally who needs the other more, who is the more dependant of the two?

1 vs. 7 (1 + 7 = 8): Successful association. Passion and love. They often share common goals and ideals the same ambition. Both are in tune. Admiration of 7 *vis à vis* 1 (creative, enterprising) and enchantment of 1 for advice, reflection, the depth of 7.

1 vs. 8 (1 + 8 = 9): If one doesn't eclipse the other, their chances of success are great. Formidable sadomasochistic relationships in both constructions and destruction. Mutual admiration and fascination. 1 will ensure respect for 8, to not to dazzle and profit from their naivety otherwise, beware of reprisals. For their part, 8 will put their cards on the table.

1 vs. 9 (1 + 9 = 10/1): Action and contemplation. Possible deal in voluptuousness, sensuality. 9 leads to a haven of peace, tranquility if 1 accepts it and the latter energizes it in return. However, 9 has a complete understanding of 1's personality but the reverse is not true. 1 struggles to understand the depth of 9. 9 understands what appears to be triviality of 1's acts. Musical environment required to vibrate in tune.

1 vs. 11 (1 + 11 = 12/3): Who will rule? Frank, sincere and constructive dialogue necessary. Mutual recognition of both parties to avoid conflict. 11 must overcome their pride and admit they need 1. In exchange, 1 must respect the living space, the spirituality and the sometimes utopian humanism of 11. 1 acts according to themselves, 11 acts as a transmitter towards others who follow or don't follow.

1 vs. 22 (1 + 22 = 23/5): The king and the republic. Impossible marriage. Between pontificating, pragmatic, serious 22 and 1 sweeping all their principles aside to serve their achievement, everything opposes them. Except that 1 gives way to the pressures and demands of society in the community.

2 vs. 2: An association without wave, marked by tranquility, peace, understanding to the full extension of the fires. The big risk is a lack of motivation. Non energizing aspect but allowing some material growth.

2 vs. 3 (2 + 3 = 5): Respect between the two parties. Mutual acceptance and understanding. Productive dialogue. Common life principles. 2 providing 3 with comfort, security, peace and 3 responding through intellectual stimulation and an organization of life which is pleasant for 2.

2 vs. 4 (2 + 4 = 6): Pragmatic meeting between the two complementary ways of operating. 4 brings material security to 2 and 2 reassures them. Sense of family and shared interests. Acquisition of property. Lasting and constructive understanding. Classic couple.

2 vs. 5 (2 + 5 = 7): Mutual and magnetic attraction. One not being insensitive to the charm of the other but real difficulties staying together in the long term. Utopian relationships. 2 does not have 5's eccentricity and 5 is bored with 2's conformism. On the other hand, children can bring them closer even if their vision on education diverges.

2 vs. 6 (2 + 6 = 8): Harmonious and constructive relationships. Common views. Complementary ways of operating. Support, moral quality, family. However, there is a risk of them locking themselves away in their common universe or forgetting themselves. May share the same points of view in relation to their role in society.

2 vs. 7 (2 + 7 = 9): Harmonious relationships in relation to the home and life together, but more delicate when it comes to objectives to be reached unless they are common commercial or artistic goals. Ancestry of 7 which can sometimes get bored of 2's lack of depth. In return, 2 may find that 7, is too introspective, complicates life and is not really present every day. No open conflict so far, rather favorable.

2 vs. 8 (2 + 8 = 10/1): Life can be harmonious if 8 is able to live their life even the hidden part. All material aspects are favored. 8's ability to generate a form of abundance suits this couple. 2 is not necessarily insensitive to 8's unbridled sexuality. The intimate side of 2 combines well with the secret taste cultivated by 8. 2 however, expects that 8's authority is in the service of the group and not themselves.

2 vs. 9 (2 + 9 = 11): Possible conflict between 2's conformism and 9's spiritual or idealist quest. Harmonious however, in terms of humanistic views, 2's potential to get involved and cooperate harmonizing well with 9's potential to give and help. On the other hand, 9 is sometimes fleeing *vis à vis* the constraints of existence, while 2 is preoccupied by the management of everyday life.

2 vs. 11 (2 + 11 = 13/4): Or all or nothing. Positive if 2 accepts 11's personality without backward-thinking (common consensus) or impossible marriage. In all cases, original but laborious association. 2 has the ability to adapt to 11's singularity, but the reverse is less evident, except for 11 finding ways to express themselves outside of 2's framework.

2 vs. 22 (2 + 22 = 24/6): Common interests, stability pact, the desire to build. 22 reassures 2, who in turn provides them with softness and well-being. Sustainable construction. Good combination able to make the perfect couple. Searches for balance between the antagonism of their personalities. 22 builds the house. 2 decorates it and makes it nice.

3 vs. 3: Castor and Pollux. Complicity, communication through dialogue, creativity. Very good understanding. Young character. Association sometimes lacking maturity. A lot of movement. Sincere quest for harmony, complementarity.

3 vs. 4 (3 + 4 = 7): Organizing and pragmatic mind. Favorable for any association of a socioprofessional character. Understanding less evident in emotional relationships, married life. 4 doesn't like 3's cerebrality and excitement. 3 doesn't like a form of paralysis in 4.

3 vs. 5 (3 + 5 = 8): Energy and stimulation. Mutual taste for new explorations. Discovery. Common outside interests. Does not like family tranquility. Anything that affects the mind, meanderings of the psyche brings them together. Fairly frequent rivalries (3 doesn't like 5's utopias and 5 sometimes complains about their preconceptions and analysis of everything). Association generating nervousness.

3 vs. 6 (3 + 6 = 9): Run after me and I will catch you. Commitment possible but never total. The duality of each number is expressed through this association. And something is missing. Certainly found in exchanges but the association is not very constructive due to lack of foundations.

3 vs. 7 (3 + 7 = 10/1): The extrovert and the introvert. Possible consensus on common objectives. But possible conflict through opposition between 7's faith and deep convictions and 3's excessive "mentalization". 7 blaming 3 for their lack of ideals and 3 countering with 7's lack of realism. However, favorable to all aspects relating to education and knowledge. They say the same thing in a different way.

3 vs. 8 (3 + 8 = 11): Is that possible? Yes, provided that each person exercises mature to accept the other person for their differences. In this case, original and creative relationship. Otherwise, 3's probity and sociability does not accommodate 8's hidden extravagances well and in this way manages things in a rather rigid manner. As for 8, they will find that 3 lacks depth.

3 vs. 9 (3 + 9 = 12/3): Placid and constructive couple where each person lives in a different place. 3's mind works totally differently from 9's psyche and yet there is mutual attraction, leading to a good harmonization of relationships. Difference does not mean antagonism in this case. Common interest in the exploration of things related to the mind through different approaches. Mutual respect. Moreover,3's sociability energizes 9's humanism.

3 vs. 11 (3 + 11 = 14/5): Passion, fireworks, explosion. 3 is stimulated by 11 while keeping a critical mind *vis à vis* their actions. 11's susceptibility may be adversely affected by 3's critical analysis. However, they come together through common investigations and projects. Private and family life not really favored. Need to conserve their passions.

3 vs. 22 (3 + 22 = 25/7): Ambivalent aspect. All that is technical and pragmatic favors leaving little room for feelings and sensitivity. 22's conformism may be appreciated by 3 but it is different from their pessimism. As for 3, there is the risk that they will disrupt 22's search for tranquility and natural reservedness. On the other hand, 3 may an excellent spokesperson for 22.

4 vs. 4: To live happily, live hidden. Association with a monotonous appearance, reserved view from the outside, but enabling a significant increase in material goods. Quest for nature, a peaceful and constructive life. Pursuit of well-being. Strong commitment to work values. Principles. Stubbornness. May not see the wood for the trees.

4 vs. 5 (4 + 5 = 9): How can 4 live peacefully with 5 extravagances and taste for exploration? How can 5 accommodate 4's fixity and life principles? Incompatibility between 4's material aspirations and 5's thirst for discovery. Understanding is therefore only possible at the expense of compromise and mutual concessions. In this case, the association can combine method and exploration.

4 vs. 6 (4 + 6 = 10/1): They share common interests. A desire to build, to achieve together. No blatant antagonism. Quest for harmony and consensus. A taste for art, well-being, the good life, aspects of tradition. Favored family life. Aesthetics.

4 vs. 7 (4 + 7 = 11): Matter and spirit. Able to get along on the condition of respecting the other's deep personality because everything separates them. 7 is very admiring of 4's abilities to construct and materialize what they desire (making them more confident). 4 can be enriched by 7's the deep faith and convictions. A marriage of spiritual and material quests as well as the resulting peace.

4 vs. 8 (4 + 8 = 12/3): They share sensuality and a taste for earthly pleasures. Creativity. Association favoring financial and material success. Opposing each other when one conjures up deep, even unspoken instincts in the other (jealousy, persecution). Destructive in case of conflict. All good or all bad.

4 vs. 9 (4 + 9 = 13/4): Constructive association, beneficial in many areas. Shows a quest for harmony, consensus. Not looking to make waves. Can provide mutual support. 9's anxiety and fear of life fades due to 4's protective side. 4 is not insensitive to 9's spirituality and their quest for a good life.

4 vs. 11 (4 + 11 = 15/6): Very strong opposition and antagonisms. Common ground difficult to find. Works only if 4 is willing to unconditionally accept the domination and/or independence of 11's action. 11 will in return accommodate 4's placid side. So the association is favorable particularly on the professional front.

4 vs. 22 (4 + 22 = 26/8): Favorable understanding. Achievement of material and financial objectives. Search for the pleasures of life. A taste for a form of retirement, calm, tranquility. May not be able to shine through originality but the association is strong and durable.

Propensity to isolate and overprotect themselves. Attachment to ancestral values.

5 vs. 5: Dynamic understanding but without much depth. A multitude of common points allows for an exhilarating life, shared experiences, but there is an overall lack of achievement or objective realization. Utopia. Difficult to strike a balance between deep friendship and Love with a capital L. Scattering. Instability.

5 vs. 6 (5 + 6 = 11): Great complementarity, even complicity. 6 leads to 5's harmony and discipline, who in return brings the spice of life to 6. Despite everything, 5 may have difficulty coping with 6's life principles that it considers to be too fixed. 6 finds it hard to accommodate 5's fickleness which may lead them to flee responsibilities.

5 vs. 7 (5 + 7 = 12/3): Rivalries. Discords. Two ways of experiencing independence. 7 has trouble understanding 5's expanding universe and conversely, 5 doesn't understand 7's introversion. Convergence and affinities possible as long as they take the time to exchange and are driven by common objectives. 5 has a capacity for expression that 7 does not. The latter is more introverted and deep.

5 vs. 8 (5 + 8 = 13/4): Common attraction to mysteries and "the hidden face of the moon" in general. Two medium numbers. Stimulation for all kinds of games of life, overruns. However, 5 can be bothered by 8's not always clear appetites (8 likes to establish their power) and 8 finds it hard to accommodate 5's humanistic scruples and instinct of freedom when it comes to exploring.

5 vs. 9 (5 + 9 = 14/5): Consensus and mutual respect. Quest for the good life. Harmonious understanding but risks the "unspoken" so as not to deceive and damage their relationships. Do not see themselves as adversaries. Need to explore both with a different approach and the desire to live in a non-confrontational manner. Aware of this need to make concessions, the sweetness of life is found.

5 vs. 11 (5 + 11 = 16/7): If they do not kill each other, they can go far. Complementarity in the action and willingness to get over themselves and social structures. Intelligence and understanding characterize this union, but strong impulsivity. Who will lead the other? Association promoting the dynamic in all sorts of areas. Be careful that 5's desire for freedom is not hindered by 11's need for success.

5 vs. 22 (5 + 22 = 27/9): Difficult association but mutual respect and understanding. Difficulty between 5's exaggerated optimism and 22's pessimism. Attraction to worldly pleasures even if they experience them differently. Can share a common ideal of society. However 5's desire for freedom eludes 22's understanding who wants more than anything to be materially fulfilled.

6 vs. 6: A lot of dialogue, many exchanges. Quest for harmony. Favorable to married life, to family life based on well-established life principles, on a sharing of responsibilities. Common willingness to structure, improve, cheer up. Be careful not to let yourself be taken over by the critical thinking of the other person. Difficult to cross over a certain distance that separates them.

6 vs. 7 (6 + 7 = 13/4): Difficult association on points of detail. Not conversing in the same place. 7 is sometimes too absent, too far away from 6's desire for realization of objectives. For their part, 7 may find 6 to be too down to earth. Difficult for 6 to mix in their desire for love with this 7 who is rather independent and introspective by nature. However, sharing common interests when it comes to the willingness to harmonize their lives.

6 vs. 8 (6 + 8 = 14/5): Mutual attraction to two different worlds. Constructive association. 8 can rely on 6's probity if they manage to accommodate their secretive nature. Better if 6 doesn't know anything of 8. However, 6 appreciates the protection provided by 8's material fallout. In the face of a problem, there are divergent approaches: 6 demonstrates flexibility here where 8, may seek to force through.

6 vs. 9 (6 + 9 = 15/6): They feel indebted to a lot of things, while being rather distanced from the other's concerns. They visit each department but don't go to the same place. 6 risks blaming 9 for their rivalries and a form of inconsistency. 9 is rather indifferent to 6's daily concerns. However, they may find themselves doing charitable work because they both driven by the notion of service.

6 vs. 11 (6 + 11 = 17/8): Constructive association provided that one is not dominated by the other. Favorable in a hierarchical context. 6 can support 11 enormously (rigor, discipline, placement, structure) who in turn opens them up to other possibilities. 11 may, however, be explosive faced with criticism from 6.

6 vs. 22 (6 + 22 = 28/10/1): Great complementarity in the service of common objectives. Willingness to build in the long term on the right footing. Understanding of the agreement. Method and efficiency. May however, lack a bit of fantasy. Leads to sometimes being a bit too homely. Ideal for building shelters of all kinds (children, animals etc).

7 vs. 7: Need to have a life ideal and common objectives for each other. Need to feel mutually involved in a task. Must respect their independence, not to invent stories. Shared attraction for knowledge, education and travel, but difficulty handing over and expressing their inner selves.

7 vs. 8 (8 + 7 = 15/6): Harmonious if they maintain and share their common taste for mystery and secret. Brought together by their need to benefit greatly from the pleasures of life (money, acquisitions, well-being, sexuality etc). 8 may promote 7's who in return, will provide them with a dynamizing energy and a form of security.

7 vs. 9 (7 + 9 = 16/7): Mystical-religious or purely commercial association. Quest for peace, shared harmony, faith. Sublimation of everyday life that does not preclude a search for material comfort. Diplomacy. However, be careful not to self-indulge or to grow accustomed to artificial paradises. Need to impose a disciplined life.

7 vs. 11 (7 + 11 = 18/9): They share a vision and common objectives. Willingness to go beyond pre-established structures. Huge capacity to develop all kinds of projects. 7 can support and promote 11's initiatives who has the audacity to realize 7's aspirations. However, the association is not easy.

7 vs. 22 (7 + 22 = 29/11): Constructive association in the long term. Doesn't try to oppose. Willingness to share a love of nature, to find tranquility. 22 provides 7 with great protection, who in turn gives them unconditional support. Favorable to family life, to educational contexts. However, ensures that 7's introspection does not hamper that which 22 wants to achieve in material terms.

8 vs. 8: All or nothing association. Respect and mistrust, each being aware of the other person's strengths. The pleasures of life and material interests are the driving force behind their relationship. Destruction or sublimation. Success or extraordinary fall. Need to show flexibility.

8 vs. 9 (8 + 9 = 17/8): Shared taste for earthly pleasures and goods. Complicity. Sometimes mystical understanding. They wallow in a quiet and peaceful life. 9 soothes and inspires 8 by opening them up to a more spiritual dimension. 8 provides 9 with protection thanks to their ability to find fulfillment. They like to live slightly hidden.

8 vs. 11 (8 + 11 = 19/10/1): Productive but conflicting association. Clash of personalities. 11's independence doesn't accommodate 8's authority and influence. Common ground if everyone puts their ego aside. 8 makes 11's projects a reality and will play fair with them. Passionate relationships can be fleeting.

8 vs. 22 (8 + 22 = 30/3): Perfect understanding to achieve, realize and create. They share a common taste for all of life's material aspects and pleasures. One condition: 8 must be honest and flexible with an often tense 22. working towards a pleasant and secure family life. Conflicts relating to authority possible but very powerful association.

9 vs. 9: Consensual understanding. Gentleness, harmony and peace. Search for leisure, well-being. Spiritual quest may lead to becoming disconnected from reality. A taste for travel. Available and assistance. Intuitive communication that allows tacit understanding. Common dreams.

9 vs. 11 (9 + 11 = 20/2): Less evident association, demanding a lot of reciprocal effort in terms of understanding. They do not live in the same spheres. However, their common ground is the humanistic spirit and progressiveness that characterizes them both. 9 can temper and pacify 11's agitation. 11 can energize 9.

9 vs. 22 (9 + 22 = 31/4): Favorable and constructive association enabling a complementarity. 22 bases their life on solid foundations, which suits 9's need for tranquility. In return, 9 has faith in life, a sweetness, a confidence that will reassure 22 in what they are. They share many ideals that are achieved thanks to a mutual trust.

11 vs. 11: Unlikely association unless they share deep and lasting goals. Two giant egos one beside the other. Hence the risk of confrontation. They both need effects in equal measures, so as to satisfy their need for recognition.

11 vs. 22 (11 + 22 = 33): Conflict of authority. Diametrically opposed operating modes. 11 builds with a desire for immediate and spectacular effects; 22 builds for the long term and rather discretely, sometimes with too much reserve. They share the desire for achievement but to express it together, huge concessions are required. However, when 22's achievement is the product of 11's inspiration, the quality of the achievement is impressive.

22 vs. 22: Favorable association because they pursue the same goals. Do not allow excitement but favor long term construction. Need to provide a bit of fun. joviality to avoid falling into a form of seriousness. Solid but not dynamic.

CHAPTER VII

Interaction of numbers and forecasts

"Do you have any idea how many lives we must have gone through before we even got the first idea that there is more to life than eating, or fighting, or power in the Flock? A thousand lives, Jon, ten thousand!... We choose our next world though what we learn in this one... But you, Jon, learned so much at one time that you didn't have to go through a thousand lives to reach this one."»

(Richard Bach - Jonathan Livingston Seagull)

Numerological forecast consists of revealing a person's road map, the one that he freely chose before incarnating. This does not mean that following this path, which is largely defined by your aim in life, is inevitable. That said, distancing yourself from, or even abandoning, your life path probably requires a heightened level of awareness, i.e. the being must know who he really is. Once a person has mastered this knowledge then he can become the creator of his own reality.

At that stage, the being can choose whether or not to follow his road map. If he does not reach this stage then he may have the feeling that he is simply subjected to events. Yet, everything is perfect, everything happens as it should so that we are able to play our part and participate in the game of life.

A number is behind every letter constituting a word; it gives the word a vibration and a strength which translate the true intention of the person expressing the word. These vibrations are contained in the collective subconscious and have a definite impact on our lives, redefining on a larger scale the directions which we all collectively take. As proof of this I would like to cite the online use of tools like WebBot which are used to analyze the impact of all words used on the web on global consciousness. The results are so pertinent that some people use them to make forecasts which have proven to be accurate. This proof makes it difficult to deny that words possess an active vibration.

Each of us are gifted with qualities and faults, with a personality principally defined through the Expression, Aspiration and Potential numbers, and we are all here to walk along our own Life Paths. As we saw earlier, the latter is the fadic sum of all of the numbers contained in our date of birth and it is divided into three periods called life cycles. These cycles are collective. The first cycle, determined by our month of birth, is shared by a very large number of people. All those born in the month of May, for example, share a first cycle of 5 (as May is the fifth month of the year). This general context should therefore be nuanced by the Life Path specific to each individual. A Life Path 1 on a first cycle 5 is different from a Life Path 2 on the same cycle.

In order to further refine this period you then need to look at the Cycle and Life Path pair in the first of the four Pinnacles (fadic sum of the day and month of birth). Moreover, the sub-number behind this pinnacle (for Pamela 16 + 10 = 26/8) will add further precision to the reading.

We can go even further by observing if an inclusion modulator is referred to by these numbers. Everything that is signified by these modulators is even more important during the corresponding period. This gives the reading even more precision. At this stage, even people born on the same date no longer share the same analysis because the inclusion modulators relate to their respective surnames, first and middle names.

It is remarkable that the first Cycle 5 on a first Pinnacle 3 corresponds to 3 letters worth 5 and/or 5 letters worth 3. This means that out of all of the information collected by this inclusion chart, the interpretation of this modulator is of utmost importance particularly when describing the personality of a child during this period.

In the same way, if, in addition to a correspondence between a Cycle or a Pinnacle and the Life Path, the number in question is also found in one or more boxes of the inclusion chart, then the associated interpretations must be taken into account. For example, if a person has a Life Path 4 and a second Pinnacle 4 then not only do we need to look at which boxes in the inclusion chart contain a 4 (e.g. 4 letters worth 3), but also the number of letters worth 4. Additionally, we must not forget to check if this 4 corresponds to a challenge for the same period.

Likewise, it is important to take any correspondence with the planes of existence into account. In our example, Pamela is in a first potential 8 which reflects the 8 physical letters in his name.

Finally, when we construct the birth chart, we are already depicting the contexts and potentials that will present themselves throughout the course of a subject's life. Using this information, we are able to extrapolate the way in which a native will react in accordance to this environment. An easy way to understand this is to consider how much the weather affects our mood. Some of us like a dry sunny day in winter and others would much prefer to see the snow fall. The reasons for our preferences are often personal and not always as easy to explain as a simple interest in skiing.

Predicting in numerology is a little bit like predicting the weather. It is not easy to know in advance the precise future temperature but restricting forecasts to rounded temperatures such as -10° or +30° is a lot easier. From that point, common sense prevails.

When I read a weather report, I know what to wear so that I am not out of synch with the weather. Like in the proverb "forewarned is forearmed", the science of numbers provides a weather report of my existence. It also shows me which doors will open more easily along my path, or even those that will already be open to me. Numerology can also warn me of any obstacles that might block my path and can tell me that if a door remains resolutely shut to me then there is probably a reason. Thanks to numerology, I can avoid wasting my volition and energy trying to force this door open in vain and wait until more favorable conditions, should they occur. Numerology is the definitive effective prevention tool. Quite simply, it gives us the keys to wisdom.

However, trying to isolate a specific future fact is a delicate task. The numerologist is very quickly faced with contradictions inherent in the connections between, and the interpretations of, an overly large number of core elements. This rapidly becomes true for monthly, let alone daily, forecasts. And then there are hourly predictions to contend with! Numerological forecasts are meaningful on a year-long scale, or over the course of a few months, but are above all very dependent on the choices made by the native. As Edgar Cayce said for astrology, man is free to make his own choices within tendencies and influences that he cannot control. This is all the more true if he is conscious of his aspiration and driving spiritual force.

Before discovering which elements are useful for forecasts, you need to know that some are based on a civil year whereas others interact from birthday to birthday. In all cases it is of capital importance to organize the relevant data into a hierarchy.

The principal element is the Personal Year. This corresponds to the fadic sum of the day and month of birth and the year in question. Thus for a person born on the 14th of March 1959, 2010 will be a personal year 11 because $(1+4)+(3)+(2+0+1+0\ ) = 11$. Applying the rule that master numbers are not reduced, we retain the 11. If there is a sub-number, it must always be taken into account. A personal year 4 may by nuanced by the fact that it comes from a 13, a 31 or a 40 for example.

Once we have this information then we need to check if the Personal Year corresponds to the person's Life Path, in which case it is an important year in the fulfillment of his destiny. Next, we check if it corresponds to a current Cycle or Pinnacle and then if it has the same value as a challenge or missing number (for 11 see 2 but also 1, for 22 see 4, and less significantly, 2). We also want to discover whether the personal year is the same as the person's Aspiration, Potential or Expression number. If so, then everything signified by those core elements will be intensified. Do the same thing for inclusion even if in our example the personal year is 11 and it is quite rare to find 11 letters with the same value (except 5).

The Personal Year vibrates with the Universal Year. 2010 is a Universal Year 3 (2 + 0 + 1 + 0 = 3). In our example the combined energy is worth: 11 (Personal Year) + 3 (Universal Year) = 14/5. Although not necessarily intensified, the karmic debt 14 is present. If it also appears in other key parameters then everything related to this debt will be emphasized.

The second most important element is undoubtedly the Personal Year/Astrological House association defined by the numerologist Françoise Daviet.

From his birth to his first birthday, each individual is linked to the first astrological house, then to the 12th in his second year of life and then to the 9th, and so on. The influence of those Houses is directly related to the 12 sectors of the zodiac. Françoise Daviet also suggests that each house is related to a specific element of the numerological chart in question. Experiments have shown her method to be well-founded.

The Personal Year/Astrological House pair has a 36-year cycle. That means that if you are born in the period 3/I, you will have that same Personal Year 3/House I combination on your 36th birthday and again on your 72nd. There are 11 personal years multiplied by 12 possible houses which makes a total of 132 combinations. They are not all present during a person's lifetime and the same combination does not affect each person in the same way because it is dependent on the value of the initial Life Path. In fact, this association helps us to differentiate between the different phases of each of the 11 Life Paths. Once again, the sub-numbers of this Path must be taken into consideration as they can subtly change the significance of these periods.

For our native, the year 2010 will be characterized by the pair 11/XI before his birthday and then 11/X after his birthday. During interpretation, the link must be made between the meaning of the Personal Year and the areas relating to the astrological house that it passes through. The houses will be defined later on. Remember also that his Life Path 11 comes from a 29 but that the presence of a 20 also reveals a 2 factor.

For the sake of completeness, I must mention that other methods exist which reveal new elements, in particular those relating to transits of letters, arcana of age and year, Magi cycles and challenges and pinnacles, within the year in question.

However, at the time of writing, I do not believe that we can definitively validate those elements. There is still much research and cross-referencing to be done.

Whatever happens, if you are just starting out in numerology, stick to the above rules and you will obtain the desired outcome without getting into a tangle. A forecast should never be seen as a final verdict but rather as an inventory and a possibility allowing a person to prepare himself as much as possible for every situation. Nothing is unavoidable.

I recall a reading which revealed that the professional direction of the subject might change but, by the end of the year, I had to admit that this had not happened. However, during a discussion with this woman she admitted that she had indeed received a serious job offer from a friend who managed her own business but that she had declined. This offer could have radically changed her socioprofessional circumstances and it visibly corresponded to the numerological forecast. This is a good illustration of the fact that, while numbers make the suggestions, people act on them as they will.

For another person, the reading signaled a period in which the health of a close friend or relative would be affected. She could not see to whom that would apply because no-one in her family had any significant health problems. Subsequently, however, the subject's mother started to complain of headaches, which she blamed on her frequent migraines. The daughter, aware of the potential of a more serious illness as predicted in the chart, strongly encouraged her mother to see a specialist. This was the right decision as it turned out that there was a more serious problem which the doctor himself said could have been fatal had it not been detected in time.

You should also note that sometimes numerological forecasts which are supposed to be directly applicable to the native are actually experienced by a close friend or relative and that the subject only lives the events vicariously through that person. For example, an important love affair could concern a girl but the mother who is the subject of the chart identifies with her daughter to the point that we can be forgiven for questioning who it was that fell in love… This mirror effect is quite frequent.

Cycle Personal year/Astrological house

House	Corresponding age (birthday) Meaning								Link with that said
I	0 yo	12 yo	24 yo	36 yo	48 yo	60 yo	72 yo	84 yo	The Life Path and its sub-numbers. The signifiers with a 1 and an 11.
	Refers to the beginning, temperament, personality, physical appearance, constitution, the ego etc								
XII	1 yo	13 yo	25 yo	37 yo	49 yo	61 yo	73 yo	85 yo	The number of Physical letters. The signifiers with a 9.
	Refers to the unfathomable, inner life, emotions, religion, the occult, trials, health (psychic), hospitalizations, laboratories, monasteries, hospitals, prisons. Speaks of exile, hidden hostilities, failures. But also opens the connection with the divine, spiritual protections...								
XI	2 yo	14 yo	26 yo	38 yo	50 yo	62 yo	74 yo	86 yo	The Aspiration number and its sub-numbers. The signifiers with a 5 and an 11.
	Speaks of friends, projects, protection, social and humanitarian goals, hopes and future ideas. Also speaks of those who help and support...								
X	3 yo	15 yo	27 yo	39 yo	51 yo	63 yo	75 yo	87 yo	The Maturity number and its sub-number. The signifiers with a 22 and a 4.
	Refers to personal achievement, professional ambitions, the career, social success, reputation and honors. Speaks also of grandparents...								
IX	4 yo	16 yo	28 yo	40 yo	52 yo	64 yo	76 yo	88 yo	The Number of letters worth 9 (inclusion). The signifiers with a 7 and a 9.
	Refers to travel, adventures, ideals, religion, philosophy, studies and								

House	Corresponding age (birthday) Meaning								Link with that said
	higher education, social class, justice, laws and intelligent judgments etc								
VIII	5 yo	17 yo	29 yo	41 yo	53 yo	65 yo	77 yo	89 yo	The Number of letters worth 8 (inclusion). The signifiers with a 8.
	Refers to sexuality, money, occultism, death and rebirth, initiation, transformation. Speaks of crises, mysteries and secrets, money from others, heritage etc.								
VII	6 yo	18 yo	30 yo	42 yo	54 yo	66 yo	78 yo	90 yo	The number of Emotional letters and the 1st middle name with its sub-numbers. The signifiers with a 2 and a 6.
	Refers to harmony, temperance, associations and unions, contracts and trials, the spouse, relationships with partners, the public, competitors, struggles etc.								
VI	7 yo	19 yo	31 yo	43 yo	55 yo	67 yo	79 yo	91 yo	The first name number and its sub-numbers. The signifiers with a 6 and a 3.
	Refers to daily life, service, work, health care, hygiene, everyday health, small constraints, servants, subordinates, pets etc.								
V	8 yo	20 yo	32 yo	44 yo	56 yo	68 yo	80 yo	92 yo	The signifiers with a 1 and an 11.
	Refers to creation, recreation and procreation. Speaks of love, children, pleasures, leisure, entertainment, games, speculation, hobbies, personal expression and creativity, the father etc.								
IV	9 yo	21 yo	33 yo	45 yo	57 yo	69 yo	81 yo	93 yo	Mother's maiden name number and its sub-numbers. The signifiers with a 2.
	Refers to fertility, family, home, childhood, heritage, the birthplace then to home staff, to the attic, to treasures, to the past, to roots,								

House	Corresponding age (birthday) Meaning								Link with that said
	animals, your mother and her past etc.								
III	10 yo	22 yo	34 yo	46 yo	58 yo	70 yo	82 yo	94 yo	The Number of letters worth 3 (inclusion). The signifiers with a 3 and a 6.
	Refers to thought, studies, communication, reading, contacts and meetings realized through means of communication or movement, to small studies, brothers and sisters, cousins, friends, the neighborhood, to means of moving forward in local moves etc.								
II	11 yo	23 yo	35 yo	47 yo	59 yo	71 yo	83 yo	95 yo	The Potential number and its sub-numbers. The signifiers with a 4.
	Refers to inner talents, profit, acquisitions, personal earnings, possessions and personal values, to that which is acquired through their own means etc.								

In Personal Year 1...

P.Y. 1 / I: A good time to start something we have wanted to do for a long time. Open to all sorts of new ideas. Possible success in sport, business. Intellectual brilliance.

P.Y. 1 / II: A good time in windfalls, to restore your health/beauty. Anything related to creation is favored. Emotional meetings.

P.Y. 1 / III: A good time to move, to make new friends as well as professional contacts. Purchase of a vehicle. Desire to express their desires. Dialogue, shared easily. Renewed links with siblings.

P.Y. 1 / IV: A good time to embellish the inside. Desire to have children. Renewed contact with the family. Favorable to the creation of a business. Sudden popularity in many areas. Moves possible.

P.Y. 1 / V: A good time for anything related to the desire to please. Many contacts, outings, evening with friends. Displays a certain joie de vivre. Renewed contact with children. Success of one of them. Discovery of passionate love. Success.

P.Y. 1 / VI: A good time to put things in order in both your life and others' lives. Anything that relates to analysis, to restructuring is favored. The period may be disturbing because there is a bit too much speed for the person. It's time for them to let their hair down and to take things on without any planning.

P.Y. 1 / VII: A good time for associations and marriages or conversely divorces with difficulties managing them. Many contacts. Several proposals which are not always controlled by the subject. Good time for the appearance of artistic talents.

P.Y. 1 / VIII: A good time for many contacts in all sorts of areas, discovery of a passionate love, sudden and unexpected windfalls. Health is favored, even if medical treatment of a surgical intervention is required. Discovery of secrets, inventions. Morale high.

P.Y. 1 / IX: A good time to travel, return to studies, get a new qualification. Possibility of finding a new love abroad or with a foreign person. Success in examinations, even for progeny. A good time for writing. Appointment. Desire to get back to sports, to have a healthy life.

P.Y. 1 / X: A good time to buy property, the transformation of the home. Many administrative steps. Success in professional life, contact with the world of business, politics. Sometimes radical and sudden life changes. Renewed relationships with the father or grandparents.

P.Y. 1 / XI: good time for all kinds of contacts. Outings, travel, new adventures. Desire to have fun with no strings attached. Friendly relations are going well, but do not allow a lasting relationships. Discovery of new horizons. Feeling of total freedom.

P.Y. 1 / XII: A good time to discover new horizons but a little too agitated however, to be catholic. Romantic meetings favored, but difficulty mastering them. The commercial sector is doing well. Possibility of recovering from physical problems, illnesses. Desire to want to look after yourself, new energy to get back on track.

In Personal Year 2...

P.Y. 2 / I: Renewed popularity, contact with the family circle, which is not always easy. Forgotten conflicts may resurface. It's time to take stock of certain commitments, and change them if necessary. Beware of wild dreams and do not take anything that is said or woven for granted. Leveraging period to defuse a sometimes hectic climate in live, in association and with children.

P.Y. 2 / II: Period conducive to love, softness and embellishment. Unexpected windfalls. Commitments, success, thanks to a climate conducive to good understanding. Hardly letting your hair down, risk of giving in to indulgence. Particular attention to everything related to food. Desire to please.

P.Y. 2 / III: New links are forged. Importance of contact with siblings. Small constant and irregular moves often for business affairs or the family. Epistolary exchanges favored. Sometimes romance, adultery. Rejuvenation of the body. Possible life at two different addresses... or two homes.

P.Y. 2 / IV: A period where family interests dominate by being too heavy to bear at times. Business favored. Important place for children, animals too... Desire to procreate. Beautifying of the lifestyle. Marriage, union, signing of contracts. Possibility of moving. Water or its vicinity plays an important role.

P.Y. 2 / V: Beware of mirages and love at first sight, even if the love life is favored. The period is pleasant but hides pitfalls that must be avoided. Windfalls through gambling possible, or even presents. A period where the native wants to have fun. Children can be a source of joy. Travel, even weddings!

P.Y. 2 / VI: A period where doubt mar arise. Desire to organize their life, but sometimes lacking lucidity. Possible minor surgery. Makeover. Fragile psyche. Medical care to lavish on the family or in the professional environment. Learn to accept messiness caused by relatives. Red tape.

P.Y. 2 / VII: A period conducive to associations, signing contracts or their questioning. Delays associated with commitments already undertaken, can be completed ... Common ground. Harmony in married and family life. Artistic and creative domains favored. Musical environment. Seduction of others.

P.Y. 2 / VIII: Difficult period in terms of peace and harmony in married and/or family life. Sometimes conflicts with the mother. Separations or deaths. Bizarre or adulterous encounters. Beware of genital, sexual diseases. Death or separation can cause a profound questioning on the meaning of life. Contacts with dead people. Depression or lack of energy. Unexpected child.

P.Y. 2 / IX: Encounters with foreign people, or feeling of being invaded. Dreams favored. Be careful not to overly idealize that which holds true. Desire to discover new horizons. Period favorable to children or the spouse in terms of new studies. Distance from a loved one for professional reasons, or faraway travel. Discovery of new products in a commercial setting. In any case, keep your feet on the ground, confabulation.

P.Y. 2 / X: An aspect favorable to changes in a professional context, but a depressing period. Do not give in to the pessimism that can gain ground. times are tough in terms of authority, above all that related to superiors or the father. Contact with nature is advised. Relationships with family or with a spouse can be tense. Significance of nocturnal dreams ... taken into account. Desire to withdraw, to retreat. Important subordinates in the family circle (domestic, employees etc).

P.Y. 2 / XI: A crazy but exciting period. Female encounters are favored, travel too. Moves, travel, but despite everything a desire to settle. Female support in the fulfillment of projects. Success and popularity among friends. Luck with contacts. Be careful not to get involved in utopian projects, keep your feet firmly on the ground. The family can become a burden.

P.Y. 2 / XII: The desire to please and unite is heightened. Beware of wild dreams. A period favorable to living in peace. Contact with water is indicated ... but beware of drowning! The artistic environment is favorable. Links are renewed with family and particularly the mother. Hidden love. Do not want too much out of life... Imprisonment (symbolic or real).

In Personal Year 3...

P.Y. 3 / I: A period which may be disrupted because of difficulty taking the right path. Conflicts may arise with authority and siblings. Discussions are going well, but the outcome is not always very clear. Favorable period for the purchase of a vehicle and for small investments. Be careful when it comes to accidents. Misplaced words may cause hostile reactions.

P.Y. 3 / II: The climate may be displeasing despite a desire for harmony and peace. Romantic encounters may occur, but they need epistolary changes where a remoteness characterizes them. Desire to redo their lifestyle, to improve it. Favorable period for creativity, deep reflection on what the native wants to make their life better. Frivolousness.

P.Y. 3 / III: A disrupted period. A lot of trips, discussions. A period where the native can reconnect with siblings. Many contacts of all kinds not necessarily giving rewards immediately. A period of analysis, reflection. Desire to sing to dance, but perhaps also to see a shrink. Possible commercial or sports success. Epistolary exchanges.

P.Y. 3 / IV: Possible desire or obligation to move or to have another residence. Sometimes distance from the family home or return of persons having left. The schooling of children takes an important turn. Change of school. Adoption of an animal. Family secrets emerge. Contact with the public. Great cerebral creativity, fertile imagination. Desire to throw tantrums.

P.Y. 3 / V: Good period for success in exams for you or your children. Business is favored, success. Discussions are going well. Contacts with influential people, much movement. Events, society life. Desire to travel. Contact with the father. Life seems simple. Ideal period to learn to play a musical instrument or improve their technique.

P.Y. 3 / VI: A period favorable to putting things undertaken in the preceding months in order. Intense cerebral activity. Sometimes heated discussions. Anything that relates to writing or medicine is favored. Calm the critical mind and accept unexpected changes. Desire to play sports. Exacerbated competitive spirit.

P.Y. 3 / VII: A period of romantic encounter which forces a choice to be made. Proposals are underway but are of destabilizing. Desire to move with the loved person if possible. New associative contracts are valid. Decoration, art, beautification of the lifestyle. Discussion of contracts (employment contract for the loved person loved for example).

P.Y. 3 / VIII: Sometimes difficult news. Departure or loss of relatives. Change in the organization of life. Encounters with unusual people. Epistolary contacts with the distant. Change of vehicle or sometimes accidents. End of a period for a new sometimes diametrically opposite direction. Contact with the hereafter. Nightlife is favored. Sometimes scientific or otherwise discoveries. Beware of thieves.

P.Y. 3 / IX: A very favorable period for everything. Business, contacts of all kinds and even the desire to resume studies, writing etc. Many professional and commercial approaches. Departure abroad possible or exchanges with. Exacerbated curiosity and investigation. Beware of spreading yourself too thinly. Stay realistic in business and proposals. An enriched period.

P.Y. 3 / X: The serious is topical, fruitful but wise encounters. Ideas to implement long term projects are favorable. Real estate contacts, again about the subject's profession (professional or social advancement). Contact with professors, the elderly, tutors. Administrative steps. Signing of contracts.

P.Y. 3 / XI: Disturbed period, frequent movement and encounters with friends and their brother, if they have one. The talks are going well, learning to calm down. Desire to prove, to say everything. Travel, often by air. Excitability and brawls. Innovative ideas, rapid changes. Bizarre, strange events. Beware of accidents. Doesn't trust anything that is electric, lightning. A slightly crazy period.

P.Y. 3 / XII: A period where intuition is favored, as is a tendency towards introversion. Desire to get closer to the liquid element. Indecision in choices, but business affairs are favorable if stressful. Distraction, forgetfulness... Melancholy. Administrative approaches or minor ailments pose problems. Stay alert. Departure of a brother or sister. Possible losses. New and unnerving inspirations. Learn to calm down and to relax. Mental fatigue.

In Personal Year 4...

P.Y. 4 / I: A period marked by financial aspects. Reorganization and restructuring of the way in which the person manages their finances. Possible financial conflict with the administration or in connection with the family circle. Favorable aspect for declaring their love. Need to get rid of all that weighs them down, all that clutters life. Ideal to undertake improvement works to their home. Interest in that which relates to food. Making of very down to earth decisions.

P.Y. 4 / II: A pleasant period, favoring acquisitions, windfalls, but also romantic relationships. The conservative spirit is highlighted. Need for calm, tranquility. Quest for serenity. Homebody. Sometimes strong influence from the mother. Improvement and harmonization of the lifestyle. Manual tasks favored. Important decisions may be made to late.

P.Y. 4 / III: Disrupted period. Difficult discussions may involve siblings, if required. Frequent moves in professional or romantic terms may be difficult. Obligation to challenge and prove their values. Necessary epistolary exchanges. Favorable with respect to activities linked to image, photography.

P.Y. 4 / IV: Favorable for business and family life. Beautifying of the lifestyle. Earnings favored. Projects concerning children. Likely role of a mothering person (mother, grandmother, mother-in-law). Occasional desire to have an animal. Sometimes burdensome family obligations. Heavy atmosphere. The native can feel trapped.

P.Y. 4 / V: A period favoring elation, the desire to have fun, to think of oneself. Need to shine in socioprofessional and/or family terms. Desire to be seen at their best. The search for a certain lightness. Success in love. Overload of responsibilities linked to the expectations of relatives. Artistic environment, including musical favored. Exacerbated creativity. Desire for their children to succeed.

In case of conflict with the father, possible flattening of relationships. Importance of the surname in some contexts.

P.Y. 4 / VI: A delicate period possibly leading to its share of limitations and bitterness. Sometimes romantic disillusion or prevention of enjoying a romantic relationship. The person oscillates between a desire for the frivolous, lightness, love and a need meet their responsibilities and obligations. Favorable however, to healing. Excellent time for a makeover.

P.Y. 4 / VII: Confirmation, even fulfillment of contracts and commitments undertaking previously. Commitments characterized by their long term aspect. Take advantage of this period to achieve things (signing of contracts, loving relationship etc). Paternal or paternalistic presence and protection. Successful outcome of certain litigations. Desire to be supported. Be careful not to be too locked into the principles of life.

P.Y. 4 / VIII: A heavy period, in certain cases private. End or renewal of an old love (rediscovering a lost love). Climate conducive to conspiracies. Sometimes love or hidden decision making. Fantasies and/or exacerbated sexuality. Everything physiologically related to the genitals and the blood is to be monitored. Possible remoteness, death. Frustrations. However, a promise of renewal, a rebirth after sometimes difficult events. Possible inheritance.

P.Y. 4 / IX: Financial and property deals favored. Desire to travel far. Correspondence and/or encounter with people far away or of foreign origin. Desire to resume studies. Administrative and legal steps favored. Signing of contracts. Be particularly ware of the field of vision. A period full of love and romance. Joie de vivre. Pleasures of the table.

P.Y. 4 / X: A favorable period for the acquisition of property. Socioprofessional advancement. Recognition by their peers, but also by the father (presence, help etc). Beautification, upgrading of the lifestyle, both professionally and privately. Sometimes need to get closer to nature (mountains, among others), to experience a retreat.

P.Y. 4 / XI: A pleasant and exciting period marked by romantic and/or friendly encounters. Sympathetic support favoring the fulfillment and realization of projects. Outings and evenings out are on the program. Desire to travel as well. Renewal. Despite everything, some constraints may weigh on the smooth running of projects. Some delays are to be feared.

P.Y. 4 / XII: A period of tranquility, calm sometimes characterized by confinement, remoteness, even exile. A favorable period for business, to expanding the customer base. Difficult administrative steps. Love occurs. A romantic and sentimental period. Be careful not to become disillusioned.

In Personal Year 5...

P.Y. 5 / I: A desire to shake up that which is acquired, to question that which has been created or is going be. Meet new people, new opinions. Questioning of the environment. Increased excitability, nervousness, reactivity may lead to open conflicts. Travel. A good time to discover new horizons. Opportunities. Beware of accidents.

P.Y. 5 / II: Great creativity. Willingness to resolve conflicts, while keeping a certain distance. Harmonization of their environment. Exploration of new ways of doing things, manufacturing, designing. Favorable period for love, friendship. Possible restrictions. Sometimes slow in achieving goals. Need to show patience.

P.Y. 5 / III: A period marked by movement, contacts, openness and dialogue towards others. Beware of misplaced reactions but also of accidents. Do not overly conceal their intentions. Good period for learning and/or teaching. Risk of slimming through rather than achieving. Scattering. Favorable for outings. In some cases, conflicts with siblings.

P.Y. 5 / IV: A restrictive period. Difficulty in relation to the family (spouse and/or children). Problematic in terms of lifestyle. Prevention. Favorable period for renewing a client base. Beware of disillusions. Family/business constraints and/or responsibilities may interfere with the native's need for independence. Important role of the mother or women in the family circle.

P.Y. 5 / V: Favors relationships and the consideration of others. Culmination of new ideas. Creativity. Romantic encounters. Exaltation. Completion of an innovative project. Support and/or proposals from people may lead to success. Attraction to gambling. Everything forward-thinking and original is favored.

P.Y. 5 / VI: Restrictive period leading to some serious thinking. Need to look after their health. Ideals, horizons are limited. Analysis and introspection are favored on the other hand. Stress. The context leads to withdrawal. Consider the need to stay calm, to go out, to get some fresh air.

P.Y. 5 / VII: Disturbed period in terms of relationships, associations. Questioning. Willingness to change habits. New objectives can displease the spouse, associates. New romantic and/or associative encounters posing problems compared to the existing situation. Desire to be liked, to please loved ones. Favorable to anything related to art (great creativity).

P.Y. 5 / VIII: Discovery in every sense of the word. Sometimes updating of secrets. Things hidden may resurface. Encounters with unusual friends, not part of the usual environment. Contact through modern means of communication. Sometimes danger in relation to changes, radical, sudden, unexpected separations. Beware of fire.

P.Y. 5 / IX: A period favorable to the questioning of their achievements, their knowledge. Desire to be educated, to take long trips. Need to feel free, independent, free from the daily routine. Sometimes professional guidance. New ideas, new designs for life that the native wants to share (or even impose depending on the chart). Opportunities to grasp. Happiness is found far away from home.

P.Y. 5 / X: A period favoring a form of stability but with obligations to change surrounding structures (professional life. Restructuring). Contact with people in positions of influence. Possibility of relying on weak individuals and confidence to complete their projects while respecting a very specific path. New direction in their career. Desire to be free, to have their difference valued particularly at socioeconomic level. A form of inertia comes despite loved ones.

P.Y. 5 / XI: Great sense of freedom. Desire to have fun, travel, discover the world. Exaltation. Desire to get involved. Sometimes scattering. Excitability, nervousness to be calmed. Revolutionary, reactive mind. Optimism accompanying the person. Importance of friends, relationships. Meetings. Anything that relates to the esoteric and/or cutting-edge fields (new sciences) is favored.

P.Y. 5 / XII: A rather soft, calm, even sentimental, nostalgic period. Desire for encounters in a serene, tranquil environment. Significance of dreams, the imagination. Sometimes romantic encounter. Life sometimes wants secrets. Concessions in terms of certain limitations in their environment. However, favors meditation, introspection, retreat etc. Starting with themselves.

In Personal Year 6...

P.Y. 6 / I: A conflicting period. Difficult relationships with hierarchy. Opposition to ideas. Questioning, sometimes violent, where it is advisable to explain. Excellent for taking advantage of the rethinking of a project, realizing it again. Separation possible. Breaking and/or signing of contracts. Possible promotion in administrative, military areas and everywhere where authority is present.

P.Y. 6 / II: A rather harmonious period. Monitor finances even if on the whole the aspect helps conflicting situations. Favorable to body care, food and to caring for their health more generally. Importance of hygiene in life. If necessary, the dominance of the relationship with a sister (or any person occupying that spot).

P.Y. 6 / III: A period of intense reflection, inner questioning, analysis. Frequent small trips (sometimes to see a loved one). Desire to help others, to do a favor. Contact with siblings causing important discussions. Favorable for self-analysis, introspection and everything related to writing.

P.Y. 6 / IV: Everything related to the family, hospital is highlighted. Beautifying of their life style and/or moving house. Creativity and business favored. Desire to mother to take care of loved ones. Special connection with animals. The influence is focused on the person's close environment. Sometimes renewed contacts with the family.

P.Y. 6 / V: Success in the implementation of structures enabling the development of new projects. Pleasant period. New encounters. Consideration of the advice and desires of loved ones. Challenging relationships. Excitement for their projects. Remember to stay realistic. Ambition and success emerge. Sometimes recovery from a disease.

P.Y. 6 / VI: An ideal period for expressing feelings, their design for life and rethinking the old in order to reorganize their life. Administrative steps. Be careful not to be overly mentally agitated. A good time to care for themselves and/or to care for others. Despite oppositions, a desire to find a consensus, a common ground. Tendency towards pessimism.

P.Y. 6 / VII: A harmonious period. Flattening of oppositions. Desire to please the partner (spouse, associate etc). Everything is going well. The native arranges, demonstrates good will. Often administrative steps and/or legal advice. Marriage and contracts of all kinds. Sometimes divorce. Favorable for developing a new taste for the arts (music). Society life, outings.

P.Y. 6 / VIII: A problematic, bizarre period favorable to the reconsideration of oneself, care but disturbing in terms of the discovery of hidden things, secrets, often leading to disagreements, even separations. Remain trusting. Possible inheritance (sometimes from the spouse). Sometimes loss of a family member. Beware of accidents. Hidden loves, secrets.

P.Y. 6 / IX: A desire to learn. Favorable to learning and meeting people who share their opinions, desires. Desire to come together and share a single environment. Contact with foreign people. Sometimes sentimental journey. Interest in works of art, collections. Desire to relax without excluding new goals and the search for new horizons. Administrative and/or legal approaches.

P.Y. 6 / X: A period favorable to the improvement of their lifestyle and/or professional life. Sometimes heavy work. Socioprofessional constraints are rather heavy to bear. Things are not progressing as fast as expected. So knowing how to overcome their pessimism and make projects from the preceding years a reality. Laying foundations. Monitor the skeleton.

P.Y. 6 / XI: A rather positive period even if it causes disruptions and an inner agitation. Keep a cool head. Think things through before acting. Cutting-edge technologies and innovations can cause problems. Discussions and conflicts with some friends, not excluding happy settlements. Be discreet. Do not stagger their projects too much. Also respect the wishes of relatives.

P.Y. 6 / XII: Restrictions. A period marked by a form of duality between the difficulty in making their projects a reality (waiting, obstacles) and harmony promised if the native takes the time to slow down, rest. Love is present but so is stress because of their obligations in relation to others. Find a balance. Desire to relax, to get closer to the water... A delay in epistolary exchanges.

In Personal Year 7...

P.Y. 7 / I: An ideal period for implementing a project, finding the necessary support for its completion. Wrestling interests, rivalries. Despite everything, a presence of energy necessary to fight. Be careful not to escape reality. Do not get involved in ill-considered businesses. Do not systematically look for conflict. Stay alert. Unhoped for support. Emulation, competitive mind.

P.Y. 7 / II: Favorable to romance. Sentimentality. Harmonization of the emotional. But also a desire to beautify their surroundings, to have fun, to have money. Luck. Windfalls. Investment. Accounting. Favors the purchase of pretty things. Be careful not to become overweight and eat too much.

P.Y. 7 / III: A sometimes difficult period due to having to justify oneself, to have an answer for everything. Obligation to prove, to highlight their strategies to obtain the help of others. Favorable to training for oneself or others. Favors that which relates to itinerant business. Also difficult due to many trips (often in conjunction with business). Be careful of investments. Sometimes supported by a brother or an uncle.

P.Y. 7 / IV: A lucky period, favorable to investments, to the purchase of nearby businesses. Windfalls. Family well-being. Beautifying of the lifestyle. Desire to have fun in a family context. Sweetness of life. Appreciated presence of a woman (often the mother). Increased popularity. Intuition favored. Sometimes relocation.

P.Y. 7 / V: A period of luck. Favorable running. Good omens. Be careful not to get drunk on success. Success of children. Playfulness, fun, going out, meeting people. Brightness, recognition. Creativity highlighted. Favoring a musical environment. Everything is very tainted. Contact with very influential people.

P.Y. 7 / VI: A rather difficult period due to restrictive administrative obligations. Therefore, it is better to use this time to reorder their paperwork and their life in general. Favorable to recovery from some diseases. End of physical difficulties if relevant. Dynamism. Possible litigious regulations. Be careful not to be too haughty and distant in relation to others' difficulties.

P.Y. 7 / VII: An excellent period for finalizing contracts. Harmonization of their partnerships (couple, association etc). Favorable to healthy windfalls particularly in terms of their associations. Promotes the artistic domain. Desire to share, to make peace if necessary, to feel useful, kind. Prefers consensus to confrontation.

P.Y. 7 / VIII: A period of discovery, of changing life goals, or redirection. Travel and/or meeting new, unusual, sometimes curious people. Administrative steps, even legal. Unexpected windfalls. Desire to discover new horizons. Teaching of hidden things. Changes, the unexpected can throw the native. A favorable but strange period on the whole.

P.Y. 7 / IX: Possible professional redirection with training. A period often synonymous with a new direction in their life. Sometimes steps to be performed to promote windfalls. Desire to meet people like ourselves. Seeking support in the professional field. Importance of schooling of children. A favorable period for reviewing and/or updating contracts or committing to legal steps. The native becomes curious about their environment.

P.Y. 7 / X: Professional career favored. Advancement, promotion and enhancement of their occupation. Deals. Buying a property. Ability to get involved, to assume an overload of work, not excluding the possibility of making retreats (closer to nature, feeling calm, countryside, animals). Help & support for their children at the professional level if required. Significance of dreams.

P.Y. 7 / XI: Exciting period with a desire to break free from constraints, a desire for travel, freedom. Meeting interesting and influential friends. Unexpected things that challenge life, not necessarily negatively. Fluctuating windfalls. Do not invest in the first idea that comes along. Show patience. Favorable to the exploration of new horizons. Aid given to friends. The opposite is also true. Do not fall into the utopia.

P.Y. 7 / XII: A calm, tranquil, restful period also favoring business. Desire to escape an overly heave lifestyle. Need to get rid of constraints and disagreements present in their life. Good for meditating and spiritual meetings. Intuition favored. Desire to get closer to water. Travel in this direction.

In Personal Year 8...

P.Y. 8 / I: Emphasis on making radical, even hasty decisions. All or nothing depending on the chart. Gambling, luck building on the opportunities presented or loss, destruction. Possible disappearance literally and figuratively of loved ones. Beware of inconsiderate head butts that may lead to serious consequences. Risk of bodily injury (head in particular). End of one life cycle and beginning of another. Beware of theft, fire. Possible losses or unexpected windfalls.

P.Y. 8 / II: Discovery of hidden things in terms of love and/or hidden love. A period unfavorable to harmony of the couple. Disagreements may lead to a separation. Losing money. Ill-considered spending. But protection from a woman is also possible. Beware of health (sore throat). Anything that relates to sexuality is not favored. Beware of excess in this area.

P.Y. 8 / III: A very favorable period for anything relating to technology, relationships established with others and the clarification of many outstanding problems. Sometimes hidden secrets concerning siblings may resurface. Beware of trips, problems with their vehicle (possible change). Communication with the favored divine spheres for those who follow this path. Evenings, outings, meetings in the first place.

P.Y. 8 / IV: A difficult period in terms of family atmosphere. Family conflicts or family secrets resurface Sometimes separation, break-up, departure of a child, death, inheritance. Duty of care in some cases. Favorable for business in terms of changing clientele. Financial shocks. Expenses and/or windfalls. Expatriation or relocation possible.

P.Y. 8 / V: A period that may lead to unexpected financial gains, encounters of all kinds. Sometimes the end of a business to start a new one. Change of perspectives, of schooling for oneself or children. Desire to assert their authority, to rethink things. Need to get rid of all constraints. Claiming their freedom. Challenging oneself. Questioning of their identity, their inner self. Sometimes discovering the esoteric and its implications. Monitoring the heart.

P.Y. 8 / VI: An uncomfortable period, full of the unexpected, even bad luck. Introspection, analysis. Desire to see a shrink. Reorganizing, planning, change in strategies in both their goals and heir way of living with the impression of not controlling everything. Favorable to care, medicine, recovery from certain diseases. Difficult relationship with the animal world.

P.Y. 8 / VII: Often synonymous with break-ups, separations, divorce. In all cases, these ideas are in the air. Termination of contract and new commitment. Uncomfortable period where people make wrongs right, commitments are not always required. Premature end of certain projects or remembering of forgotten projects. Discovery of hidden things in terms of the partner (couple associate). Obligation to meet certain commitments against nature. Uncertain period where you are better to wait for good times.

P.Y. 8 / VIII: Destabilizing, sometimes conflicting period. Destruction and complete restructuring in life linked to a radical awareness. Updating of hidden activities. Sometimes discovery of new potential. Meeting strange people. Connection with the occult, death, hidden things or a desire to live secretly. End of a cycle. A favorable period for surgery. Rather pleasant from a financial point of view.

P.Y. 8 / IX: A period which may lead to litigations the outcome of which is usually favorable. An often unexpected improvement financially and/or professionally because of the appearance of support, assistance or an unexpected event. Desire to explore new horizons, changing lifestyle, to invest in new projects (finance, business, etc). Contact with the foreign. Travel.

P.Y. 8 / X: A difficult, sometimes chaotic, violent period causing professional disagreements, isolation, even to the extreme of imprisonment. Hidden things, an overload of work may characterize the native's occupation. Favorable to rebuild their home, transforming their inside, rebuilding. Disappearance of elderly people from the family circle. More frequent and intense dreams. Need to manage their heritage. Property affairs.

P.Y. 8 / XI: Explosive period characterized by anger, misplaced reactions with others, often following revelations. Favorable to discovery. Need to distance oneself may be synonymous with separation, a long journey. The desire to go to the end of the earth is strong. Separations from old friends. Discovery of new ones. Outings. Need to exhibit lucidity, to not indulge in their utopias. Monitoring the blood.

P.Y. 8 / XII: A period of exile, of separation from the environment. Difficult compared with responsibilities and difficulties linked to an overload of work through the obligation of being present to help, support. Hence a pressure causing an urge to withdraw and/or introspect. Be careful of everything related to water (flooding, drowning etc). A financially difficult period which obliges them to review their plans which may end in windfalls. Mystical communication, relationships with the hereafter favored. Do not pull the wool over people's eyes.

In Personal Year 9...

P.Y. 9 / I: An ideal period to achieve their objectives. The dynamics of ambitions are particularly favored. Important contacts. Desire to dominate the world, to consolidate their strength and willingness. Feeling of invincibility. A period favorable to claiming (lawyer, union or other activity of this kind). Desire to break with some habits, all that doesn't please, all that hinders the smooth running of their life.

P.Y. 9 / II: A period favorable to finance in general. Desire to have fun, to buy nice things. Be careful not to overly benefit from the pleasures of life, beware of excess, including those of the table. An ideal period for doing their accounts. Pleasant romantic relationships. Anything related to expression (dress, appearance etc) is highlighted. Significant female support.

P.Y. 9 / III: A period favoring the areas of communication, expression, writing. Desire to meet challenges to prove their abilities. Sometimes buying a vehicle. Education favored. Learning or training others. Flattening of some rivalries. Meeting characters playing a guiding role in life and profession. Importance of epistolary exchanges.

P.Y. 9 / IV: Bodes well for moving at both family and professional level. Looks for a pleasant lifestyle despite some constraints caused by loved ones (often family). Support and presence of women. Anything related to domestic life is favored. Desire to live near water. Visit from people living far away. Review their insurance contracts. Sometimes looking for financial support.

P.Y. 9 / V: Success in projects (initiatives, legal approaches, writing, contracts etc). Favorable contact with the foreign and/or different people from everyday life. Favorable to windfalls. Loves are happy. Pleasant period. Playful mind. Possible meetings with influential people that have an impact on the native's life.

P.Y. 9 / VI: A very favorable period for completing all sorts of projects. Desire to organize, to develop, to structure. Anything related to administrative steps, daily writings, paperwork is important. Recovery from certain diseases possible. Increased vitality. General improvement in health. Desire to cut corners, to relax their intransigent. Ability to reflect, think, organize.

P.Y. 9 / VII: Period of signatures, commitments requiring them to not get carried away, to reflect properly on the scope of their actions. Do not become deluded. Stay realistic, pragmatic. The quest and search for a peaceful climate does not always work out. Remoteness of the loved ones for different reasons (different workplace, romantic encounter etc). The professional life interferes with the private life. The period requires compromises to be made to obtain the best balance possible.

P.Y. 9 / VIII: Making their dreams a reality. Mystical support. Anything relating to intuition is favored. Listening to oneself. Extra sensory communication. Brilliance. Business favored. Return of people living far away or forgotten. Desire to travel, to explore new horizons but also to live in peace. A good period to care for their health. However, they should watch their food.

P.Y. 9 / IX: Achievement of desires, objectives. Making their hopes a reality. An often exciting period. However, pay attention to utopias. Anything related to business, studies, to financial aspects is favored. Unexpected remoteness of relatives. A generally pleasant period. Transcendence. Willingness to transcend.

P.Y. 9 / X: Socioprofessional progression favored. Increased responsibilities. A period favorable to taking sometimes political stances. Desire to build or to renovate a country house, to have a pleasant lifestyle meeting their aspirations to have a quieter life. Easing the burden of existential contingencies. Everything becomes a little easier. Sometimes a period of wage or professional status claim. Questioning of knowledge. Remoteness of a child (due to schooling, boarding etc).

P.Y. 9 / XI: Desire to conquer the world, to make their own way, to feel free, to stand on their own two feet, without god or a leader. Feeling of invincibility, total freedom. Desire to explore new horizons, to make long journeys, to go on an adventure, to meet new people. Favorable friendships in a socioprofessional context. Beware of reactivity. Do not over-revolt or react violently to anything that displeases or bothers you. Excellent period to discover other ways of living.

P.Y. 9 / XII: Search for tranquility, peace, the sweetness of life. A rather calm period where the native irons out disagreements. A philosopher's mind, more conciliatory towards their loved ones. Desire to take a vacation. Interest in places close to water. Beware of excess pleasures. Sometimes indulging. Favorable to love, finance.

In Personal Year 11...

P.Y. 11 / I: A revolutionary period. Great reactivity, sometimes violent. Desire to impose their views, ideas. Need for recognition. Desire to be free, to push the limits, to have fun, to explore all sorts of new horizons. Reckoning with their environment not excluding looking for a consensus. Beware of sudden trips. Think things through before acting. Do not do things on the spur of the moment.

P.Y. 11 / II: A period favoring success in love. Recognition. Slowing down, slowness in the fulfillment of objectives. Quest for the good life. Desire to have fun. Head butts in terms of acquisitions. Beware of overindulgent expenses.

P.Y. 11 / III: Many trips. Obligation to express their desires, sometimes to impose them through words. Strong adversity. Antagonisms. Wit, lucid. High reactivity. Words and speech are favored. Quest for brotherhood in the broadest sense of the term. Meetings and useful contacts, sometimes extraordinary. The action occurs outside of the box.

P.Y. 11 / IV: A restrictive but favorable period in terms of redevelopment of their family context. Desire to rebel. Possible relocation. New assignments. A slightly heavy presence of the mother (or a woman). Potential obligations vis à vis her. Renewed popularity. Favorable in terms of clientele. Children or animals may constitute a barrier to the person's free expression.

P.Y. 11 / V: A period with a feeling of freedom and independence. Desire to do what we want. Many contacts. Many projects. Desire to shine, to gain exposure in society, to meet people, to express their potential. Leaves little room for criticism or a contradicting mind. Passions and romantic encounters favored. A taste for music, evenings out, outings, gaming, holidays. Desire to please.

P.Y. 11 / VI: A period characterized by a form of mental disturbance. Sometimes messy ideas. A love at first sight or passion may end suddenly. Difficulty to master their organization. Antagonisms. Need to deal with wishes problems other than their own. New ideas are going well but are not finding the necessary fertile ground to develop. Learn to be calm, to control their nervousness.

P.Y. 11 / VII: Charming encounters. Romantic relationships and/or friendships favored. Desire to please their spouse, their associate. The native shows themselves at their best. Many projects and/or meetings but difficulty in choosing. Do not confuse love and friendship, difficult differentiating between the two. Desire to go out, to have fun. A good period to highlight their artistic talents. Disruption in terms of their preconceived ideas. Certain principles of life can be shaken. Awareness of the true nature of people who surround the native.

P.Y. 11 / VIII: Freedom from prohibitions. Outlaw spirit. Clarification of some gray areas in their life. Hidden loves. Desire to travel, to leave the ordinary course of life. Contact with the hereafter. A disturbed period during which questioning, breaks with daily life, profound changes can occur. Favorable to start new projects with some discretion. Contact with different, non-standard people, far away from normal life. Be careful not to make a clean sweep of everything the native has experienced up to now.

P.Y. 11 / IX: An excellent period for studying, resuming training, updating their knowledge, meeting influential people. Freedom from certain financial, legal, administrative constraints. Increased desire for freedom and independence. Beware of exaltation, which can cause a distancing from their relatives. This remoteness may also have professional or other reasons. Preoccupations compared to the schooling of children. Upsurge of militancy and demands.

P.Y. 11 / X: Period of constraints, slowing down of projects. Possible changes in the socioprofessional context but which will bear fruit later. Difficulty asserting their points of views, their desires. The desire for change is hard to be made a reality. Sense of limitations. Pessimism, bitterness. A good period to learn to relax, to take a retreat (country), beautifying their lifestyle.

P.Y. 11 / XI: Disturbed, exciting period. Be careful not to scatter yourself too thinly. The projects are well underway even if they do not become reality for the moment. Desire to emancipate oneself, to have some fun. Rejection of constraints. Travel, trips. Outings, freedom, independence, discovery of new horizons. Favorable to everything related the emotional. Meet new people and/or reunions with friends and lost loves. Sometimes powerful antagonisms with people not sharing the same aspirations.

P.Y. 11 / XII: A restrictive period. What is done does not. Feeling of being locked away, not being able to complete their projects. Disenchantment. Obligation to deal with life as it comes, to adapt to external events. However, the support of a loved one is favored. Support, love of close and disinterested people. Do not rebel, deal with it. Favorable to everything that revolves around music. Playfulness. Evenings with friends.

In Personal Year 22...

P.Y. 22 / I: A serious period. Difficult to make projects a reality. Obligation to consider their action in the long term, to integrate the notion of time. Increased responsibilities. May mean disruptions in the socioprofessional domain. Degradation of property or transformation of lifestyle. Disappearance of elderly people. Decreased vitality and yet, a resurgence of a certain authoritarianism.

P.Y. 22 / II: Meeting younger people. Often making a romantic life a reality. Desire to acquire both concrete and beautiful things. Anything that affects the aesthetic, the body, magnetism is favored. Questioning in relation to food.

P.Y. 22 / III: A restrictive period, obliging questioning. Antagonisms. Can begin a project but has trouble directing it one way or another. Meetings and support of younger people. Sometimes has the predominant role of the eldest of the siblings. Favorable to everything relating to technology, the industrial, plans. Know how to be light when needed. Renewed juvenility.

P.Y. 22 / IV: Domestic constraints. Weight of family responsibilities. Obligation to care for their family, to be more present, to engage further. Sometimes difficult relationships with the mother in general. Feeling of imprisonment. Obstacles in socioprofessional life. Learn to suspend your authoritarianism with loved ones. Life may lead to the resurgence emotions that the native does not ordinarily express.

P.Y. 22 / V: Conflicts of authority. Rivalries with the father. Misunderstandings sometimes. Desire to impose their views, ideas. Increased sensitivity. Difficult to question oneself. Feeling of not beings loved or recognized. Sometimes difficulties with children. However, favors socioprofessional development, the recognition by their peers. Renewed outbreak of their responsibilities.

P.Y. 22 / VI: A period pushing pessimism. Everything related to planning, implementation of structure, organization is favored, but leaves little room for fun. Intensity of work. Obligation to excel, to be responsible in their occupation. Adversity but ability to cope with it. Positive for analysis, introspection but also tidying, putting everything related to paperwork and particularly administrative documents in order. Sometimes frigidity.

P.Y. 22 / VII: A very favorable period for the signing of contract, taking positions, commitments. Feeling of easily being able to apply their principles of life. Support and/or influence of elderly people. Desire to help others, to serve, to do something good. Sometimes charitable works. Righter of wrongs. Long term commitment with the loved one and/or associate.

P.Y. 22 / VIII: Retreat. Introspection. Significant inner transformation. Sometimes mourning, inheritance of property. Feeling of easily perceiving people. Increased mediumship. Contact with the forces of nature. Discovery of hidden things. Stigmatization of conflicting relationships. A certain hardness in relationships. Possible surgical operation or medical treatment. Problem with animals. Exacerbated sexuality.

P.Y. 22 / IX: Consolidation of ongoing projects. Ability to help oneself using law texts and/or terms of a contract to take a stance and act, to force destiny, to impose their views, to bring others along. Increased strength of conviction. Favorable to provide the means to complete projects. In some cases, resignation, retirement, loneliness and/or misunderstanding. Constraints due to approaches requiring distance from the usual course.

P.Y. 22 / X: A quiet period, favorable to meditation, to life in the country. Peace. Construction, real estate, contact with nature. Sometimes distance from family life. Solitude. Political positions. Commitments in occupational structures. Reorganization in their profession (change or transformation of premises). Do not lapse into a form of authoritarianism and/or intransigence.

P.Y. 22 / XI: A disrupted period. Questioning but despite everything the presence of influential friends. Difficult to retain their knowledge in a period of significant change. Sometimes obliged to cope with trips, travel, meetings which nevertheless turn out to be profitable. The native brings a lot to their friendships. Great ability to help those around them.

P.Y. 22 / XII: A period of exclusion, forced retreat, isolation. Favorable to meditation, contemplation. Loneliness not necessarily experienced in a negative way. The native distances themselves from social life, from everyday life. Back to basics. Feeling of heaviness also. Things are not moving. High demand for loved ones to be helped. Spiritual period. Watch out for water leaks, floods.

CHAPTER VIII

Comparison of different methods

"They are not right by simple virtue of so many of them being wrong!"

Michel Colucci

It goes without saying that a new method provokes interest if, and only if, it is backed up by proof. As we have seen, the Maia method does not take the subject's birth surname into account but his biological mother's, which in fact is the same thing for those who were registered under their mother's surname.

In order to compare and verify the effectiveness of the Maia method, we are going to study some famous dead people: a famous director (amongst other things), a head of state, a world famous singer and a visionary writer. Since using the mother's birth surname modifies the numerological personality markers, we will focus on character, aspiration and potential.

Apart from the reading for the first figure in which me and Michel will give our own interpretation, the numerological analyses have been created using the interpretation engine of the latest version (5 at the time of writing) of the online software Numeyoga. It is clear that the computer program has no knowledge of the historical dimension of these characters. It simply delivers an analysis based on the interpretation of the Aspiration, Potential and Expression numbers calculated using all of the first and middle names declared at birth and the mother's birth surname.

Orson Wells
born on the 06/05/1915
to a mother with the birth surname Ives

Aspiration 8 - Potential 11 - Expression 1
Missing numbers : 2, 3, 7 & 8

The reading of this famous person's numerological chart is irrefutable proof of the pertinence and effectiveness of the Maia method. While it seems pointless to specify that he was a brilliant American director, actor, writer, producer and scriptwriter, we must do so in order to find the parallels between his life and the numerological reading. This passionate and particularly inventive man managed to revolutionize every aspect of the seventh art with great gusto. He did not hesitate for a second to deviate from the beaten path and this brought him great notoriety. It should not be forgotten that he received many laudatory reviews even though the public at the time were not yet able to apprehend or appreciate this cinematographic revolution. This is proof that he was ahead of his time and that he never hesitated in his exploration of new horizons. He was without a doubt a pioneer and the Maia method is going to reveal this personality, and much more besides, in his chart.

First of all, we think it is necessary and indispensable to stress that his life path 27/9 reveals a true humanist nature, an extreme sensibility and a natural empathy, all of which allowed him to apprehend the world in a holistic way. This trait made him a non-combative person who did not seek to force his point of view on others or make them follow him. The natural diplomacy of 9's and their ability to overcome obstacles was extremely present in this figure who remained nonetheless mysterious. Throughout his life he always strove, whether consciously or not, to be impalpable and difficult to apprehend. Most of us in possession of a revolutionary method would want to impose it on others, but this was not the case for him. He expressed his sensibility much more through artistic expression that through the vindication of his discoveries; he showed rather than imposed. This figure is, and will remain, mysterious and in any case that is what he left us with. The indefinable mysterious intuitive and inspired nature of this source element is strongly emphasized irrespective of the method used because it is linked to his date of birth.

The "traditional" method taking into account his first name Orson (he has no middle names) and his family name Wells would reveal a person with an Aspiration 22, a Potential 9 and an Expression 4. However, this does not at all correspond to this person's innovative mind. The classical method portrays an entity who does not in any way want to question the established way of doing things (4 and 22 are static and conformist numbers, the exact opposite of revolutionary). This would mean that Orson Wells was a conformist who did not want to rock the boat. Frankly, that description does not resemble him in the slightest.

On the other hand, the Maia method, which takes into account his mother's maiden name Ives instead of Wells, reveals an Aspiration 8, a Potential 11 and an Expression 1.

It is not possible to disagree that under the cover of a diplomatic and consensual 9 lurked an assertive spirit which denounced society's mistakes and in particular its power struggles. No doubt his karmic memory knows more than anything the effects of greed which makes people want to impose their own points of view on others. The 8, in this particular case, reveals a quest for power that was no doubt present in his previous lives. Therefore he, more than anyone, thanks to his natural empathy, had a sharpened awareness of it. In any event, this is what he managed to convey through images.

As for the 11, it highlights his inventiveness, his verve and his ability to explore previously unexplored cinematographic territory. This master number contains energy; it wants to free itself from the weight of tradition. In short, it wants to explode. Once again it is useful to emphasize that the karma linked to this master number will multiply the number of back roads punctuating this great man's career and life. Despite his determination, he will face many obstacles and overwhelming incomprehension from his contemporaries.

His Expression number 1 pushed him to start projects and impose but this virile expression (1) does not always complete what it has started. Pioneering 1 often starts things but only rarely finishes them, tending to rely on other people to finish the job… Therein lies one of the aforementioned back roads. Furthermore, Orson Wells, in his time, had too many opponents to be able to rely on his juniors or even his colleagues. 1's are innovators and, whether or not they recognize it, they need to be surrounded by people who believe in their projects. That is why Orson Well makes us think of an unfinished work.

Nevertheless, for some people, he remains a sort of "foo fighter" (of Martian origin?) who beat many new paths that he was the only one to explore in his lifetime and that he did all that only for himself. He did not impose them on others, no doubt due to a lack of obvious support but more because of his true nature 9. It is not always easy to understand geniuses!

General de Gaulle
Charles André Joseph Pierre Marie
born on the 22/11/1890
to a mother with the birth surname Maillot

Aspiration 1 - Potential 1 - Expression 11
No missing number

This man was gifted with a complete personality, driven by an independent mind and a proactive nature. The leader in him carefully controlled his path; he was determined to fight anything that anyone tried to impose on him and he never deviated from his route. Who could deny that those character traits belong to him? Consequently, as we know that number 1 represents this personality type, it seems impossible that it would not appear in this man's chart. Any numerologist, even one with little experience, would be excited to see the strength of the numbers revealed by the Maia method. I do not know of any other numerological combinations better able to define him. Aspiration and Potential 1!

The French method, with its analysis based on the first name Charles and the birth surname de Gaulle, reveals an aspiration number 2 (opposed to 1), a Potential 5 and an Expression 7. Suffice it to say we are no longer talking about the same person!

The American method, which, in addition to the birth surname and first name, takes into account all of the registered middle names, reveals an Aspiration 8, a Potential 6 and an Expression 5. We still have not seen the number 1. Using these methods we obtain charts in which we can of course find corresponding points but which contain too many contradictions. However, with General de Gaulle, we are intrinsically approaching the archetype of number 1 which is associated with the astrological signs Aries and Leo. He is also a leader symbolized by the master number 11 (two further 1's). This is an easy way of showing the strength of the new method presented in this book. And here is the proof.

The expression number 11 revealed by the Maia method characterizes the strength, willpower and exceptional determination of this man. He is always driven by the need to strive for greater things, in accordance with his thirst for morality and fairness. He is independent, knows what he is doing and does not like anybody else telling him how to act.

He is at the helm and is capable of taking to the open seas in a second but, as he is hard to predict, it is sometimes difficult to follow him. His vitality is proportional to his ability to keep promises. He is determined and opinionated and can easily maintain a calm exterior even in times of internal turmoil. He is much more emotional and tense than he appears. He sometimes becomes angry but quickly returns to his ideal image of generosity and goodwill.

He is influenced by his past but seeks to distance himself from it in order to be more authentic. He is eternally dissatisfied because he sets himself unattainable targets. He is extremely demanding which sometimes makes him disagreeable.

With an Aspiration number 1, his deepest desire is to forge ahead by proving how efficient he is. He distinguishes himself through his originality. He can count on the help of others to succeed. He is at ease when the winds change, even if it is for the worse, because 1's like adversity as it gives them the opportunity to courageously promote their aspirations and advance situations and to find in this action the recognition they are seeking.

Was de Gaulle not this grand 1 marching down the avenue des Champs Elysées when his country was liberated?

His Potential number 1 indicates that he wants to throw himself into grand-scale projects, to be the one who makes the decisions and succeeds, sometimes at the expense of his personal life. He loves beautiful things, is particularly fond of a comfortable life and is sensitive to his own feelings yet he sometimes feels that something is missing. However, he has the means to be financially autonomous through his own initiatives whilst also keeping in mind that he needs professional independence in order to give the best of himself.

A General de Gaulle without a single number 1 in his core personality numbers? It would make no sense!

Edith Piaf
Edith Giovanna
born on the 19/12/1915
to a mother with the birth surname Maillard

Aspiration 6 - Potential 4 - Expression 1 (10)
No missing number

Internationally renowned, Edith Piaf's career is the very image of her desire to always move forward, despite the numerous hard knocks that she experienced along the way. The numerological analysis carried out using the Maia method describes the personality of the singer and actress perfectly, her sharp sensibilities and her ability to overcome obstacles.

A person with an Expression number 1 is strong-willed, ambitious and shows authority. She is confident that she has the means to succeed and will have the opportunity to fulfill her potential. She is driven by passion (*is passion not the central theme in Piaf's songs?*). She knows how to organize, guide, direct and take initiative (*Edith Piaf mentored many young artists including Yves Montand and Georges Moustaki, to name but two*). She will blossom in a career in which she will assume the role of leader or at least one in which she is independent. She has a tendency to project a father-role onto her husband which could cause problems.

While external events may render her dependant on others (*Edith Piaf's life was punctuated by knocks*), a personality with an expression 1 can always depend on its own intuitions and creativity to manage situations (*Edith Piaf sang in Paris during the German occupation and evokes the resistance in songs containing double meanings such as "tu es partout" (you are everywhere)*). She may have problems with hierarchy, with the powers-that-be tarnishing her fame and/or limiting her influence for a period in her life (*the assassination of, amongst others, the night club owner Louis Leplée who was the first to discover Edith, was at the origin of a scandal that overshadowed the early days of the young singer's career*).

The Aspiration 6 describes a person who deeply desires to live responsibly and on an equal footing with her close friends and family. She is appreciated for her kindness and availability. She is looking for other people who share her values. The more her partner resembles her in this quest for affection and dialogue (e.g. someone with the same aspiration number 6), the stronger the couple will be, whatever happens in her lifetime. A person with this aspect often finds great love through friendship. She is sensitive to the gestures and attentions of others, is never at rest and knows how to give the best of herself (*did Jean Cocteau not say of Edith Piaf on his deathbed that he had "never known someone less mean with her soul. She did not spend it but lavished it; she was throwing gold out of the windows"?*) That said, she is characterized by a sort of naivety, thinking that nobody would ever really think bad thoughts about her. Devoted, she seeks approval for her actions in the eyes of others. More than other people, she needs to be loved (*this expectation probably took hold of Piaf in her miserable early childhood*).

In practical terms, with a Potential number 4, the person gradually succeeds because she is hard-working, organized and patient. Others can count on her. She knows how to show integrity and respect for the rules. It is all a question of timing and the day will come when she will be able to demonstrate her skills in an activity that suits her (*this is exactly what happened to Edith Piaf who achieved her goals despite her difficult beginnings*).

This person is not always at ease with material affairs. She is frightened of not having enough and so puts all her energies into feeling financially secure. Despite some difficulties and set-backs, she manages it. She must try to avoid any pointless and badly thought through expenditure in order to maintain a balance.

She loves surrounding herself with useful objects (e.g. books and tools) and so it is likely that she will manage to construct a home that meets her expectations because, for that person, these things are necessary for her to express her potential and blossom. Her environment must resound with nature, countryside and roots. Family life holds a particular importance for her, whether this comes from her real family or the one that she creates for herself.

Jules Verne
Jules Gabriel
born on the 08/02/1828
to a mother with the birth surname Allote de la Fuÿe

Aspiration 11 - Potential 11 - Expression 22
Missing number: 8

If there has ever been an inspired or visionary writer, it is this man. Wherever it is found in a chart, 11 expresses creativity, inspiration and the ability to depict the things which lie outside of reality. It is not surprising to find this number in the Aspiration, the Potential and even the Life Path of Jules Verne! As if that wasn't enough, remember that 22 represents the realization of visionary potential; this is the Expression number of this great author.

A 22 in Expression reflects a character that is aware of his strength and potential. He tries to prove in his potential the things he knows he is capable of doing. Gifted in the art of performance, his pride and ambition are his driving forces. He is rarely satisfied and never stops realizing his projects with patience, an eye for detail, depth and determination. He only acts when he is sure of what he is doing. He hates doing anything that goes against his convictions. In fact, he is of the same mould as those who need to construct things based on their personal and sometimes visionary ideas.

Behind the calm and prudent aspect that seems to characterize him at first glance, he suffers from anxiety issues. Furthermore, these difficulties affect his joints and he may suffer from all sorts of epidermic reactions and allergies linked to his worries. He embraces his opinions fully and with honesty. These opinions may incite the reprobation of others as they are often very blunt (*Jules Verne was criticized for his anti-Semitism*).

He is sure of himself and knows how to use psychological pressure to achieve his goals even though he cannot stand others using blackmail against him. It is certain that in his lifetime he will manage to leave his mark by becoming a model or a precursor within his chosen domains (*it is difficult to say otherwise about Jules Verne!*).

This is a figure driven by an Aspiration 11 who has a powerful need to go where his inspiration dictates. He knows how to see the positive side of every situation because everything helps him to evolve. His close friends and family can count on him because he is sincere and faithful. For this reason he attracts people worthy of interest who are spiritually evolved and often share his values. Some of them will help him along his path. He certainly has a well-developed ego but, over time, he will find a balance and will work for the collective good.

A lack of affection may characterize his childhood leading him to be independent and requiring a lot of personal space but also looking for affection, tenderness, warmth and comfort. He probably develops ambivalence towards his parents, love for his mother but jealousy and/or resentment towards his father generated by a desire to replace him.

His outlook on the world leads him to live as harmoniously as possible with nature and the elements. He could be active in movements that promote this idea (e.g. ecology or naturism). His soul urge will also result in a love of travelling with friends (*travel and adventure are main themes in the work of Jules Verne*).

In a practical way, the Potential 11 fills him with a real ambition equal to the esteem he has for himself and for his capabilities. This type of character never doubts. Inspired by a role model, his principles flow naturally from what he thinks is his duty. He does not always say what he thinks, as if a higher being sometimes tells him to accept things in silence.

He is generous and open but this does not make him less selective in his choice of activities, discarding anything he deems insignificant and mediocre. He is focused on progress and does not stop investing all of his energy into improving his plans which end up exhausting him and preventing him from devoting his energies to a personal life. Furthermore, his socioprofessional activity will be characterized by a transformation, which could happen suddenly and unexpectedly, or which could follow legal complications. His persistence and mental strength will lead him to success at the end of his path which will also result in material and financial stability. He can expect undreamed-of profits. It must be remembered that his emotional balance goes hand in hand with a full purse. He must also learn not to spend beyond his means.

These few examples go to show that there is no doubt the Maia method yields surprising results. The depth of analysis goes well beyond the apparent personality defined by the assumed name and patronymic. It is remarkably accurate and I beg you to believe me when I say that I have tried every way possible to find fault with it because it turns the established methods of numerology on their heads.

When I realized that my friend Michel's discovery, once it was validated, was going to significantly change things, I began to evaluate the results of dozens of close friends. Using my software, I did numerous searches on all of my files to find out if the significance of a number was appropriate to the subject's personality. In this way, me and Michel were able to verify the accuracy of the interpretations of dozens of close friends and celebrities.

This pertinent and meticulous research enabled us to honor the orders we had received for readings. While it is clear that a chart generated by the software can never rival one cast by a seasoned professional, the simple act of taking the correct parameters into account for the reading had remarkable consequences.

Many people were genuinely amazed, even dumbfounded, by the revelations obtained. The relevance of the perspective disturbed more than one person. Their opinions on numerology became much more than simple amusement.

A few readings, and truth be told very few, were quite violently rejected. It was easy for us to see why in light of their analyses. As if by magic, we discovered that these people had a combination of numbers which made it difficult for them to hear these truths.

It was easy to observe that the strong reaction of certain subjects matched the level of their disappointed narcissism or their superiority complex. They tended to see the reading as a judgment without appeal. This is possibly because the number revealed them in their entirety without leaving room for compromise. It is up to the native to gain self-awareness and to reconsider the way in which he lives in order to go beyond the stage of the eternal victim.

Henceforth we will all be able to identify our character traits and the attitudes at the origin of conflict in order to implement the means necessary to achieving harmony in our lives. From now on the Maia method will allow each of us to identify ourselves in a numerological reading. It is no longer a privilege reserved for those few people who were given their mother's surname at birth!

Of course, it is never going to be easy for people to admit that the data taken into account to construct a reading before this discovery did not fully correspond to the demands of the science of Numbers. For this reason, I am well aware that there will be resistance and rejection.

But surely this discovery deserves to be seriously studied as objectively as possible by anyone passionate about numerology. For my part, I find it stupefying to see how intensely it reflects the true nature of the being.

The study of known personalities is a good exercise if you need convincing. I have only reported the findings of three such personalities in this book but I have studied many more. It naturally requires some research in order to find out precise information on the real name of the person and the birth surname of his/her mother.

CHAPTER IX

The veil is lifted

"Every one of us is born with a destiny and we must complete the tasks we are given in this world. A long time before I was conceived, it was decided that part of my destiny would be to convey all of these things. This is why I have come here to speak to you."

White Bear (Hopi Indian) "Kasskara and the Seven Worlds"

I have chosen to write a few words to end this book as a chapter rather than in the form of a conclusion. It would be very presumptuous of me to attempt to draw a line under the study of the science of numbers.

There are indeed many paths left to explore and improve upon e.g. the interaction of numbers, the real effectiveness of transit, the preponderance, or not, of the official alphabet used to register the birth over the 26 letters of the Latin alphabet (English and French) for Germans, Italians, Spanish, and so on. All in all I am asking you to take a fresh look at numerology in light of the Maia method. We hope that skilled numerologists will participate in this reconquest and we are keen to help this work in whatever way we can.

It is an undeniable fact that it was common sense that drove us and allowed us to write this book and it is also this common sense that is whispering to us that we do not have all the answers, that it is possible to see effects without necessarily knowing the causes.

Whether we are talking about the science of numbers or the science of stars, mistakes have been made and passed on, more often than not in good faith. We hope that this book will allow some of those mistakes to be corrected.

Other works will follow.

As a final point, I want to thank my friend Michel Pirmaïer from the bottom of my heart for his guidance. Without him, this book would never have existed. I also want to mention my friend Desline for her warm welcome when I was carrying out research on the history of numbers and letters.

Thanks to you, and many others, the revelation has begun.

Appendix 1

MAJOR LATIN ALPHABETS AND THEIR LETTER/VALUE
CORRESPONDANCE TABLE

English/French Alphabet								
1	**2**	**3**	**4**	**5**	**6**	**7**	**8**	**9**
A	B	C	D	E	F	G	H	I
J	K (11)	L	M	N	O	P	Q	R
S	T	U	V (22)	W	X	Y	Z	

Spanish Alphabet								
Traditional classification before 1994								
1	**2**	**3**	**4**	**5**	**6**	**7**	**8**	**9**
A	B	C	CH	D	E	F	G	H
I	J (11)	K	L	LL	M	N	Ñ	O
P	Q	R	S (22)	T	U	V	W	X
Y	Z							
Since 1994								
1	**2**	**3**	**4**	**5**	**6**	**7**	**8**	**9**
A	B	C	D	E	F	G	H	I
J	K (11)	L	M	N	Ñ	O	P	Q
R	S	T	U (22)	V	W	X	Y	Z

Italian Alphabet								
1	**2**	**3**	**4**	**5**	**6**	**7**	**8**	**9**
A	B	C	D	E	F	G	H	I
L	M (11)	N	O	P	Q	R	S	T
U	V	Z						

Portuguese Alphabet								
1	**2**	**3**	**4**	**5**	**6**	**7**	**8**	**9**
A	B	C	D	E	F	G	H	I
J	L (11)	M	N	O	P	Q	R	S
T	U	V	X (22)	Z	K ?	W ?	Y ?	

Note : K, W and Y are now included. If they have the same rank
than in English, use the English/French alphabet

German like English Alphabet with Ä Ö Ü ß at the end of the alphabet								
1	**2**	**3**	**4**	**5**	**6**	**7**	**8**	**9**
A	B	C	D	E	F	G	H	I
J	K (11)	L	M	N	O	P	Q	R
S	T	U	V	W	X	Y	Z	Ä
Ö	Ü	ß						

Another way for German Alphabet...								
1	**2**	**3**	**4**	**5**	**6**	**7**	**8**	**9**
A	Ä	B	C	D	E	F	G	H
I	J (11)	K	L	M	N	O	Ö	P
Q	R	S	ß	T	U	Ü	V	W
X	Y	Z						

In case you think Ä, Ö, Ü and ß have that placement
Otherwise, if you consider that umlauts have been formed by the merger
with the vowel E you can define :

$$Ä → AE → 1+5 = 6$$
$$Ö → OE → 6+5 = 11$$
$$Ü → UE → 3+5 = 8$$
$$ß → SZ → 1+8 = 9 \text{ or } ß → SS → 1+1…$$

Dutch Alphabet								
1	**2**	**3**	**4**	**5**	**6**	**7**	**8**	**9**
A	B	C	D	E	F	G	H	I
J	K (11)	L	M	N	O	P	Q	R
S	T	U	V (22)	W	X	Y or IJ	Z	

Appendix 2

EVOLUTION OF THE LATIN ALPHABET

Hebrew	Greek	Latin	Emerging	In the beginning	Value III BC	Value I BC	Today
aleph (1)	alpha (1)	A	Since the beginning	1	1	1	1
bèt (2)	beta (2)	B	Since the beginning	2	2	2	2
guimel (3)	gamma (3)	C	Since the beginning	3	3	3	3
dalèt (4)		D	Since the beginning	4	4	4	4
hé (5)		E	Since the beginning	5	5	5	5
		F	I BC			6	6
		G	III BC		6	7	7
hèt (8)	heta (8)	H	Since the beginning	6	7	8	8
youd (10)	iota (10)	I	In the beginning I and J are the same letter	7	8	9	9
		J	Dissociated from I to 16th century				1
khaf (20)	kappa (20)	K	Since the beginning	8	9	1 (10)	11
lamed (30)	lambda (30)	L	Since the beginning	9	1 (10)	11	3
mèm (40)	mu (40)	M	Since the beginning	1 (10)	11	3 (12)	4
noun (50)	nu (50)	N	Since the beginning	11	3 (12)	4 (13)	5
aïn (70)	omicron (70) omega (400)	O	Since the beginning	3 (12)	4 (13)	5 (14)	6

Hebrew	Greek	Latin	Emerging	In the beginning	Value III BC	Value I BC	Today
pé (80)	pi (80)	P	Since the beginning	4 (13)	5 (14)	6 (15)	7
kouf (100)	goppa (90)	Q	Since the beginning	5 (14)	6 (15)	7 (16)	8
rèch (200)	rho (100)	R	Since the beginning	6 (15)	7 (16)	8 (17)	9
chine (300) tsadé (90)	sigma (200) san	S	Since the beginning	7 (16)	8 (17)	9 (18)	1
tav (400) tèt (9)	tau (300) theta (9)	T	Since the beginning	8 (17)	9 (18)	1 (19)	2
vav (6)		U	In the beginning U and V are the same letter	9 (18)	1 (19)	2 (20)	3
		V	Dissociated from U to 14th century				22
		W	Seen in the 12th century				5
samè'h (60)	xi (60)	X	Since the beginning	1 (19)	2 (20)	2 (20)	6
	upsilon (400)	Y	I BC			3 (21)	7
zaïn (7)	zeta (7)	Z	I BC			22	8

Note: the rank of a letter and therefore the value that is associated with depends on its appearance in the common language or date of its formalization? In the case of W, and as found in our studies of historical figures, it seems more compelling to consider the influence of a letter from its first appearance in the language. In the same way that new words in a language have their own life long before they are formalized in a dictionary

Appendix 3

CORRESPONDANCE
ENNEAGRAM PROFILES/NUMBERS

Profile number in the enneagram	Dominant Regression Glorification	Dominating number of the profile
1	Perfection, precision Anger, shame Honesty, serenity	4
2	Concern for others, Help Pride, Flattery Humility, freedom	2
3	Production, competitor, liar, megalomaniac Authenticity, hope	1
4	Creativity, enthusiasm Jealousy Superficiality Originality, balance	3
5	Monitoring, Research, avarice, greed Non-attachment, omniscience	7
6	Loyalty, Knowledge Fear, cowardice Faith, courage	9
7	Freedom, change, Intemperance, gluttony Simplicity, joy	5
8	Power, control Lust, impudence Innocence, truth	8
9	Mediation, agreement Laziness, indolence, Harmony, love	6

Bibliography

AVERY Kevin Quinn
The Numbers of Life: The Hidden Power in Numerology / DMS / 1977

BROOKE THOMSON M.A. Leeya
The Wisdom of Sound and Number / IUnivers / 2006 / Lincoln USA

BUESS Lynn
Numerology: Nuances in Relationships / Light Technology Publications / March 1991
Numerology for the New Age / Light Technology Publications; 2nd edition / December 1978

CAMPBELL Florence
Your days are numbered / Devorss Publications / 1931 / Marina del Rey USA

DECOZ Hans with MONTE Tom
Numerology Key to your inner self / Avery Publishing Group / 1994 / USA

DUCIE Sonia
The complete illustrated Guide to Numerology / Element Books Limited /1999 / USA

GOODWIN O. Matthew
Numerology The Complete Guide (Volume 1: The personality reading) / 1981 / Newcastle Publishing Company, INC / North Hollywood, California
Numerology The Complete Guide (Volume 2: Advanced personality analysis and reading the Past, Present , and Future) / 1981 / Newcastle Publishing Company, INC / North Hollywood, California

MILLMAN Dan
The Life You Were Born to Live: A Guide to Finding Your Life Purpose / HJ Kramer / 1993

Table of Contents

Made in the USA
San Bernardino, CA
26 May 2014